*LARREY: Surgeon
to Napoleon's Imperial Guard*

LARREY: *Surgeon*
to Napoleon's Imperial Guard

ROBERT RICHARDSON

Quiller Press
London

First published 1974
This edition published 2000
by Quiller Press Ltd.
46 Lillie Road,
London SW6 1TN.
Copyright © 1974 and 2000
Robert Richardson.
The moral right of the author
has been asserted

ISBN 1 899163 60 3

Printed in Hong Kong
by Colorcraft Ltd.

Contents

Contents

Foreword

Napoleon was dying, a tightly guarded prisoner on a tiny island, half-lost amid the lonely reaches of the South Atlantic. In mortal agony, he still could shape his last will and testament as precisely as he had planned his great campaigns.

To one bequest among the many to friends and faithful comrades-in-arms, remembered from their years of glory and high deeds, the Emperor added a special salutation:... *to Chief Surgeon Larrey, 100,000 francs. He is the most virtuous man I have ever known.*

Dominique Jean Larrey, Baron of the Empire, Surgeon-in-Chief to the Imperial Guard, later Surgeon-in-Chief to the entire *Grande Armée*, Commandant of the *Légion d'honneur*, Knight of the Order of the Iron Crown, was indeed a man of virtue: faithful, competent, fearless, always ready — even eager — to 'choose the hard right, rather than the easier wrong.' (From the *Cadet Prayer*, United States Military Academy.)

One of the most expert surgeons of his day — he apparently was the first to successfully amputate a leg at the hip joint — he also was an imaginative, forceful military medical officer. The mobile ambulance service he developed seems to have been the first such organization since the great days of the East Roman empire. Beyond that, there was his sense of duty toward his fellow soldiers that always brought him forward onto the battlefield, whether the Guard was actively engaged or not. Napoleon praised him as a truly honest man, who spared neither himself nor his assistants and would unhesitatingly get generals out of bed if the sick or the wounded of their commands were not receiving proper care. And he cared for all the wounded, whether friend or enemy, with equal devotion.

It is difficult for us — accustomed to antibiotics and kidney transplants — to realize the conditions confronting Larrey and his comrades. Having no conception of pathogenic micro-organisms (in vulgar parlance 'germs') they must fight invisible enemies and could only guess at the causes of most diseases. (For example, Dr. Richardson shows the feared 'Madrid colic' to have been lead poisoning: Larrey concluded that it resulted from individual susceptibility to the local climate.) Even Larrey would not risk an operation requiring the opening of the abdominal cavity. Moreover the Army's *Intendance* (Administration), the civilian administrative service that controlled medical supply, hospitals and evacuation of the wounded, was usually inefficient and too often corrupt. Larrey's letters to his wife echo his constant struggles with it.

It must be admitted that Larrey's *Mémoires* and letters are not accurate military history. He was obviously too busy with his wounded to consider the details of the fighting that produced them. He did not accept opposition easily, dubbing the universally esteemed Marshal Bessières, ad hoc Commander of the Guard, 'presumptuous' — Bessières, with some knowledge of surgery, having been a medical student, apparently had offered suggestions!

Larrey's rewards were various — from Egypt, a ruby ring (grabbed by Prussian troopers after Waterloo) and twelve beauteous female slaves (passed to his assistants; Larrey's virtues included marital fidelity). From Napoleon — besides the awards of the *Légion d'honneur* and the Iron Crown — he received, after Eylau, the Emperor's own sword to replace one looted while Larrey laboured among the wounded, and in 1809 a barony in northern Germany (lost in 1813). But beyond such worldly tokens, there was the affection of the *Grande Armée, grognard* and conscript, marshal and camp-follower alike. During the worst of the 1812 retreat soldiers protected and fed him.

Bravery and devotion were common virtues among the men of Napoleon's *Grande Armée*. This book presents the life and career of one of their bravest and most devoted, Baron Dominique Jean Larrey, Surgeon-in-Chief of the Imperial Guard, whose skilled scalpel served his Emperor better than any sword.

'If the Army were to erect a monument of the memory of any one man,' declared Napoleon, 'it should be that of Larrey. All the wounded are his family.'

John R. Elting
(Colonel, USA-Ret.)

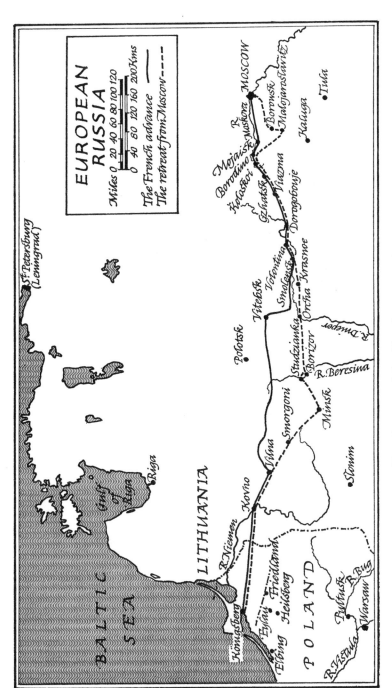

Sketch map of the Russian campaign

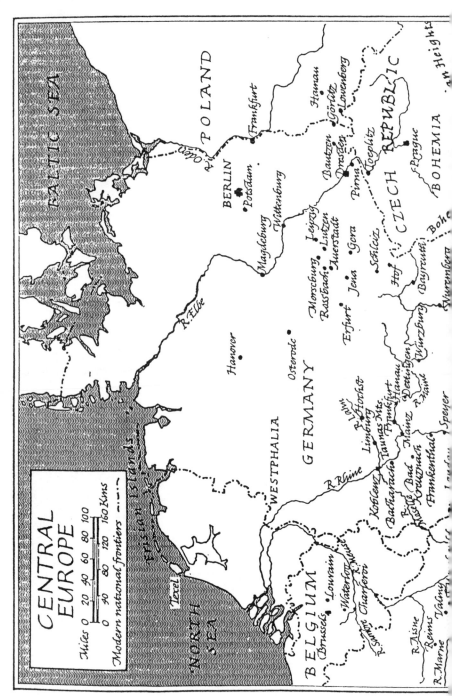

Sketch map of Central Europe

Sources and Acknowlegment

My main sources were Larrey's own published works; the unpublished collection of his letters, documents, and other material in the Wellcome Institute of the History of Medicine, London; Dr Paul Triaire's 'official' biography (1902); and Dr André Soubiran's more recent biography (1966) for which he had access to material released since 1902 (though he was apparently unaware of the collection in the Wellcome Institute).

The Larrey collection in the Wellcome Institute (identified in the Notes at the end simply as Wellcome) consists of: (1) letters to his wife (from Milan, 1797; Egypt, 1800-1; the Prussian campaign, 1806-7; and the Austrian campaign, 1809); these were formerly in the Bibliotheca Lindesiana of the Earl of Crawford and Balcarres until purchased by Sir Henry Wellcome in 1930. (Extracts from a few, probably no more than half a dozen, of these letters have previously been published in a variety of places.) (2) Letters to his daughter (from Boulogne, 1805; Berlin, 1806; Spain, 1808; the Austrian campaign, 1809; Paris, 1811; Moscow, 1812; and the campaigns of 1813 and 1814). (3) Larrey's 1813 campaign journal—a small notebook. And (4) other miscellaneous material relevant, in one way or another, to Larrey.

Larrey's own published works consist of the four volumes of his *Mémoires de Chirurgie Militaire, et Campagnes*, 1812-17 (referred to as *Mémoires* in the Notes); *Relation Médicale de Campagnes et Voyages de 1815 à 1840*, 1841 (referred to as *Campagnes* in the Notes—this book can be considered as the fifth volume of the *Mémoires*); and a large number of books and articles (the more important surgical ones only are listed in my Bibliography, and the only one referred to in the Notes is *Clinique Chirurgicale*,

1829. Larrey was prone to repeat the same case history in different publications).

Larrey's *Mémoires* are a confused and jumbled account of events interspersed with travelogues, nature notes, historical notes, and medical essays, from which personal details, frustrations, financial worries, trials, tribulations, and controversial matters have all been stripped away. Thus the essence of Larrey has to be found in his correspondence and notes.

Triaire's and Soubiran's books and, to a lesser extent, Hassenforder's 1957 article are valuable published sources of much original Larrey material unpublished during his lifetime. In my Notes I have given detailed references to these works where appropriate and indicated also the original sources. Other brief references in the Notes are to be found in full in the Bibliography to which I have added, for this revised edition, some suggested Further Reading dealing particularly with military matters.

The translations are my own; in the process I have edited the text severely, sometimes very severely, and have avoided the Revolutionary calendar. However, on no occasion am I aware of having altered sense or fact; indeed, my object has been to make the meaning of the 18th/19th-century original absolutely clear to a reader today.

Finally I am deeply grateful to Colonel John Elting not only for writing the Foreword to this revised edition, but also for drawing my attention to a number of military errors and, in particular, for his help in clarifying some of the Napoleonic quasi-military ranks employed in the Medical Services.

Introduction

The cold that night was intense. With the windshift to the north-east the misery of the retreating army grew deeper. And, to add spiritual insult to physical injury, the sign of God's displeasure formed and faded on the northern horizon. There, a comet had appeared, its long perpendicular tail a rod of chastisement. The terror of superstition took hold of them. Yet to many the omen seemed pointless; their plight could hardly be worse.

Barring the line of retreat was the part-frozen River Beresina, the only bridge already destroyed by the Russians, the far bank heavily defended and out of range of the French guns. The French feinted; leaving a token force to create the impression of imminent attack, Napoleon moved his army a few miles north and built two bridges across the river. At dawn, as the comet disappeared, the crossing began. The Imperial Guard and two corps reached the west bank without incident. Then, as the heavy artillery began to cross, one of the bridges gave way. The first signs of panic appeared; the tenuous thread of discipline was stretched to breaking point. Suddenly it snapped. The Russians had broken through the rearguard and their cannon balls were scything through the mob around the bridgeheads. The second bridge was now a virtually impassable bottle-neck of wrecked carriages and guns. Men fought in desperation; those knocked down were trampled to their deaths. Horses and drivers were crushed under their overturned wagons. The shouts and screams were heard in horror-struck silence by those already across.

Then, from the very centre of this ghastly, stricken mêlée, a voice rang out: 'It's Monsieur Larrey. He must be saved!' The cry was taken up with an urgency that stilled the terror: 'Save him who has saved us!' From the little oasis of calm an organized ripple moved towards the bridge as Larrey was carried across the heads of the soldiers to safety.

★   ★   ★

Baron Dominique Jean Larrey was Surgeon-in-Chief of the Grand Army on the Russian campaign, yet this alone cannot explain the extraordinary devotion, akin to love, that he inspired in Napoleon's soldiers. As an operator he was incomparable but, perhaps more important in an age when surgeons were reviled, he showed true compassion to which was allied a rare combination of courage, initiative, loyalty, and moral integrity. The fact that the morale of Napoleon's army was maintained for so long in the face of such concentrated and seemingly endless carnage owed much to the inspiration of this one man.

But there was a more enduring quality to his greatness, for he awakened mankind's conscience to the inhumanity of war. Before him, the military machine was all-important, nothing was allowed to interfere with its efficiency—one simply cleared away the mess after the game was over. As Pierre François Percy so truly remarked in 1799, when Napoleon Bonaparte was getting into his stride, 'One would believe that the sick and wounded cease to be men when they can no longer be soldiers.'[1]

Tragically, though, it still took many years for the military mind to accept that, in the 18th century, warfare had altered and with it certain priorities. Nevertheless, once Larrey had stamped the mark of compassion on the military scene nothing could ever be the same again; he had made change inevitable.

In the 300 years since the shining armour of chivalry had been so sorely dented by the invention of cannon and fire-arms, armies had grown bigger, battles were fought over larger and larger areas, and casualties were numbered in thousands rather than hundreds or even tens. With few exceptions, notably Ancient Rome, medical officers were not found in armies before the 18th century; surgeons who went to war did so as the body servants of monarchs and the nobility. The rank and file either looked after themselves, were tended by local inhabitants, or were treated by itinerant charlatans and camp-followers. Logistically speaking, battle casualties were no real problem; they either tagged along with the baggage wagons or were abandoned. Their significance was on a par with the score chalked up beside a dart board. (Sickness was another matter entirely, as communicable diseases could, and did, influence the outcome of a campaign. Until their cause was discovered in the second half of the 19th century, little could be done to bring them under control—though here again Larrey showed remarkable foresight by the exercise of what to us today would be regarded simply as common sense.)

The attitude of the soldier himself throughout this period is seen in a story told by Ambroise Paré, one of the handful of worthwhile military surgeons before Larrey. In a stable at the siege of Turin in 1537 he found three soldiers 'leaning against the wall, their faces completely disfigured; they were unable to see, hear, or speak. Their clothes were still smouldering with the gunpowder that had burnt them.' An old soldier came in and asked if there was any hope of curing them. Paré answered, no. So the soldier 'calmly cut their throats. Seeing this great cruelty, I told him he was a wicked man, but he said he prayed to God that if ever he should be in a like case someone would do as much for him.'[2]

The first European monarch to organize help for the wounded soldier was Queen Isabella of Spain who, in about 1487, produced bedded wagons to carry the casualties to large hospital tents at the end of the battle. Her grandson, the Emperor Charles V, continued the good work. He stationed his doctors among the rearguard with orders to do their best to remove the casualties to a safe place and there dress their wounds. After the action the sick and wounded were sent to the baggage train if they were fit to travel; otherwise they were left behind in the nearest town. But this was too much bother for commanders during the next two centuries and medical organization reached a miserably low ebb.

The Duke of Marlborough stemmed the rot with a deep concern for all aspects of the welfare of his troops. At Blenheim, in 1704, after his superbly conducted march across Europe, he went to great pains to show his surgeons where to assemble the wounded. How much this was due to humanitarian motives and how much to a desire to keep them out of the way is problematical, since both French and English generals were forever complaining about the interference of the wounded with their battle plans. Whatever the case, hospital tents were erected at a distance behind the lines, and there the surgeons waited until the casualties walked in or were carried along by comrades glad of an excuse to leave the fighting. From the tents, the wounded were taken to hospitals set up in nearby towns.

At Dettingen in 1743, John Dalrymple, the Earl of Stair, anticipated the Geneva Convention by more than a hundred years. Sir John Pringle, his physician, tells us that the Earl 'proposed to the Duke de Noailles, of whose humanity he was well assured that the hospitals on both sides should be considered as sanctuaries for the sick, and mutually protected. This was readily agreed to by the French General. . . . This agreement was strictly observed on both sides all that campaign; and tho' it has been since neglected, yet we may hope, that on future occasions, the contending parties will make it a precedent.'[3]

Humanity was indeed ill-served throughout the wars of the remainder of the 18th century, and with Rossbach (1757) a hitherto uncommon element of real hatred came into the fighting. Vast armies, their attendant artillery and enormous baggage trains churning the roads to quagmires, needed space to manoeuvre and fight, and battlefields covering as much as ten square miles were not unknown. Battles that began as though on the parade ground ended in chaos, tumult, and mud. And throughout the whole bloody shambles the military machine had complete priority. During the Penninsular War, even the Duke of Wellington would allow nothing to interfere with the movements of his army. Casualties were a confounded nuisance and the regulations governing their disposal were founded on this credo.

These regulations required that the ambulances—huge, cumbersome vehicles, known as fourgons, and needing four horses to draw them in the best of conditions—together with their surgical personnel should wait about three miles in the rear. After the engagement, the wounded were collected at a convenient spot to which the fourgons proceeded with all possible speed. All possible speed! Bogged in the mud by their own weight, obstructed by artillery and wagons jammed in confusion, they never arrived in less than 24 or 36 hours, by which time many of those they were designed to help were already dead or beyond hope. Many, too, were left on the field, prey to the camp-followers who swooped down like vultures to strip, rob, and mutilate—friend or foe, dead or alive, it made no difference.

With the wars of the French Revolution the situation became completely out of hand. Something had to be done, but it needed a man of quite exceptional qualities, not least of which was the strength and the will to stand up to the might of military authority. That man was Dominique Jean Larrey.

At the heart of the matter lay the status of the army medical service.[4] This was not an autonomous corps but, in France, came under the wing of the 'Administration de la Guerre' at whose head was the Minister of War—though it would be more realistic to say that the Administration had its claws in the medical service and was not going to let go. The reasons for this date back to the 15th century when military hospitals had been run by civilians for what they could get out of it, not for love. To put a stop to this extortion, Louis XIV had placed the hospitals under military administration. The decree of January 17, 1708, then simply regularized an existing state of affairs. Unfortunately, the relationship between doctors and administrators, never very happy, became positively bitter when the Administration acquired service status and so ranked with the artillery, the engineers, and—the original sole combatants—the infantry and the cavalry. The decree of January 1, 1747, put all medical officers under the orders of the commissaires. Chief surgeons did, however, have a certain say until a Ministerial Regulation of 1796 took away the last semblance of their authority—the establishment and running of military hospitals,[5] the organization of ambulances, and the movement of casualties became the responsibility of the Administration and their local representatives, the civilian 'commissaires ordonnateurs', roughly the equivalent of contemporary British commissaries or modern quartermasters.

Adding to the complexities of the problem was the status of the medical officer himself. Socially, this was low and the conditions of service did nothing to attract the best type of man. Pay was poor and, particularly on active service, irregular. Combatant officers lined their pockets handsomely with the spoils of war—indeed, *it* was expected of them—and they petitioned their sovereign for rewards for services rendered. Decorations, favours, honours, land, and great sums of money were heaped upon those whose sole interest was self. This was the way of life and a man was considered a fool if he did not conform.

Then came the Revolution with its Liberty, Equality, and Fraternity. Fine ideals maybe, but alas they ignored human nature: so far as warfare was concerned it was truly a case of 'plus ça change, plus c'est la même chose'—only more so. In such a situation an idealist could only be his own worst enemy, and Larrey was an idealist. Life in the army medical services of the Consulate and the First Empire was not easy anyway, but for a humane surgeon who would not conform and who believed in the principles of the Revolution it could be crucifying. Larrey found petitioning for rewards he maintained were his due a distasteful practice (hence his chronic financial difficulties); in treating his casualties, he took the wounded in order of their surgical need regardless of rank or even nationality (which did not go down at all well with those who were more equal than the rest); and he had the unthinkable temerity to interfere with the military machine (thus incurring the implacable enmity of the Administration).

If there is any truth to be found in Heine's remark that, terrible though war may be, it yet displays the spiritual grandeur of man daring to defy his mightiest hereditary enemy—Death, we must seek it among those who defy death, not to take life but to save it.

1. *The Shoemaker's Son*

The Seven Years' War had placed a severe financial burden on France and had reduced her prestige abroad. She had lost Canada and her conquests in Germany, and was hamstrung elsewhere. Her navy was no longer to be reckoned with; her army was beaten, demoralized, and leaderless. Yet, in less than a decade of the end of the war in 1763, Napoleon and most of the men who were to become his marshals and carry a disordered France to the pinnacle of military glory were born. One is tempted to believe in a biological need that, in some strange way, Nature was able to satisfy.

Far away in the south, in the remoteness of the High Pyrenees the countryfolk knew little about the affairs of government and cared even less. The foothills were farming country and the local population poor but with their own high moral standards and an unswerving loyalty to each other. Into this community, in the little village of Beaudéan, Dominique Jean Larrey was born on July 8, 1766. His family had lived in the district for generations— as tough and rugged as the Pyrenean mountains themselves.

The first Larrey to take up medicine was Jean-François, the great-grandfather of our Larrey. He became the senior surgeon of the town of Tarbes, a few miles to the north. One of his sons, Dominique, followed in his footsteps and practised surgery, also in Tarbes. The other, Jean, stayed at Beaudéan to work the family fields. He in turn had two sons. Liking what he saw of brother Dominique's standing as a surgeon, he sent the younger, Alexis, born in 1750, to study medicine at Toulouse, where later he played a most important part in the education of his two nephews. The elder son, another Jean, was originally intended to stay at home to help his father; but his health was poor and he became instead a master shoemaker.

B

Jean the shoemaker married Philippine Perès and they had three children: a girl, Geneviève, born in 1760, Dominique Jean, and Claude François Hilaire, born in 1769. Dominique Jean was christened on the day of his birth at the turreted village church set in the hillside. His Christian names were almost inevitable, though had there been any doubt it was resolved by the choice of godmother—Dominique Jeanne Piéra.[1]

When he was old enough, his mother sent him to the village school run by the young Abbé Grasset. The resources of a parish priest in a village of some six hundred souls were limited, but in one respect his tutorship was of immense value in shaping Larrey's character, as he gave him a belief in God and a deep love for his fellow men. Like many country boys, Dominique had an insatiable curiosity about the world around him and seemed to have an instinctive understanding of nature. One particular pleasure was to accompany his mother to market in Bagnères de Bigorre, a town two or three miles away that had boasted a spa since Roman times. On the way she would weave the most wonderful tales of fantasy and of folklore interspersed with gems of practical knowledge. But all these happy delights came abruptly to an end when Dominique's father died and he was sent to his uncle Alexis to continue his education. On May 10, 1780, a sad little boy of thirteen in his Sunday best set off northwards down the rocky track on the 70-mile walk to Toulouse.

Alexis Larrey, Surgeon-in-Chief to the local hospital[2] and a corresponding associate of the Royal Academy of Surgery in Paris, had two sons of his own, both destined for the medical profession, yet not for one moment did he regard the addition to his family as an imposition. Before long though, he realized that, despite the efforts of the Abbé, Dominique's cultural and classical education left something to be desired: a term or two at the College of Esquille would not come amiss. When the rougher edges had been smoothed away he himself gave his nephew an excellent grounding in medicine and surgery. He was well rewarded, for Dominique was an outstanding pupil and at nineteen won first prize among the students at the hospital; the following year he was again first in the examination for house surgeon, and shortly after his twentieth birthday he defended his thesis on the surgery of bone caries with such brilliance that the University of Toulouse awarded him a medal bearing the arms of the city.

To say that Larrey was typical of his race would be to do him less than justice. In fact, all the physical and mental qualities of those people found an almost exaggerated expression in the man. He was short, probably shorter than the average, but this was apparent only when he stood in a crowd, and indeed it then came as something of a surprise. His body was handsomely put together and, although he later became stocky, in his younger days there was a slim elegance to his bearing and movement. Throughout his life he wore his thick black hair long, curling down the nape of his neck and on to his shoulders. ('Every time I cut my hair,' he noted in an unpublished part of his memoirs, 'although I took the precaution of leaving it more than two inches long, I experienced many slight indispositions and my mental and physical functions did not return fully to normal until it had again reached its usual length.')[3] His hands were large and strong—reflecting the needs of his chosen career—and his brown eyes were truly the mirrors of his soul—profound intelligence; a practical sympathy for those less fortunate than himself; a truthfulness that could be embarrassingly frank; utter integrity; and a pride and a stubbornness that came to the surface when confronted with an authority that was at odds with his beliefs and wishes.

For nearly a year he continued to work in Toulouse, but was unable to settle. He felt the need of wider experience and advanced training that only Paris could offer. And his youthful spirit was responding to the call of Liberty. So, armed with a letter of introduction from his Uncle Alexis to Antoine Louis, permanent secretary of the Royal Academy of Surgery, he set out on the long walk—public transport was not for him; it would make too deep a hole in his already shallow purse.

Larrey arrived in the capital and presented himself to Louis who told him to enrol for a course of instruction by Pierre Joseph Desault at the Hôtel Dieu. This was sound advice, for although the Hôtel Dieu was grossly overcrowded (up to six in a bed and with sanitation to match), Desault was a great surgeon and certainly the finest teacher of his age. But a course of instruction was all very well; Larrey had to live. Paid jobs were few and far between and the competition intense. Nevertheless, he applied for one at the Hôtel des Invalides, only to be told after what seemed an interminable wait that he lacked practical experience. The situation was becoming desperate when, at the beginning of August 1787, Louis, in his capacity of secretary of the Royal Academy, announced a public examination for the appointment of a number of assistant naval surgeons at Brest.

The chance of a square meal and perhaps of adventure was too good to miss, and even though he had doubts about the delights of life at sea, Larrey entered for the examination. He was successful and once again took to the road, this time with M. Lescot, an officer of the auxiliary naval medical staff, for company. On the way they stopped at the little village of Bourg Hersent, near Laval, to visit the birthplace of Ambroise Paré. One anecdote that made a particular impression on Larrey concerned the occasion when Paré was smuggled into the besieged town of Metz in 1552 at the urgent behest of the Duke of Guise. The mere fact of his presence there had a remarkable effect on morale: 'Now if we are wounded, we cannot die; Paré is among us.'[4]

'When I entered the house,' Larrey afterwards confided to Lescot, 'I was overcome by a strange emotion, almost of worship. I had the feeling that at any moment I might see the great man himself.'[5]

By the time the two men had reached Brest on October 4 events in the world outside had already lost Larrey his first appointment. The fleet at Brest had been equipped for the Dutch, but as Holland had made peace with England orders arrived for its disbandment. In consequence practically all the assistant surgeons were discharged from the service. A few ships—mainly those needed to safeguard French commerce at sea—were, however, still allowed to be armed and Larrey was one of a small number of surgeons retained by the board of health to complete the complement of these vessels.

He was posted as first surgeon to *Vigilante*, an 18-gun, copper-bottomed corvette of 350 tons,[6] commanded by Captain Saques de Toures who was under orders to winter in port. Enforced idleness was never to Larrey's liking, and without more ado he organized a series of lectures on anatomy and surgery for the students and medical fraternity of Brest.

In April 1788, de Toures received orders to set sail with the first wind for Newfoundland where *Vigilante* was to act as a fishery protection vessel. Larrey at once detailed a complete supply of medicines, dressings, and surgical instruments to be brought aboard,[7] and made a close inspection of the ship, checking particularly on the ventilators and air pumps. The concept of preventive medicine in those days was a dim blur; but Larrey realized instinctively the vital importance of maintaining health if morale and efficiency were not to suffer. Yet even more feared than contagious disease was the scurvy. No one knew its cause, so Larrey conformed to the contemporary recommendations and made the men wash frequently with water and vinegar, had their drinking water laced with vinegar and brandy, and kept them active when on watch—whatever other effect these measures may have had, they had none on scurvy which could fairly confidently be relied on to appear after two months at sea.[8]

Throughout the six-month voyage, Larrey had 24 of *Vigilante*'s crew of 123 on his sick list. At least half had suffered from scurvy and some had been dangerously ill. This sickness rate was rather above average, but morbidity and mortality figures in 18th-century navies, particularly in peace-time, are notoriously hard to come by, and comparisons are difficult because of inconsistencies and unreliability. Nevertheless, Larrey did well to contain minor outbreaks of smallpox and typhus and to complete the voyage without the loss of a single man from disease.

Much to his relief the corvette was laid up in Brest and he had no difficulty in getting his discharge. Turning his back on the ocean, he set off inland for Paris where destiny awaited.

2. *Le Déluge*

Larrey's France was a country so taut in its mind for reform that release could come only from a cathartic physical convulsion of its body. Larrey himself was firmly on the side of those who sought to bring order out of confusion and to abolish privilege that had not been earned. He had been born with freedom in his soul and believed passionately that all men should have the right to follow their chosen path. But, unlike so many who cried for liberty, he recognized that freedom and responsibility went hand in hand.

When in November 1788, Larrey reached Paris, he felt rich. For the first time in his life he could jingle the livres in his pocket and be his own master for a few months. So off he went to the Hôtel Dieu where Desault took him on as a trainee surgeon. This allowed him the time to attend lectures in other hospitals, among which were those given by Raphael Bienvenu Sabatier at the Hôtel des Invalides, an establishment for old pensioners. He was greatly impressed by the surgical qualities of Sabatier and when the post of assistant surgeon at the Invalides fell vacant in March 1789 he applied for the job. But despite coming top in the competitive examination, Larrey was not appointed. The Minister of War had the patronage of the hospital; he also had a favourite. Sabatier was incensed at the loss of an outstanding candidate but was powerless to act against the Establishment. Larrey's ego was sorely bruised.

During the first half of 1789 Paris only occasionally erupted in violence. But in July rumours of troop movements in the city increased the anxiety and seriously upset the tottering economy. The people milled aimlessly around in half-hearted protest against they knew not what, until sections of the mob clashed with troops who opened fire—and then they knew. Protest became revolt. 'Aux armes!' On the night of July 13/14 they looted the armourers' shops and, with a courage that surprised even themselves, several thousands assaulted the old moated arsenal of the Invalides and fought their way out with muskets, powder, and cannon. And leading the medical students in revolt was Dominique Jean Larrey.

'I put myself at the head of these young men—they numbered 1,500,' Larrey wrote in a part of his memoirs that he later deemed it wiser not to publish, 'and we were the first to march against the tyrants. Unhappily, we were unable to obtain muskets. However, everyone armed himself as best he could and we marched through the night inciting the populace to rebellion. On the morning of the fourteenth we armed ourselves at the Invalides and turned our steps towards the Bastille.

'If we did not have the honour of mounting the first assault, it was only because the immense crowd before the gates prevented us, and not because we lacked either the enthusiasm or the courage. We were nevertheless able to organize the first guard-post.'[1]

In less than four hours the 'impregnable' fortress fell. The head of the governor, Bernard René Jordan, Marquis de Launay, was raised aloft on a pike as the seven prisoners, one a madman, were freed to the hysterical shouts of the crowd. With their bare hands the mob then completed the destruction that fire had begun. Stone by stone the looming symbol of all they hated and feared was razed to the ground. Liberty had triumphed over oppression, though by no stretch of the imagination was it a victory for enlightenment over the powers of darkness.

All these tumultuous events produced a goodly crop of casualties, and many shattered wretches limped, crawled, or were carried to the Hôtel Dieu where Desault took advantage of the situation to teach his students about gunshot wounds, in particular about excising all dead and dying tissue and removing all foreign bodies from a wound — a procedure now referred to as débridement. In Larrey's day, however, débridement meant the incision through a band or layer of fascia to relieve tension in swollen underlying tissue such as muscle, or an incision to open up a puncture wound. Larrey soon appreciated the practical significance of both procedures.

When limbs had been injured and the patient was a candidate for amputation, Desault always held back. Like pretty well every other surgeon he believed that a delay allowed the man to recover from the shock of wounding and become reconciled to the coming loss. This philosophy derived from the views of Jean Faure. After the French victory at Fontenoy in 1745, the Royal Academy of Surgery had offered a prize for the best-reasoned answer, based on practical experience, to the bothersome question: 'Should one amputate immediately in cases of gunshot wounds, or should one delay?' Almost 300 soldiers wounded in the battle had had amputations, and only 30 had survived. Ten of these had been operated on by Faure after a delay of 15 to 20 days.[2] No one looked closely into the true reasons for the heavy mortality rate and Faure won the prize medal. The earlier experience of Richard Wiseman was ignored. In 1676 he had written:

'But amongst us aboard in that Service [naval], it was counted a great Shame to the Chirurgeon, if that Operation was left to be done the next Day, when Symptoms were upon the Patient, and he spent with Watchings, etc. Therefore you are to consider well the Member, and if you have no probable hope of Sanitation, cut it off quickly, while the Soldier is heated and in Mettle. But if there be Hopes of Cure, proceed rationally to a right and methodical Healing of such Wounds; it being more for your Credit to save one Member, than to cut off many.'[3]

Larrey, a hundred years later, came round to this way of thinking when he saw the unhappy outcome of Desault's delayed operations —a high mortality rate and a long and stormy convalescence for those who survived. As his experience grew, he became emphatic in his condemnation of delay, the sole exception being when there was a chance the limb might be saved—and this was not the reason why others delayed operating.

But if Desault's policy was wrong, his technique was admirable and followed the principles laid down by Henri le Dran in the early 1730s. Having emphasized the importance of trying to save the limb, le Dran wrote, 'When we are obliged to perform the Amputation of a Limb, we must endeavour to preserve enough of the Muscles and Skin, and to saw the Bone so near, that the Flesh which is cut may, if possible, cover it again, and speedily unite.'[4] (Moreover, he said, the amputation should always be made in the sound part of the limb.)[5] This was the three-cut technique that Larrey adopted with such conspicuous success. It was quick and simple: three circular cuts were made at progressively higher levels to form an inverted cone. With this technique the raw bone end was deep in the stump and lower-limb stumps, when healed, were well suited for fitting to a wooden leg.

The method, in those days, was a considerable improvement over the usual French technique of cutting flaps which led to numberless inconveniences. (Flaps, nevertheless, did have a place when the amputation was through a joint, since they then healed quite satisfactorily.) And it was vastly superior to the common German and Russian practice in which the limb was simply sliced off at a level and the skin pulled down and sutured tightly to close the wound. The resulting agonizing tension invited infection, gangrene, and a terrifying mortality rate.

In the early days of the Revolution surgery and the pursuit of liberty fought on equal terms for Larrey's attention. The students were frequently under arms and always ready to go into danger. In fact, Larrey spent the whole of October 1789 on guard duty at Versailles. But as time moved on he realized that his surgical ambition was best served in hospital, and when the job of assistant surgeon at the Invalides fell vacant again at the beginning of 1790 he abandoned the barricades. This time the Minister of War had other matters on his mind and, with Sabatier's help, Larrey successfully claimed the appointment—but all he received in return was food and lodging. To get some money he worked for a while as a demonstrator at the practical school for anatomy[6] attached to the University, and also accepted the post of district surgeon for Saint-André-des-Arts.

The declaration of martial law at the Champ de Mars on July 17, 1791, resulted in a multitude of casualties that gave Larrey a chance to show Sabatier his true worth. Consequently when, a short while afterwards, Larrey was called up for service in the Navy Sabatier was not best pleased and used his considerable influence to have his naval commitments brought to an end. When Larrey returned from Brest—where he had spent two anxious months—Sabatier welcomed him as his personal assistant, with the pay and full responsibilities that went with the post.

For nearly two years Larrey came under the influence of Sabatier, an extremely cultured man, and during this time much of his provincial gaucheness was worn away. The older man was instrumental, too, in guiding the direction of Larrey's private life—but quite unintentionally. Sabatier's ruling passion was for musical soirées and on a late autumn evening in 1791 he invited his assistant to one of these entertainments. Larrey followed Sabatier's Italian arias with some contrasting folk songs from the Pyrenees. Standing there at the pianoforte, he was conscious of one pair of eyes that never left his face the whole time he was singing. The next performer was the owner of these eyes, and it was Larrey's turn to watch, his pulses racing, convinced that she was playing the piano for him alone.

After the music, Sabatier introduced Larrey to the other guests. '. . . M. and Mme René Leroux de Laville and their daughters . . . Charlotte Élisabeth . . .' 'Charlotte.' Larrey's world stood still. What was Sabatier saying? '. . . Minister of Finance . . .' But 'Charlotte' was all his mind could take in. His emotions tumbled over themselves. He was no stranger to the fascination of women, and had been impressed with the beauty and elegance of the English girls he had met at St John's in Newfoundland; but none could compare with Charlotte. In the instant he fell completely under her spell; heart, body, and soul. Larrey, the young provincial doctor with no clear prospects, was in love with a daughter of King Louis' Minister of Finance, and— miracle of miracles—his love was returned.

There were three daughters in the Laville family (a fourth had died as a child) and all were incredibly beautiful. To anyone other than Larrey, Émilie, the eldest, was physically the most attractive, but Charlotte had a charm of manner all her own. She was twenty-one and even more gifted as an artist than as a musician. Her father encouraged this artistic talent by sending her to study under three of the greatest painters in Paris—David, Gros, and Girodet. Like Émilie, she excelled with portraits.

After that momentous evening at Sabatier's, Larrey and Charlotte met whenever they could. At first the Laville parents raised no objections, because they believed their daughter was merely infatuated with the good-looking surgeon. But when Larrey asked their permission to marry Charlotte they became antagonistic. What had he to offer their daughter? Nothing. No position; no money; nothing. The impasse was resolved—temporarily at any rate—by the outbreak of a war that was to last, on and off, for twenty-three years.

In October 1791 the Legislative Committee had taken over the work of the National Assembly. It was composed of the most fervid revolutionaries whose speeches thoroughly alarmed the King of Prussia and the Emperor of Austria. The time had come, these monarchs reckoned, to take active steps to rescue their royal brother from his plight. As they assembled their armies and began the march to the west, the French made what was perhaps one of the craziest declarations of war in history. The country had no army worthy of the name. Its troops were few, lacking in equipment, and shot through and through with insubordination. The crack regiments, consisting largely of foreigners such as the Swiss, had either been slaughtered in defence of the King, or had been disbanded only to cross the frontier and find employment with the armies of Prussia and Austria. Many of the officers, drawn from the aristocracy, had fled the country to enlist in the émigré forces. With a few exceptions, discipline did not exist, and the soldiers, infected with the fever of revolution, did only what it pleased them to do.

Nevertheless, even an army such as this needed its medical officers and Larrey was conscripted a second time at a salary of 250 livres[7] a month. Sabatier, now consultant to the Army of the North, used his influence with the War Minister to get him a posting where his skill would not be wasted.

At the end of March 1792, Surgeon-Major Larrey took leave of his Charlotte, both vowing eternal love, and set off to join the Army of the Rhine. On April 1, he reported to the headquarters of Marshal Nicolas Luckner at Strasbourg.

3. *The Rhine*

Allons, enfants de la patrie
Le jour de gloire est arrivé!

At the time when Claude Joseph Rouget de Lisle—an officer and a royalist—dedicated his *Battle Hymn of the Army of the Rhine* to Marshal Luckner, the day of glory had certainly not arrived. Admittedly, as the hands of the clock turn it was not far away, but in that short period the honour of France was dragged through the mire of a terrible summer.

War was declared on April 20 and floods of Carmagnoles poured out to the frontiers to defend their newly won liberty and equality. They swelled the numbers of the already demoralized armies and well nigh destroyed them in the process. By mid-September they had been pushed back to within 130 miles of Paris. Charles François Dumouriez, recently given command of the Army of the North, decided the time had come to make a stand. He deployed his force among the wooded hills and treacherous marshes of the Argonne—an ideal defensive position—but unfortunately the Duke of Brunswick broke through where he had been least expected and Dumouriez retired on St Menehould. Meanwhile François Christophe Kellerman was marching from Metz to link up. On September 19 he advanced beyond Dampierre's Camp—where Dumouriez had intended him to halt—crossed the River Aube, and took up his position on the plateau of Valmy. Here he was unpleasantly close to the enemy, drawn up on the surrounding heights of La Lune, and dangerously separated from Dumouriez.

The allied commanders decided to attack the nearest French positions first, and, as the autumn mists slowly cleared the next morning, Kellerman's men saw the might of Europe descend into the valley to drive a wedge between their army and that of Dum-

Dominique Jean Larrey, by his friend Anne Louis Girodet

Larrey's two-wheeled ambulance

Larrey's four-wheeled ambulance

ouriez and then sweep them to their slaughter at the hands of the waiting Prussian cavalry. Scared beyond anything and unsure of their comrades standing by their side, the French yet stood firm. The Prussian artillery opened fire and was answered by the famous French cannonade of Valmy. Then the Prussian bayonets began their assault on the plateau. The French infantry wavered; Kellerman, whose horse had been shot from under him, dashed into their ranks. His cry of 'Vive la nation!' was, incredibly, taken up by battalion after battalion. Alone, this display of enthusiasm would not have demoralized the Prussians, but they were sick men. Short of supplies and short of clean water, they had drunk from the stagnant marsh pools and gorged themselves on the grapes—still unripe after a long spell of wet weather—from the champagne vineyards north of the Marne. Dysentery, already rumbling, blasted their guts. They were incapable of the uphill charge, and slowly fell back to their old positions. Thus does disease sway the fate of nations.

King Frederick William harangued them mercilessly, but by the time he personally led a second attack Kellerman had been joined by Dumouriez and a jubilant French army threw the Prussians back in disorder.

That night Goethe, a spectator of the battle, remarked to his friends in the Prussian camp: 'From this place, and from this day forth, begins a new era in the history of the world; and you can all say that you were present at its birth.'[1]

The victory at Valmy not only made men of the French rabble—though it took considerably longer to turn them into efficient soldiers—it also changed the whole concept of warfare. Gone were the almost parade-ground battles of the 18th century fought in the open to a set pattern and with their emphasis on methods rather than men. Overnight, a nation had taken up arms and thus possessed a seemingly endless supply of fighting men. Unaware of the gentlemanly manner of conducting war, these troops fought whenever the occasion demanded, exploiting the nature of the countryside to the discomfiture of their enemies. They learnt to live off the land so that they could move rapidly and largely dispense with slow, cumbersome supply trains, and they relied heavily on field artillery to shake the morale of the opposing troops.

But above all, in the early years of the French Republic, this new force was fired with a tremendous sense of patriotism.

The Army of the Rhine was fortunate in escaping much of the insubordination rife elsewhere, despite having had a rapid succession of commanders. Its advance guard on the west bank of the Rhine had already been pestered by émigré forces under the Prince of Condé, so, when the news of Valmy arrived, Adam Phillippe Custine, the recently appointed commander, decided to get his own back and advanced northwards to cross the river at Speyer. He left Wissembourg on September 29 with 20,000 men, and, with a speed that was possible only because of discipline and enthusiasm, surprised the Speyer garrison at their early morning exercises—they only just had time to get back inside and shut the gates. Custine's demand for surrender was answered by gunfire. After all, there were 40,000 men in the garrison and a ball or two fired in anger at the cowardly French would soon send them packing. It did not.

Custine immediately invested the town and launched an attack. As soon as the Austrians saw that he was in earnest they surrendered and threw open the gates. Yet despite the seeming ease of victory, many Frenchmen were wounded and most of them died—completely unnecessarily in Larrey's opinion, as regulations denied them immediate aid. But military regulations or not, Larrey was determined to alter the state of affairs. The two prime requirements were immediate treatment and prompt evacuation, and in the coming weeks he set his mind to puzzling out how these could be achieved.

On October 15, Custine resumed his march and arrived before Mainz on the eighteenth. This stronghold withstood the siege three days longer than Speyer before the garrison capitulated and the French army was welcomed by the town band and the general rejoicing of the pro-revolutionary populace. Here, Custine decided to wait on events. They did not keep him waiting long.

Towards the end of November, news came that the King of Prussia had regrouped his forces and was advancing on Koblenz from the east. Custine therefore set out with part of his army to intercept him. First he marched east along the River Main to secure his own rear; he then turned north through the Taunus

Mountains until he came to Limbourg on the River Lahn. Here the advance guard under General Jean Nicolas Houchard ran into trouble in the shape of its opposite number. Houchard drove the Prussians back, but soon found himself in deeper water than he had bargained for. The enemy called up numerically superior reinforcements which compelled him to withdraw from the field under cover of darkness. Throughout the whole episode Larrey chafed impotently at the bonds of authority that kept him, a useless spectator, well to the rear. He could do nothing for the wounded who were left to non-existent Prussian mercy. But he could do something for the wounded of the future. Initially he had thought of rescuing the men in panniers slung on horses, but one or two attempts had proved the impracticality of this. Now he knew the answer.

Obtaining temporary leave of absence from Houchard, Larrey returned to the main body of the army which had fallen back to a good defensive position on the Main between Hochst and Frankfurt. He immediately sought out Custine and the quarter-master-general, Jacques Villemanzy, and with no beating about the bush stated the problem and his solution. The advance guard, said Larrey, was supported by flying artillery which was extremely mobile and could be called up at a moment's notice. He was therefore seeking their authority to construct an ambulance along similar lines—a flying ambulance.[2]

Custine was fifty, an aristocrat, and a professional soldier. Larrey was twenty-six, a provincial doctor, and had been in the army only a few months. There was a time when Custine would have sent anyone packing who came to him with such a hare-brained scheme. But times had changed. The Terror was under way and it would never do for the National Convention to learn that one of its generals had turned down a plan for helping its citizens. This doctor seemed safe enough, but he had a quiet air of determination about him, and these days you could never be too sure.

Larrey obtained his authority. He knew what he wanted. His ambulance had to be a carriage; well sprung and capable of being drawn swiftly like the flying artillery by two or four horses. Under his guidance, and with Villemanzy's willing help, a few of these vehicles were ready in a very short space of time. Then proudly, riding at the head of his first flying ambulance, Larrey rejoined Houchard's advance guard up in the mountains behind Königsberg.

Conditions there were rough. Snow was falling heavily and Houchard's men were mainly the first volunteers from Paris to reach the Rhine army. Houchard was unhappy; he really wanted trained troops to hold a pass against a strong force of advancing Austrians. Fortunately the Carmagnoles made up for what they lacked in experience, clothing, and weapons by the fire of patriotism in their bellies. They imagined themselves as second Spartans at Thermopylae, prepared to suffer the same fate if need be. And they very nearly had to. A deserter, like Ephialtes of old, betrayed the French and led the Austrians around their position. But Houchard was not to be a second Leonidas. He attacked suddenly at the enemy's weakest point and forced an opening for a precipitate, but well-ordered retreat in conditions so appalling that he had to call a halt in a mountain hamlet. Eventually, half-frozen and with stomachs empty, the advance guard rejoined the main army.

During the engagement a number of French had been killed and 30 wounded. Here for the first time, Larrey dressed[3] the wounded on the field of battle, exposing himself to terrible risk in a fight that was no set piece, but a break-out in foul weather over broken, mountainous terrain. What is more, his ambulances carried them all back to safety.

Things now began to go badly for the French, faced as they were by the vastly stronger allied armies of Prussia and Austria. The garrison at Frankfurt unexpectedly surrendered and was put to the sword for its pains. Custine fell back on Mainz, leaving Houchard still in the mountains where Larrey and his ambulances served to good effect in many minor but bloody encounters.

In January 1793, a strong body of allies crossed the Rhine at Bacharach. Leaving a garrison in Mainz, Custine marched west and found these enemy troops in possession of the forts and strongpoints of the mountainous Kreuznach area. He dislodged them one at a time, but could take no advantage of his successes because of his numerical inferiority. Slowly, fighting all the way, he retreated on Frankenthal.

Houchard, covering the retreat from the heights of Altzey, was attacked on March 30 and almost surrounded. Despite a vigorous counter-attack, the day was saved by Custine who sent up reinforcements of flying artillery and himself arrived at the head of a light cavalry charge. The enemy retreated, and Larrey for the first time amputated on the field—an operation he could perform in, literally, one or two minutes.

The wounds that led to the need for amputation were, in the main, those caused by musket- and cannon-balls, cannister-shot, bombs, and shells which all severely damaged the tissues. Musket-fire had this effect up to about 30 or 40 yards; over 250 yards it was little more than a nuisance—in consequence muskets were usually discharged at close quarters. The violent effect of cannon-fire was retained up to a 1,000 or so yards. The shattered nature of the resulting wounds had important surgical consequences.

The limb was numb and the muscles relaxed for a few inches above the injury; this meant that amputation through healthy tissue could be done with very little pain. The wounded man was shocked, pale, with an almost imperceptible pulse, and a low blood pressure that helped to stop the bleeding. As the hours passed, the muscles above the injury became rigid and extremely painful; the shock passed off, the blood pressure rose and bleeding started again; the state of the arteries in the wound began to deteriorate so that control of haemorrhage became more difficult; and infection began to gain a hold. Should the patient be evacuated before the amputation was done, the bumping and jarring of the wagon made the broken bone ends grate horribly together. All too often the wounded man arrived dead.

Immediate amputation had overwhelming advantages to which, however, the contemporary surgeon was completely blind as a result of his training and tradition. Apart from being relatively painless and technically easier, it converted a bloody, dirty mess into a well-ordered surgical wound that would travel well—indeed many of Larrey's patients recovered so rapidly that they were able to walk or ride away, even hundreds of miles back to France.

Larrey had two further reasons in support of his actions. First, hospitals were dangerous places where fever and gangrene were rife.[4] A soldier who arrived already amputated and with his wound on the way to healing stood less chance of falling foul of these diseases. Secondly, should the casualties have to be abandoned they could defend themselves against thieves and murderers. The wounds did not need re-dressing for several days, and if the men fell into the hands of unskilful surgeons—a not uncommon happening—their operation was done.

When Larrey reached Wissembourg and discussed his enthusiasm for immediate amputation with his colleagues they would have nothing to do with it and advised him most strongly not to submit a paper to Paris for publication. By no means discouraged, Larrey agreed. He would simply wait until his results had convinced the doubters.

The Army of the Rhine now came in for another shake-up of its senior officers. Houchard was sent to command the Army of the Moselle, and was replaced by General Landremont. Custine was ordered to the Army of the North to restore discipline and morale after the desertion of Dumouriez to the allies, and was succeeded by General Alexandre Beauharnais who at once decided to resume the offensive and marched out to raise the sieges of Landau and Mainz. On July 20 he came on the enemy and prepared to give battle. For two days the armies glowered at each other before action was joined. It was a bitter fight in which Larrey showed his mettle in more ways than we would expect of an army surgeon today—the Geneva Convention did not originate until 1864.

On one part of the field a group of French soldiers had had enough and were scattering to safety. Larrey galloped after them with drawn sword, calling down upon them the wrath of God for deserting their posts and leaving their comrades to be slaughtered. His own courage was known to them and shamefacedly they returned to the fray.[5]

Later, Larrey spotted four Carmagnoles who had fallen, wounded, in an attack on a Prussian battery, and were being stripped of their clothes—this was but a prelude to the Prussian habit of cutting their throats. At the head of five dragoons, given him as an escort by Landremont, Larrey charged and routed the Prussians. The wounded men were quickly put in the flying ambulance, though not before coming under fire from the battery. By great good luck not one man and not one horse was hit. Back in the safety of a sheltered gulley, Larrey operated on all four with complete success.

'These brave Republicans,' Larrey noted in his journal, 'with many others on that day, found their safety in the flying ambulance which was now known throughout the entire army for the immediate help it could bring in all battles.'[5]

After the battle, which the French won, Beauharnais wrote in his dispatch to the National Convention in Paris:

'Among those brave men of intelligence and action who so brilliantly served the Republic on this day, I cannot ignore the adjutant-general, Bailly; Abbatouchi[6] of the light artillery; and Surgeon-Major Larrey with his companions of the flying ambulance, whose indefatigable care of the wounded eased the suffering of mankind on such a day, served the cause of humanity itself, and contributed to saving the gallant defenders of our country.'[7]

These sentiments, warmly applauded by the Convention, were a landmark in history, since never before had a military surgeon received formal acknowledgment of his services from his general and his government. But Larrey—and indeed the entire medical service—was in greater need of more material recognition.

He had had to leave behind in his billet in Mainz all his books, the bulk of his instruments, and his clothes. When he learnt that the house had been burnt down and all his possessions lost, he carefully listed every item and put in a claim to the War Ministry for 2,000 livres which he backed up with glowing testimonials from Villemanzy and Landremont. The Council of Health in Paris endorsed the claim, but before Larrey received an answer he lost in action everything he had left except the clothes he was wearing. In desperation he wrote again to the War Ministry begging for some reimbursement otherwise he would be unable to keep body and soul together. Eventually Villemanzy was authorized to pay him 300 livres, a meanness which so upset the quartermaster that he showed Larrey the Ministry instructions clearly indicating that payments could only be made to medical officers on the authority of the Minister of War.[8] Petty though this may seem it was typical of the whole attitude towards the medical services and was merely the opening shot in the life-long battle between Larrey and the Administration.[9]

In spite of Beauharnais' victory, Mainz had surrendered and the French were now in a most awkward situation, particularly as their commander was recalled to France where a ghastly triumph was being prepared for him. Under his replacement, General Carlin, the army was forced back, in a series of frightful battles, to Wissembourg where it was utterly routed by a surprise attack in which Larrey was slightly wounded in the left leg and only just manged to escape capture. But once again a victorious army failed to follow up its advantage, and the French were able to rally at Strasbourg. Here the Army of the Rhine was amalgamated with that of the Moselle under twenty-five-year-old General Lazare Hoche who sallied forth and in a glorious 17-day campaign of uninterrupted fighting carried all the enemy fortresses, raised the siege of Landau, and drove the allies back across the Rhine. Throughout, Larrey was attached to the advance guard which, on Landremont's recall, had come under the command of General Louis Desaix whom Larrey was proud to number among his greatest friends.

Desaix wrought havoc among the Austro-Prussian army, forcing it back to Mainz; but severe weather made a siege impracticable and he decided instead to go into winter quarters. The following February (1794) Larrey was sent by the representatives of the people to Paris under orders to complete the organization of his flying ambulances, and to establish them in the other armies of the Republic. Their usefulness had been proved beyond doubt in the Army of the Rhine.

4. *Toulon Return*

Larrey arrived in Paris in some trepidation. The Terror was reaching its climax and his humanity towards all wounded, be they French, Prussian, Austrian, or émigré, had not passed unnoticed. His services may have been appreciated but this did not guarantee his safety. Luckner, Custine, Houchard, and Beauharnais had all been guillotined on their recall to the capital. And on April 6, shortly before Larrey's return, Danton himself was executed. It was healthier to be with the army than in Paris.

France had certainly changed in the two years Larrey had been away. The first flush of enthusiasm for war had passed. Volunteers no longer came forward in sufficient numbers to satisfy the needs of a nation at arms, and the Committee of Public Safety had introduced conscription enforced by fear. The resulting mixture of the best and the worst in France was being gradually welded into an organized fighting force through the drive and ability of Lazare Carnot the member of the Committee of Public Safety charged with the direction of the armies.

Medical officers had to be found to look after these huge armies. At the outbreak of war in 1792 there had been about 1,400, mostly volunteers, but many had been lost from wounds or disease. To fill the gap and supply the growing demand the National Convention placed all qualified doctors, health officers, and pharmacists, between eighteen and forty, at the disposal of Carnot. By 1794 there were 10,000 serving medical officers.[1] Yet, by a decree of August 12, 1792, all the eighteen medical faculties and fifteen medical schools in France had been abolished—they were privileged institutions. Unfortunately the Revolutionaries had no idea how they were to be replaced. War, however, made some sort of action essential, and the first step was taken by the National Convention towards the end of 1793. A Central Council of Health at the War Ministry authorized the teaching of medicine at four military hospitals in Lille, Metz, Strasbourg, and Toulon.

After this promising start, matters rapidly grew worse and worse. In February 1794 the Council of Health set up Schools of Health with the sole object of churning out 'officiers de santé' to serve as medical officers in the armies. The result was deplorable. The training of these men was superficial; their medical education as such was non-existent; and if they could pay for it, they got a licence without difficulty. The morale of the medical service crumbled. The one desire of worthwhile officers was to get as far away from the hospitals as possible and into the field. Here, at least, they might be able to escape from the Administration or find a quartermaster of the calibre of Villemanzy who was motivated by a desire to help the sick and wounded. This situation was responsible for the appalling state of the general military hospital during the Napoleonic era (and for many a long year afterwards).

As soon as Larrey reached Paris he was summoned to the War Ministry and told to forget about the organization of his ambulances. What, he wondered, was coming next? Report back to the Army of the Rhine? Prison? Memories of Custine, Houchard, Beauharnais—fine officers, courageous soldiers, loyal friends—flashed in his mind. Was he to join their battles along the banks of some other Rhine? But no; he was handed his commission as chief surgeon of the expeditionary force to Corsica and ordered to report with all speed to Toulon.

Larrey was overjoyed. He now held an important position and his future seemed assured. His immediate problem though was whether M. Leroux de Laville would see things in the same light. During the past two years M. and Mme Laville had hoped to distract Charlotte's thoughts from Larrey by encouraging her to meet other more eligible men, but her love was not to be shaken. So now they recognized, in the two young people before them, the inevitable. They would stand in their way no longer. Larrey managed to delay his departure for Toulon by a few days, and at eight o' clock on the evening of March 4, 1794, he and Charlotte were married at a civil ceremony in the Paris Town Hall before the sacred flame of Liberty. They had both desperately wanted a church wedding, but the Revolution had swept all that away.

The next morning, anxious to shake the blood-stained dust of

Paris from their feet, Larrey and his wife set off south by post-chaise. Completely unaffected by any sense of urgency, Larrey made a leisurely detour to Toulouse to see his uncle. Charlotte was an immediate success; so much so that when April arrived and Larrey thought it advisable to move on, he was persuaded to leave her with the family until his return. When he at last reported to the expedition's headquarters no one seemed aware of his dilatoriness and he was simply told to embark the dressings and instruments he would need, and then proceed to Nice where the squadron was to take aboard the land forces. As soon as it was ready, the squadron put to sea, met the blockading British fleet, and scurried back into harbour. The rescue of Corsica from the British would have to wait a while.

Among the staff at headquarters was the desperately thin officer who the previous year had played a prominent role in the capture of Toulon from the Royalists and the British. Although the two men met, Larrey dismissed his future emperor with the brief note, 'I saw General Bonaparte for the first time.'[2]

For five months Larrey fretted with inactivity until in the autumn he was invited to replace the two elderly surgeons in charge of the surgical services of the army in eastern Spain. He leapt at the offer—particularly as the journey would take him through Toulouse. Spurred by the prospect of action, his enthusiasm whetted by the reports of his brother, Claude, now a surgeon of the first class and on leave from Spain, he stayed only a few days with his wife before riding over the border into Catalonia. Here he was present at the taking of Figueras and endured the terrible winter-long siege of Rosas where the French besiegers suffered equally with the Spanish besieged.

When the port eventually fell Larrey returned to Figueras, where a deputation arrived from the Spaniards to negotiate a peace. This was the signal for the Committee of Public Safety to order him back to Toulon to rejoin the Corsican expedition which was fitting out afresh.

The expedition still showed no signs of departure so, as the past winter had proved a strain on his health, Larrey obtained permission to go to Paris. On the way he collected his wife and as soon as he reached the capital, on May 1, he reported to the Council of Health and was given 40 days sick leave on account of 'a skin condition resulting from an acute illness, and pains in the head'. [3] His convalescence was, however, interrupted during the last week of May when, true to form, the Faubourg St Antoine erupted in violence. Troops were sent in to restore order and Larrey took it upon himself to organize ambulances in support.

At the end of his leave he was ordered to report, yet again, to Toulon. This time he took Charlotte with him. By now the expedition to Corsica had been postponed indefinitely and Larrey's job became simply the surgical direction of the hospitals in Toulon. But events were shaping themselves in Paris.

The National Convention had elected Paul Barras, a ci-devant count, Commander-in-Chief of the Army of the Interior. Shortly after, on October 4, 1795, he was faced with a great mass of royalist sympathizers strengthened by several batallions of National Guard from different parts of Paris converging on the seat of government. Barras had no choice but to call upon a young general whose guns had impressed him at the seige of Toulon — General Bonaparte. On October 5, Bonaparte met the mob with two eight-pounders and broke them with a whiff of grape-shot. As his reward, he collected Barras's mistress Josephine, widow of General Beauharnais, and, in February 1796, two days after his marriage, command of the Army of Italy.

Early the next year, 1796, Larrey was recalled to Paris by the Minister of War to occupy the chair of anatomy and operative surgery at the new school of military medicine at Val-de-Grâce. [4] His friends at Toulon tried to persuade the authorities to countermand the order and have him appointed chief medical officer for the port, but to no avail. So, with good wishes speeding them on their way, Larrey and his wife, now pregnant, returned to the capital.

But before long Larrey again came up against the Administration with an unpleasant bump. A certain Citizen Bodin, a representative of the people, wrote, in August 1796, to the Minister of War accusing Larrey and the chief surgeon, by name Noël, of having fiddled their appointments. Joseph Athanase Barbier had, he said, a far better operating record yet he was only a junior surgeon. Larrey and Noël were incensed and at an inquiry Barbier admitted having given the information to Bodin who had accepted the figures as true. However, mud sticks, and when, a few days later, Noël went on a month's holiday, who should be appointed his deputy but Barbier. Larrey was furious. Despite pleas by Charlotte and his surgical friends to keep quiet and ignore the insult, he wrote to the Minister of War stating the facts and asking for justice to be done. In reply, he was informed that his objection was ill-founded.[5]

Then, even before his first course in anatomy was completed, Larrey was uprooted yet again. This time the order from the Minister of War came at the request of the Commander-in-Chief of the Army in Italy. Villemanzy, the quartermaster-general to the army, had been Larrey's advocate since the days on the Rhine; he clearly appreciated the military significance of efficient casualty evacuation and strongly advised Bonaparte to have Larrey attached to his troops. So, on May 1, 1797, Larrey left Paris to join the victorious army of beggars that had crushed the Austrians in Northern Italy. But he left with a heavy heart. Charlotte had given birth to a son who had lived only a few short weeks.

5. The Flying Ambulance

The fighting was done when Larrey came to Italy. A half-starved army, motivated by an excess of revolutionary zeal, had swept down the Alps into the Plain of Lombardy to liberate their oppressed neighbours from the yoke of Austria. Their commander did not see the campaign in quite the same light. His objective was conquest and the furtherance of his own ambition. But he was the last one to let a little matter of semantics trouble his conscience. By superb generalship he beat the Austrians at Lodi, Arcola, and a host of lesser engagements, finally bringing them to their knees at Rivoli in January 1797. In so doing he had created a triumphant army that with General Bonaparte at its head, would dare anything for the glory of France.

Bonaparte did, nevertheless, free the people of northern Italy— of their works of art and of vast sums of money which he sent back to France by the wagon load and to the delight of the Directory. These five men were aware of the threat to their authority posed by the victorious general, yet it was a risk they had had to take. They believed they could control him. How wrong they were!

If the Directory did not know its Bonaparte, Bonaparte certainly knew his Europe. Spain was an ally of France. The Austrian Netherlands (Belgium) was in French hands. The third partitioning of Poland, in 1795, had ceased to be a distraction for Austria and Prussia, and Prussia was more concerned with gaining territory in the east and was at peace with France. Austria and England were thus the only serious challengers to French domination in Europe. Bonaparte realized quite clearly that the way to Austria, the first of the two to be tackled, lay through the back door of Italy. His initial victories in Lombardy made Sardinia and Naples sue for peace, and by the time he had shown his mettle at Rivoli, the Prussians saw the light and gave up all their land to the west of the

Rhine—much to the disgust of the Austrians who had been beating the French on the other side of the river.

When Larrey reached Milan towards the end of May, the preliminaries of peace had just been agreed at Leoben in the Austrian Alps. (A few months later, in October, the Treaty of Campo Formio between France and Austria was signed giving the Austrian Netherlands and Lombardy to France. As compensation, Austria received most of the free State of Venice which had been completely innocent of any part in the hostilities.)

Bonaparte himself had returned to Milan where he now made his headquarters. Despite the armistice, Larrey was ordered to prepare his flying ambulances as the General had in mind a direct attack on Austria across the Alps. But when Villemanzy invited him to come on a tour of the whole army to organize a complete system of casualty evacuation and base hospitals and to ensure that the medical staff was adequately trained, Larrey jumped at the opportunity.

They set out on May 25 for the north-east of Italy, and during the next two and a half months managed to bring some semblance of order to the filthy, insanitary, overcrowded, and disease-ridden conditions they encountered in most of the garrison towns. The army had an innate ability to turn its quarters into pig-sties. Its sick were left to rot. But rising above the physical squalor was the stench of corruption, and nowhere more so than in Milan. On his return, on August 15, Larrey wrote to Charlotte:

'Truly, before my arrival here the name of humanity was outlawed; it was banished into dark and fearful corners. It is of course pointless to talk of any sort of aid on the battlefield, but how did our gallant and loyal soldiers fare in hospital? No one can tell you better than the honest Villemanzy who visited them with me. Don't ask me to spell out their ghastly fate, it would break your heart and you would weep: even the thought of it fills me with despair. Good God, if only I could tell you that these brave men were now well! They are better, but one has always to be there to prevent abuses.'[1]

The Italians had bribed the Administration not to commandeer their monasteries and other large buildings for hospitals. The French quartermasters had accepted the arrangement eagerly and had compounded their crime by selling provisions, medicines, dressings, blankets, and paillasses to the local inhabitants.[2] The medical officers themselves were not blameless in this respect, and Bonaparte was moved to remark: 'It's a market place here, everything's for sale.'[3]

In his letter (of August 15) Larrey bemoaned his own honesty; many others were making fortunes whereas he had to look for every way possible to reduce his expenses and he warned Charlotte that she must do the same. This very real need for economy was a theme he kept returning to in his letters. Another was his marital faithfulness:

'Since my arrival in Italy, I have not had more than a week's rest. . . . Judge for yourself whether I have time to occupy myself with women who interest me not at all, and then you will know that here there is no one else. . . . Dream love, how I adore you. I think only of you, I live only for you, and all my longings are centred on you. Today you again entered into my soul; you won me and captured me with bonds that will last for ever; Larrey will always be your worthy and faithful lover.'

And he was as good as his word. No other woman ever came between them, though there must have been times when Charlotte could have wished for a more tangible rival than her husband's work. Larrey allowed nothing to interfere with what he believed to be the best for *his* sick and wounded and in Villemanzy he had a valuable ally. Shortly after their return, the Quartermaster-General set up a board of health which gave Larrey a free hand to proceed with organizing the evacuation of casualties. The heart of this organization was the flying ambulance proper—the vehicle —but for this to have life, it needed the support of a complex system, both medical and military. The medical staff of the army had no military rank and consequently no military authority; they were little more than civilians in uniform. Because of this, Larrey took great care to include elements from the army to give authority to his 'ambulances' in the field.

One 'ambulance' consisted of 340 men in three divisions with the chief surgeon in command, an arrangement that had the full approval of the Quartermaster-General and of Bonaparte.

A division of 113 men was made up as follows:[4]

A senior surgeon, who commanded the division.

Two assistant surgeons.

Twelve under-assistant surgeons, two of whom were to serve as pharmacists.

A lieutenant, serving as commissary officer.

A second-lieutenant from the military police, also acting as assistant commissary officer; nevertheless, he probably acted more in his primary function of maintaining order in the unit.

A mounted company sergeant-major [first sergeant] as chief clerk in charge of records.

Two mounted corporals as assistant clerks.

A mounted trumpeter who carried the surgical instruments.

Twelve mounted medical orderlies, to include a farrier, a bootmaker and a saddler.

A company sergeant-major [first sergeant]; another chief clerk.

Two supply sergeants as assistant clerks.

Three corporals as assistant clerks and for general duties.

A drummer in charge of surgical dressings. Twenty-five foot medical orderlies.

Each division (variously referred to by Larrey also as 'troops' or 'ambulances') had twelve light and four heavy vehicles. These required:

A company sergeant-major [first sergeant] in command.

A sergeant, second-in-command.

Two corporals, one of whom was a farrier.

A trumpeter.

Twenty supply train drivers. Until 1807 these probably were civilians hired by the contractor who provided the army's transport — though in 1796-97 Napoleon, far from Paris, had militarized the Army of Italy's trains.

'The uniform of the surgeons attached to the ambulance was like that of other army surgeons. They carried a lightly ornamented, black morocco pouch, or cartridge box, divided into several compartments to hold a case of surgical instruments, various medicines, and the articles necessary for giving immediate assistance to the wounded on the field of battle. They wore a sword—for decoration and defence—and a black leather belt.

'The uniforms of the administrative officers were of different colours and ornamented according to their rank. The commissioned officers had epaulets.

'The medical orderlies wore a short uniform jacket with a red woollen sash that served, in case of emergency, to carry the wounded; their shakos were of black felt, ornamented with leather and brass. The mounted orderlies were issued with short cloaks and hussar-type boots; each man carried a black leather knapsack containing one or two trays, a tin mug, two blankets for the wounded, and everything necessary for attending to a wounded horse. They wore a small sabre suspended from a chamois leather belt. The medical orderlies on foot had greatcoats and wore stout shoes with black cloth gaiters. They carried leather bags holding reserve supplies of surgical dressings.

'The uniform of the 20 soldiers attached to the vehicles was cut along similar lines, though simpler and made of coarser cloth. The different ranks of these men were indicated by the colour of their collars and lapels and by the ornamentation of their jackets.

'The trappings of a horse belonging to a medical officer consisted of a French saddle with a saddle-cloth the same colour as that of the uniform of the rider and edged with gold braid to an extent depending on the grade of the officer. Instead of pistol holsters, I supplied them with two saddle-bags the flaps of which were also edged with gold braid—these bags proved far more useful than holsters. A small leather portmanteau was also fixed to the saddle; it contained dressings and could be opened easily without disturbing its holding straps. The trappings of the medical orderlies' horses were generally similar, though inferior in quality and ornamentation.

'Each division had twelve light, well-sprung carriages (flying ambulances) for the transportation of the wounded. Eight of these had two wheels, and were designed for use in flat country; the other four had four wheels and were intended primarily for use in mountainous terrain.

'The small carriage resembled an elongated cube, curved on the top. It had two small windows—for ventilation—on each side, and double doors at both ends. The floor of the carriage could be slid easily in and out along the side beams and over four central rollers. It was furnished with a horse-hair mattress and bolster, both covered with leather. The side panels were padded for about a foot above the floor. Four metal handles were set into the wood of the floor to take the straps or sashes of the orderlies when these were used as stretchers. The wounded could be dressed on the sliding floors if the weather was too bad for this to be done on the ground. The carriage was about 44 inches wide, and could carry two patients lying at full length. Lining the sides were several pockets to hold bottles and other necessities for the sick. These carriages, drawn by two horses—one ridden—combined solidarity with lightness and elegance.

'The four-wheeled carriage was longer and wider than the two-wheeled version, although of essentially similar external design. Inside, however, the floor and its mattress were fixed. The padding and pockets were the same, but the left side opened for almost the whole of its length by two sliding doors, so that the wounded could be laid inside. Four men could be accommodated, though they had to lie with their legs slightly bent. Small windows were provided at intervals. A wheel-barrow slung underneath served a number of useful purposes; there was a place at the back for carrying forage. The carriage was drawn by four horses, with two drivers. Manœuvrability was increased by a swivelling front axle.

'(When the army was fighting in rugged mountainous country we found we could not do without mules or pack-horses equipped with panniers to carry the materials for dressings, the surgical instruments, medicines, and so forth.)

'We set up an administrative committee with the members chosen from among the medical and administrative officers of each division. The order of march, internal discipline and policing, and the duties of every individual were laid down in special rules.

'The function of the organization was to rescue the wounded on the field of battle and, having given first aid, to transport them to the first line of hospitals.

'A secondary duty was the removal of the dead for burial. This job was given to the unmounted medical orderlies under the direction of the military police lieutenant who was authorized to requisition the labour from the local inhabitants.

'These ambulances can follow the most rapid movements of the advance guard. When necessary, they can separate into a great many subdivisions, as every medical officer is mounted and has at his command a flying ambulance, a mounted orderly, and everything necessary for giving the earliest assistance on the field of battle.'[5]

Thus did Larrey describe one of the greatest things, in principle as well as in practice, that has ever happened to military surgery. But in his pursuance of humanity he could not help treading on the wrong people's toes; in the instructions to his officers he wrote: 'The casualties rescued by the flying ambulances will be assembled with all speed at a central point where the most seriously wounded will be operated on by the Surgeon-in-Chief or, under his direction, by a competent surgeon.' This was fine, but he continued: 'We will always start with the most dangerously injured, without regard to rank or distinction.'[6]

While in Milan, where he established a school of surgery and gave the first clinical lectures, Larrey visited Bonaparte's headquarters at the castle of Montebello. Something had happened to the pale, pimply officer that Larrey remembered from Toulon. The man who had shared hardships with his Republican soldiers, now shared the fruits of conquest with his officers. Bonaparte had beaten the best in Europe; the army, from the highest to the lowest, recognized his authority with worship; his own government recognized it with alarm; and other governments recognized it with fear. And Bonaparte wore the mantle of his authority with the ease of a born sovereign.

The castle was more a glittering court than a military headquarters, thanks largely to Bonaparte's womenfolk. Intelligent and ambitious, they allowed no one to forget their relationship to the victorious general—gracious and frivolous Josephine, who took immense pleasure in being called 'Citizeness Bonaparte'; Élisa, the eldest sister and the most like her brother in character; Pauline, outrageously beautiful and aware of it; Caroline, already at fifteen married to the dashing Murat; and, dominating the whole Bonaparte family, Madame Letitia, their mother.

Paying court to the array of beauty assembled at Montebello were the princes, dukes, and marshals of tomorrow, dazzling in their new uniforms; still, perhaps, unsure of reality but determined to live a dream life to the full—Berthier, in his mid-forties older than most, and Bonaparte's extremely able chief of staff; Murat the incomparable horseman; beloved Lannes, promoted in the field at Millesimo the previous year; Duroc with the baby face; moustachioed Lasalle; Junot, a sergeant at Toulon; Marmont; Augereau; Masséna; . . .

In striking contrast were the sombrely clad scholars, professors of the arts and sciences, whom Bonaparte was gathering around his person. Even at this early stage he was imagining himself as another Alexander of Macedon and was certainly not going to be outdone so far as the gathering and dissemination of culture were concerned.

When Larrey entered the strange world of Montebello Castle he was vaguely perturbed at the portent of all this magnificence; it seemed that here was the rebirth of one of the things the Revolution had been about. But the General welcomed him with favour and asked all the right questions about his flying ambulances. Bonaparte could inspire an unswerving devotion that was blind to all his faults and injustices; and, like so many before and since, Larrey was enticed into the web. He fell completely under the spell of the man, a spell not even death could break.

At Montebello Larrey received orders to report to the headquarters of the advance guard under the command of General Jean Baptiste Bernadotte at Udine. Here he met his old friend Desaix who was on a tour of Bonaparte's battlefields and asked Larrey to accompany him to Trieste. As Desaix wished to remain incognito the two men set off in civilian clothes by post-chaise and with but one servant, an arrangement that suited the General better than it did the surgeon.

At Monfalcone, Larrey was most upset by the insolent behaviour of some French officers, also travelling to Trieste, over the post horses which were in short supply. Desaix took the whole affair quite calmly and afterwards, when Larrey apologized on behalf of the officers who had discovered their rank, he merely said:

'What, my dear Larrey, are you still worrying about that? I had forgotten the matter as soon as we were outside the door.'[7]

Desaix's reason for going to Trieste and the immense interest he took in the port and the men-of-war, which he was seeing for the first time, puzzled Larrey—he did not find out until later that the General had been given a leading role in a projected sea-borne invasion. At the end of the day they returned to their inn where they dined amid a large company composed chiefly of Austrian generals and staff-officers. Supposing the two Frenchmen in civilian dress to be from the Administration, these officers loudly praised the French soldiers and the generals who had gained immortality. After discussing the brilliance of Bonaparte they moved on to Desaix who had covered himself with glory on the Rhine. The subject of these eulogies quietly rose from the table and slipped away, dragging a reluctant Larrey after him.

By now it was the middle of October: the Treaty of Campo Formio was signed; Desaix returned to France; and Bonaparte began a tour of inspection of his army with the advance guard at Udine. Larrey, who had been carrying out daily manœuvres with the first division of his ambulance, put on a dramatic performance for the Commander-in-Chief. Bonaparte was duly impressed.

'Your work is one of the greatest conceptions of our age,' he complimented Larrey. 'It alone will suffice to ensure your reputation.'[8]

The second division in Padua also went throuth its paces before the General who thoroughly approved the details of the individual carriages as well as the military competence of the whole organization. He ordered 100 livres and a testimonial to be given to Larrey together with a grant of 2,400 livres to be used in the next campaign—needless to say Larrey never received the money. As a more personal mark of his regard, Bonaparte commissioned a portrait of Larrey from Andrea Appiani who had recently painted the General.

Great credit for Larrey's success must, however, go to Villemanzy who, in view of the appalling administration of the army medical services, was quite exceptional in encouraging the surgeon's schemes.[9] It was largely thanks to his recommendations that when Larrey returned to Paris he had the praises of the Commander-in-Chief ringing in his ears.

But the domestic interlude was short lived. He had scarcely started the winter course in anatomy at Val-de-Grâce when orders came for him to join, as one of three surgeons-in-chief, the army preparing for the invasion of England. He was to be attached to the right wing, commanded by General Desaix, with its head-quarters at Lille. As he was on the verge of setting out, these orders were countered by fresh ones. It was back to Toulon yet again.

'Little did I think, when I received the government order to join the Mediterranean expedition at Toulon, that I was destined to follow the French army, under the command of General Bonaparte, into the richest and most interesting country of the world.'[10]

6. *Army of the Orient*

Larrey was in his thirty-second year when he was appointed Surgeon-in-Chief to the mystery tour gathering in Toulon. The exciting years, the years of glory and disaster under Napoleon Bonaparte, were about to begin. They were years in which many were to make their names immortal, and many, many more were to prove their mortal nature. Although Larrey had already produced the innovations—in treatment and administration—on which his fame now rests, he needed the coming wars to make that fame secure. The seeds he had sown required his ability and cool, competent hands to bring them into flower; but this could happen only in the harsh soil of war.

Yet though he accepted the challenge of active service, he always hated having to leave Charlotte—more especially now as she was six months' pregnant. 'I am worried about the possible length of the coming expedition, particularly as I am ignorant of its destination and purpose,' Larrey confided to his journal while on his way to Toulon. 'My heart is sad; I have left behind a wife whom I love and cherish. When shall I see her again? That is something I can neither foretell nor guess.'[1]

Larrey made the journey in company with René Nicolas Dufriche Desgenettes, the army's Physician-in-Chief. The paths of the two men were destined to run parallel for much of their careers and they became for a long while firm friends, each with a tremendous respect for the qualities of the other, though they came from widely different backgrounds. Desgenettes was thirty-four, the son of a property-owning lawyer in Alençon and of a minor noblewoman; he was, in reality, Baron Des Genettes, but times being what they were he had dropped his title and modified his name. He had, anyway, Revolutionary sympathies and had occasionally taken part in public demonstrations. Desgenettes was an extremely able and courageous man, but—probably a result of his upbringing—he was easy-going and lacked the drive and determination of his surgical colleague.

The two doctors arrived in Toulon on April 3, 1798, where they found the preparations for the expedition well advanced, though no one who could tell them where it was bound. But there was no time for speculation. Orders were issued to the senior medical officers to recruit the assistants they would need and to procure all necessary stores—neither easy to estimate when working in the dark. However, Larrey played safe and wrote to the medical schools of Montpellier and Toulouse asking them to send him as many trained surgeons as possible. The response was immediate; every eligible man volunteered and by the time the expedition was ready to sail Larrey had under his command 108 surgeons for his ambulance divisions as well as the surgeons attached to the different units of the army.

The force these surgeons were to serve was about 33,000 strong, consisting of 44 battalions of infantry, 28 squadrons of cavalry, and some 4,000 artillerymen and engineers. (The total number going to Egypt was over 20,000 more than this, as it included Bonaparte's staff, the members of the Commission of Arts and Sciences, seamen, marines, and naval gunners.)

Part of the expedition was leaving from Italy and thither Larrey dispatched the requisite number of surgeons. Those remaining in Toulon were given the task, essential before every campaign, of preparing wound dressings—30 chests-full—and of attending the military hospitals for practical instruction by Larrey's senior surgeons.

Larrey himself commandeered all the surgical instruments and equipment he thought he would need, as well as a large number of easily transportable folding stretchers. In the process he flouted the instructions laid down by the Administration which, emanating as they did from Paris, were completely out of touch with reality. Larrey knew what he wanted and how to get it quickly—and to hell with regulations. When Bonaparte arrived on May 9 he thoroughly approved of his Surgeon-in-Chief's display of initiative, but considered it wise that the situation should be regularized. Accordingly he asked Larrey to send him a note. 'Citizen general' (Larrey wrote),

'When I arrived in Toulon on your orders, I found that I would require a far greater latitude than had been obtained from the Minister if I was to organize properly the service you required of me.

'To attain this end, it was necessary to set aside the usual regulations. The Minister's department cannot, at this great distance, judge our need and only hampers our operations. We hope you will save us from reproach by approving our conduct.'[2]

On May 13 the expedition began to embark. Larrey carefully distributed the men and equipment of the ambulance divisions among the principal ships in such a way that, should the fleet be split by accident or design, there would always be adequate surgical cover for the troops on landing. The surgeons attached to the army units, each with his own instruments and dressing kit, were spread throughout the convoy; no ship carrying a hundred or more men was thus without a surgeon.

While Larrey had been organizing the surgical side, Desgenettes had been busy looking after the medical arrangements. Between them they had gathered everything necessary for equipping and supplying the hospitals of wherever it was they might be going, and all these stores were put on board one of the three hospital ships. The fate of this vessel taught Larrey a lesson he never forgot. She was sunk by the British at the Battle of the Nile and the loss of her cargo later caused great distress and inconvenience. It was the last time that Larrey put all his eggs in one basket.

In the evening of the nineteenth the Toulon roads presented a fine sight as close on 200 ships set sail into the gathering dusk. The quayside was packed with cheering, waving citizens, and everywhere on land and sea bands were beating out their tunes of glory. The focal point of the whole affair was the departure of *Orient*, Admiral François Paul Brueys' flagship and the temporary home of the Commander-in-Chief, his personal staff, the principal members of the Commission of Arts and Sciences, and the senior physicians and surgeons. At long last the French had managed to get an expedition out of Toulon, but it was thanks to a convenient gale that some days previously had blown the blockading British fleet in disorder towards Sardinia. By the time Rear-Admiral Sir

Horatio Nelson had repaired the damage to *Vanguard*, his flagship, Bonaparte had slipped away. No matter what was about to happen on land the key to the whole situation lay in the command of the sea, so when Nelson discovered what had happened, he set off in pursuit. But before the game of hide-and-seek was ended Bonaparte had reached his destination. He did, however, spare a week to besiege and capture Malta. On June 18, the expedition, now swollen to almost 400 ships, with an escort of 14 ships of the line and 40 frigates, left the island and set off eastwards for—as everyone had guessed—Egypt.

On the evening of July 1 the fleet anchored in the bay of Marabout, about 12 miles west of Alexandria. Bonaparte was advised against landing immediately as there was a strong wind blowing and a heavy sea running, but he could not risk the British appearing and, besides, he wanted to surprise the Turks before they could organize their defence. Good luck was with them as boat-load after boat-load reached the beach without serious mishap. The only anxious moment was when the popular General Maximilien Caffarelli, in command of the engineers, managed to get his wooden leg tangled up in the rigging and fell overboard. Larrey leaped into the sea and dragged him through the surf to the safety of dry land.

Ten thousand men—the divisions of Kléber, Menou, and Bon —formed up in three columns on the flat, desolate shore of Africa, and at three o'clock in the morning began their march across the sands to Alexandria. Larrey attached an ambulance division to each column, himself marching with the centre close to the Commander-in-Chief and in a position where he could keep an eye on all three ambulances.

Alexandria capitulated before the day was through. Its defenders were no match for the French—particularly when they had the bit of liberation clamped firmly between their jaws—and, one way or another, the liberation potential was high as the inhabitants were made up of four principal races: Mamelukes, Turks, Arabs, and Copts.

To emphasize his point Bonaparte issued a proclamation to the besieged Alexandrians:

'We have no quarrel with you. We wish only to free you from

the oppression of the Mamelukes. Surrender now and I assure you we shall respect your religious faith and your customs.'[3]

The Turkish commander agreed with these sentiments and by the time darkness fell the harbour and all the forts of the city were securely in French hands. More than 500 Arabs and Turks had been killed in the fighting, and many more than this had been shot when found with arms in their possession. The French had 250 wounded, including the second-in-command, Jean Baptiste Kléber, who received a scalp wound above the right temple, but one nevertheless that exposed the bone.[4] Larrey, heedless of the danger, was close behind and able to give immediate first aid—with the General sitting at the foot of Pompey's column. During the assault Jacques Menou was wounded six times as well as being thrown from the top of the ramparts. The Revolutionary generals certainly knew how to lead from the front.

By now the entire expeditionary force had been disembarked and preparations were rapidly made for the march on Cairo. But first Bonaparte looked to his lines of communication. He was still extremely worried about the possibility of losing his fleet to the English and, as he considered the Alexandrian anchorage vulnerable, he sent Admiral Brueys to Aboukir Bay. The Admiral was instructed to dispatch a squadron up the Nile to rendezvous with the land forces and then to anchor in the bay—but if there was doubt about the safety of the anchorage he was to head for Corfu. To complete this part of the operation and secure his rear, Napoleon sent General Charles Dugua along the coast to take Rosetta, which he did without trouble.

Having a pretty shrewd idea of the conditions they were likely to meet on the march, Larrey had aquired some camels to carry many of the stores and provisions for his own ambulance division. But on the evening before the army left, these camels were filched by the quartermaster. Bonaparte knew of this, but did not intervene. The immediate needs of the military for transport took precedence over all else and Larrey had no authority to complain. So, accepting the situation philosophically, he divided the necessities among his officers and men.

On July 6, with Kléber left in command at Alexandria, the march on Cairo began. Instead of going round by Rosetta, Bonaparte took a short cut across the desert to Damanhur, apparently unaware that his troops would be unable to live off the land and that they were still unacclimatized.

'The main body of the army, without provisions or water, entered the arid desert and on the fourth day of a terrible march reached Damanhur. Never had an army experienced such great hardships and such acute privations. Scorched by the rays of a merciless sun, we marched on foot for mile after endless mile across the burning sand amid unrelieved desolation. Only with difficulty were we able to find a little stagnant water in pools that were scarcely liquid. Parched with thirst and overcome by the heat, the strongest soldiers collapsed under the weight of their equipment.'[5]

The appearance of mirages added to the distress and, for some, the disappointment of reality proved the last straw. When Larrey reached these men in time he was able to revive many with sips of water, laced with brandy, from the leather bottle he always carried with him. Death, to those he could not save, came gently. One soldier in his dying moments told him, 'I feel myself in a state of inexpressible happiness.'[6]

Not so fortunate were the stragglers. Despite Bonaparte having kept his word in Alexandria, his message of liberation seemed not to have had the desired effect on the local inhabitants. Bands of Arab horsemen continuously hovered around the marching column and attacked the strays, killing them on the spot or carrying them off to be painfully disposed of at leisure. Among the first to go in this manner was one of Larrey's surgeons who had fallen back to give first aid.

And Damanhur did little to relieve the despondency. It had been—and was to be again—fertile country, but under the Turks the Nile had gradually silted up and the desert had encroached upon its banks. The village was a miserable place and although Bonaparte's thousands could slake their thirst, the food they found was utterly insufficient for their needs. But at least they had a a brief respite from the merciless desert march, and the few who had been wounded had their injuries dressed.

To cap their troubles Bonaparte was kicked viciously in the right leg by his Arab horse. The damage was more than mere bruising as it appears likely there was active bleeding into the tissues. Larrey released the blood through a small skin incision, applied a dressing, and did his best to make the General rest. But Bonaparte would have none of it—if anything he was even more energetic than usual. Larrey could not insist; he simply dressed the injury twice a day and prayed. His prayers were answered and by the time Bonaparte reached the Pyramids the wound had healed completely.[7] Normally, Larrey would have left the dressing undisturbed for a few days, but the importance of his patient compelled him to interfere frequently to check that all was well— a clouding of judgment that might easily have invited the very complications he feared.

From Damanhur, the army set off directly for the river about 20 miles to the east. It came in sight, like a Promised Land, at El Rahmaniya. For two days the army paused, gathering its strength from the waters of the Nile and from the abundance of water-melons. Two events brought the halt to an end. The first was the arrival of the squadron from Aboukir with General Dugua's men (including Desgenettes) aboard. The second was news that a Mameluke force was drawn up in battle order at Shubra Khit a few miles further south. Bonaparte at once gave the order to march and as dawn broke on July 13 the two armies came face to face.

The engagement began as a river battle between the French squadron, which had accidentally outdistanced the land forces, and a blockade of Egyptian gunboats aided by shore batteries. Things at first went badly for the French. They lost most of the sick and wounded (who had been transferred to the ships at El Rahmaniya) and a quantity of stores and ammunition. But when the land battle began the tables were turned and the Mamelukes learned what they were really up against. Their commander, Mourad Bey, had seriously underestimated the quality of his opponent and had committed only about 4,000 of his cavalry. These men, fighters born and bred, charged the French in a wild, courageous mass. Yet individual valour was no match for the discipline and tactics of a European army, and what was left of the Bey's horsemen retreated south in disorder.

Later, when Bonaparte inspected the field dressing station,

and mindful of the fate of Larrey's transport, he was surprised to see operations in progress and no lack of dressings. His amazement grew when he found rum being given to the wounded, as he believed all spirits had been lost in the river battle. When Larrey explained that the rum had been given by Jean Baptiste Bessières from his personal store, he replied,

'Bessières is truly a kind-hearted man; and you, Larrey, because of your foresight, are always performing miracles.'[8]

The army continued along the west bank of the Nile delta, harassed all the way by bands of Arab horsemen and tormented by the burning heat. Every evening they washed away the fatigue of the day in the river, but they still had to sustain themselves on endless water-melons and what little grain they could find and grind by hand. On the afternoon of July 21 they came to the Pyramids where Mourad Bey had regrouped his forces and prepared a reception worthy of his adversary.

In the centre were 10,000 Mameluke horsemen, the heart of the Egyptian army, their richly jewelled clothing and equipment sparkling in the sun, their vicious Damascus sabres flashing like white-hot flames. On their right the fortified camp of Embabeh, with the river immediately behind it, was in the confident hands of the Turkish infantry and the fellaheen. On their left were the Pyramids and several thousand Arab horsemen. In all, some 60,000 men, arrogantly confident of victory, awaited the sweaty, tired, and hungry French. But the sight was what the heroes of Italy needed to rouse their jaded spirits. It was also what Bonaparte needed to prove that his genius in Italy had not been a fluke.

'Soldiers, you are about to fight the tyrants of Egypt. Remember, fourteen centuries will be watching you from there,'[9] and he pointed to the top of the Great Pyramid of Cheops. The answering cheer rippled the long sleep of the dead.

Desaix, on the French right in command of his own division and that of Jean Louis Reynier, was ordered forward to drive a wedge between the enemy centre and left with the object of enveloping and isolating the Mamelukes. Mourad Bey saw at once what the French intended and unleashed 8,000 of the best horsemen in Egypt on a dramatic but undisciplined charge. As if by magic the advancing columns of infantry were transformed into squares and in complete silence awaited the onslaught. It was an unnerving experience for the Mamelukes who had never before encountered this sort of defence. Time and again they threw themselves with increasing desperation at the impenetrable walls of French musket-fire and bayonets, but all they achieved was their own slaughter. At last they broke off the engagement and retired on their original positions, only to find that the French centre, under Dugua, was in their rear. In utter confusion, what remained of a fine body of courageous individuals, fled south.

Meanwhile, Louis Bon and Menou had taken Embabeh at the point of the bayonet—a task made easy by the discovery that the guns all pointed in one, fixed, direction—and had driven the survivors into the river where some succeeded in reaching the east bank and the army of Ibrahim Bey at Cairo. But as old Ibrahim was not prepared to wait and suffer the same fate as his colleague, he gathered together his treasure and his slaves and made off for Syria just as fast as his camels would carry him.

The Battle of the Pyramids gave Egypt to the French. They inflicted extremely heavy losses on the Egyptians, particularly the Mamelukes, at a cost to themselves of about 30 killed and 250 wounded. Larrey, with his ambulance division, was close to Bonaparte and the headquarters staff in the middle of Dugua's division. As always, he treated and dressed anyone, friend or foe, who needed his skill. This display of humanity astonished the Mamelukes since it was completely foreign to their own code of conduct, yet—and this is something not generally expected of such a people—they were most appreciative of kindness. As the tide of battle moved on, a minor bey, mortally wounded in the belly and lying beside his dead horse, appeared in the headquarter square. Larrey came to his side and, kneeling down, tenderly dressed the ragged gun-shot wound. The bey removed a magnificent ruby ring from his finger and gave it to Larrey saying,

'I have no more need of this; look after it carefully.'[10] It was his talisman, and Larrey wore it until it was torn from him at Waterloo.

After the battle Bonaparte wanted to show his special appreciation of Larrey's work and, since medical officers were ineligible for

rrey's camel pannier

rcy's ambulance

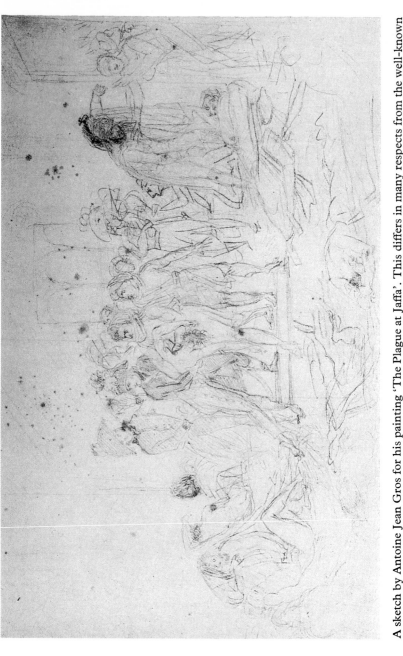

A sketch by Antoine Jean Gros for his painting 'The Plague at Jaffa'. This differs in many respects from the well-known final version. In particular Bonaparte is here shown helping to move a corpse; in the painting he merely extends his

the pecuniary perks that came the way of combatant officers, he had to act indirectly.

'I beg you,' he wrote to the Directory in Paris, 'to pay a gratuity of 1,200 livres to the wife of citizen Larrey. He has rendered us, in the middle of the desert, most excellent service by his assiduity and zeal. I know him to be the best qualified medical officer to be in command of an army's ambulances.'[11]

On July 25 Bonaparte crossed the Nile and took possession of an undefended Cairo. In spite of its dejected appearance the city was immensely rich and Larrey had no problems in luxuriously fitting out a number of buildings as hospitals. To these he brought the sick and wounded from Giza. Among their number was twenty-eight-year-old General Étienne Mireur who, in distinguishing himself at the recent battle, had received a slight sabre wound of the right shoulder which Larrey had dressed. By now well on the way to recovery, he was sent by Bonaparte with a message to Admiral Brueys telling him to sail immediately with the entire fleet to Corfu, where he was to pick up reinforcements of men and materials and return to Egypt.[12]

But the luxury of Cairo was not to be enjoyed just yet. There was work to be done. Desaix was sent after Mourad Bey's disorganized force. General Honoré Vial was sent north to Damietta to take the town and to explore Lake Manzala. Bonaparte himself first saw to the affairs of government, protecting—as at Alexandria—all the local habits, customs, and religions. Severe punishment was meted out to any of his soldiers who broke the rules and failed to respect either institutions or persons. Then, on August 5, at the head of part of his army, the Commander-in-Chief set out in pursuit of Ibrahim Bey with Larrey in charge of the accompanying ambulance division. The Bey was defeated at the battle of El Salhiya and in high spirits the expedition returned to Cairo. Egypt was now unquestionably theirs. But Fate had a cruel shock in store for them. The first news Bonaparte received when he entered his headquarters was of the Battle of the Nile. On August 1 Nelson had sailed into the shallows of Aboukir Bay on the landward side of the unsuspecting French fleet and blown it, for all practical purposes, out of existence. General Mireur, with the order that would have saved it, had been killed by Arabs.

'The death of this young warrior', Larrey wrote, 'was the cause of the loss of our fleet, of the capture of Malta, and, consequently, of the loss of Egypt, for the dispatches that Mireur was carrying concerned the defence of Malta and the reinforcement of the army of the Orient. One can readily judge how profound was the tragedy caused by the death of this envoy not only to our army but to the whole of France.'[12]

7. *Shackled by Unbreakable Chains*

'We no longer have a fleet,' said the Commander-in-Chief. 'Ah well, we will either have to stay in these lands, or make a grand exodus like the ancients.'[1]

In gaining a country, Bonaparte had lost an empire. The English, with their infuriating habit of winning when it really mattered, had cut his communications with France. His plan of hitting at England through India—which served only to mask his dream of out-Alexandering Alexander—lay shattered beneath the waters of Aboukir Bay. His disappointment was intense, yet before a day or two had passed he had risen above it and was organizing all manner of cultural and scientific schemes and laying preliminary plans for his departure. He certainly had no intention of remaining in Egypt and the only way of getting back to France was round the eastern end of the Mediterranean through Syria and Turkey, fighting if he could not negotiate a peaceful journey.

On August 20, 1798, he brought the Institute of Egypt into being with the object of documenting every conceivable facet of Egyptian life from the remote past to his own day. This kept the scholars happily employed and disinclined to worry about their isolation from France. Desgenettes and Antoine Dubois (the doctor on the Commission of Arts and Sciences) were the founder members representing medicine and surgery, though subsequently Larrey was elected to fill the gap left by Dubois' being invalided home early in October with an 'obstinate dysentery'. Larrey took this opportunity to send a letter to Charlotte.

'If you only knew, my dearest Laville, the extent of our privations and miseries and what I have suffered during this unhappy expedition. Dubois will put you in the picture. But Fate is not done with us yet! I am one of those who are shackled by unbreakable chains to the chariot of the modern Alexander; and so long as it pleases him to lead, all who are united to him are bound to follow. I share his career, though where it will take me or what its limits and perils I have no means of knowing.'[2]

Larrey's loyalty to Bonaparte and his sense of duty helped him to overcome his bouts of despair. But the morale of the army had fallen to a very low level after news of the Battle of the Nile reached Cairo, and the generals in particular were most disgruntled. They had been prepared to follow Bonaparte through the familiar hardships of Italy when it had been victory all the way. The hell fires of Egypt were another matter entirely; reality was a rude shock to their systems, and now that all seemed lost, confidence in their leader was ebbing fast. On the verge of mutiny, they sent General Alexandre Dumas—a giant of a man in size, courage, and reputation and the father and grandfather of the famous Dumas authors—to confront Bonaparte with their demand that the Directory should recall the army.

Bonaparte received Dumas alone. With a calculated display of icy anger he dominated the interview; so much so that the other left without saying why he had come. Bonaparte had shown the generals beyond doubt who was master. Nevertheless, a number of senior officers tried to get home on medical grounds. To deal with the situation, Bonaparte gave Larrey and Desgenettes the unenviable task of sitting as a board to assess the merits of each case. In an atmosphere of corruption both remained untouched and were furious when one general attempted to bribe them with a magnificent Turkish saddle for Desgenettes and a beautiful Damascus sword for Larrey.

'What do you take us for?' Desgenettes cried. 'Take away your gifts, and be good enough to address them only to those as capable of receiving them as you are of offering them.'[3]

There were, however, all too many soldiers who had earned their repatriation for medical reasons. Quite apart from those disabled by war wounds were those blinded by ophthalmia, a mixed infection that appeared among the troops shortly after their arrival in Egypt and one that continued to be a menace until they left the country.[4] From time to time the disease assumed epidemic proportions, as it did among Desaix's troops in their pursuit of Mourad Bey. This division had an extremely hard time since the Mamelukes decoyed them into long, futile marches into the desert, but eventually the two forces met at Sediman where the French won a decisive, though not an easy, victory.

The news of Desaix's victory and subsequent conquest of Upper Egypt helped restore morale in Cairo, and on the surface everything seemed to be going as well as could be hoped. Underneath trouble was brewing. A large number of Mamelukes had infiltrated the city in disguise and at daybreak on October 21, 1798, they fell on the French with savage ferocity. By good fortune General Dominique Dupuy, Commander of Cairo, had discovered what was afoot and was ready for the uprising, but as he led the first counter-attack he was mortally wounded. Larrey, following close behind, gave first aid.[5]

This deed could well have saved his own life, since when he reached the main hospital he found, to his horror, the bodies of his two senior surgeons, Roussel and Mongin, among a mangled, bloody pile at the gate. 'They indeed succeeded in causing the asylum of the sick to be respected, but it was at the expense of their own lives.'[6]

The French quickly and ruthlessly brought the situation under control. They themselves had 40 wounded in the whole affair but 12,500 Egyptians of all races perished—a slaughter that, for a time, effectively squashed further thought of rebellion throughout the country.

Roussel and Mongin were buried in the grounds of the hospital and, in a spasm of Gallic emotion, Larrey ordered a fulsome epitaph to be inscribed on a wall: 'You who come here to study the secrets of our art, go tell our fathers that we shed our blood as heroes.'[7]

More practically, he wrote letters of sympathy to their fathers, both medical men, and of recommendation to the inspector general of the medical service. He also wrote to his Uncle Alexis, since Dupuy and a medical officer killed at Sediman had come from Toulouse and had been personal friends:

'I am profiting from the departure to France of about 50 soldiers, permanently disabled on account of complete blindness or the loss of limbs, to send you my news and to charge you at the same time with carrying out a sad mission to the parents of General Dupuy and citizen Luent, medical officer. This young surgeon

E

died of wounds received at the battle of Sediman fought on October 7 between Desaix and the forces of Mourad Bey. I enclose his death certificate which I ask you to give to his family with my own deep regrets and those of his comrades. Will you also give them the sum of . . . , the proceeds of the authorized sale of his effects.

'With regard to the unhappy Dupuy, my friend; his name is found inscribed in the list of heroes who shed their blood for the conquest of Egypt and, in consequence, for the prosperity of the Republic. I had myself just passed through the blood-thirsty mob that had attacked him when I came upon him calling for my help. He was in the gravest danger as a lance-thrust had caused a large wound which had cut the axillary artery and opened the left side of his chest. All his blood was gushing out. I gave him first aid, but nature made fruitless all my efforts to recall him to life. Several moments later he died asking me to remember him to his family. Will you, my dear uncle, console them and ease their grief.

'His death, and that of several other true friends whom I had the misfortune to lose on that day, has been avenged. The army is now secure and all is calm and peaceful. Everything points to the colony becoming established without difficulty and under the happiest of auspices. So far as the expedition itself is concerned, I don't know whether its sole purpose was the conquest of Egypt; time alone will show us.

'For myself, although my family calls, the well-being of the service demands that I stay at my post until the end of the expedition. Please reassure my wife and give her all the consolation that you can: you will increase my gratitude and the sincere affection that I shall always bear you.'[8]

Towards the end of January (1799) Bonaparte ordered Larrey to check on the surgical staffing of the regiments and demi-brigades and to ensure that the senior positions were held by those with the highest grade and the longest service. It was now no longer enough for the ambulance divisions to be the only effective—and more or less independent—source of casualty evacuation; surgical efficiency, at both practical and administrative levels, had to be sustained throughout the army. Larrey had almost convinced Napoleon Bonaparte that military medicine was an essential part of warfare. Nevertheless, hard on the heels of his order Bonaparte directed that a young surgeon should be promoted. Larrey's reply firmly, yet gently, put the general in his place.

'There are only 60 places for surgeons of the first class in all the Republic. These places are allotted to those who, besides enthusiasm, courage, long service, and outstanding talent, possess a profound knowledge as revealed by practical examination.

'Citizen Couste has neither the experience nor the knowledge required to pass this grade. However, his conduct is praiseworthy and he is zealous in the treatment of the sick in his hospital; but the answers he gave in my examination of the medical officers of the eighteenth demi-brigade were not of the same merit as those of Citizen Vattat. Moreover, this officer has served for longer and has practised surgery with distinction for 30 years. I have charged him with the surgical direction of the aforesaid corps.'[9]

He got away with it. In fact, the possibility that he might not have done never entered his head. But a few days later he was faced with a far more serious problem—plague.

'In correspondence from Alexandria, Damietta, and Mansura, I learned that a malignant fever, with carbuncles or buboes in the groins and axillae, had appeared in these towns and was on the rampage. It was particularly bad in Alexandria where several naval medical officers had died. Two or three cases had already appeared in Cairo; one of these was a soldier of the thirty-second demi-brigade who was admitted to hospital with a blackish pimple on his lip which, in two or three hours, became a carbuncle. He died the next day.

'I hurriedly removed the body as it bore all the appearances of plague, burnt the man's personal effects and bedclothes, and ordered the room where I had isolated him to be fumigated. I was convinced he had died of plague and told only my colleague, the Physician-in-Chief, of my fears. Nevertheless, I took the step of sending a circular letter to all surgeons of the first class telling them to care for patients with this fever in their usual manner, but to take precautions against contagion.'[10]

Ideas about the nature of plague were utterly confused, although official policy at the start of the campaign in Egypt was to ignore it and hope it would go away. This explains Larrey's action; though, being a sensible fellow, he hedged his bet. Later, when the disease became epidemic in the army he was extremely annoyed with himself and everyone else for having taken this ostrich-like attitude. It was while he and Desgenettes were busily sweeping the unwelcome disease under the carpet, that Bonaparte made his intentions known. The French army was to make a grand exodus through Syria. Everyone busied himself in preparation.

'As the coming expedition seemed likely to be perilous and difficult, I believed we would have a large number of casualties. The means of transporting them was my first concern, for it was necessary not only to dress the wounded on the field of battle, but also to carry them beyond the reach of the Arabs and to save them from the horrors of hunger and thirst to which they would be exposed if not evacuated promptly. The camel was the only means of conveyance the country offered. I therefore ordered a hundred panniers to be made, two for each camel and constructed in the form of a cradle that hung on each side of its hump by elastic straps. Their design was such as not to impede the animal. When a removable footboard was in place, a pannier could carry a man lying at full length.'[11]

However, before leaving for Syria Larrey had one self-imposed task to perform. Some while previously an English frigate had run aground off Alexandria. The officers and crew were regarded as prisoners-of-war and incarcerated in the dungeons of the Cairo citadel where they were kept without light in a foul, overcrowded cell. Many were sick. Larrey visited them often and tried to persuade the governor to improve their condition, but General Pierre Dupas, a hard, callous man, refused. Larrey, with no intention of leaving such a situation behind him, went to Bonaparte. The treatment of the English was inhuman, he said, particularly as an unkind fate and not an act of war had put them where they were. Eventually he managed to talk Bonaparte into ordering their repatriation.[12]

'Then, confiding the supervision of my department in Egypt to Citizen Casabianca, a surgeon of the first class, I set out with General Bonaparte and his staff.'[13]

8. *Exodus*

The march that Bonaparte intended should take his army from one end of the Ottoman Empire to the other and on through the Balkans to France began on February 9, 1799.[1] Dugua was left behind in Cairo, Auguste Marmont in Alexandria, Menou in Rosetta, and Desaix in Upper Egypt. A mere 13,000 men—the divisions of Kléber, Bon, Lannes, and Reynier—took their farewells and departed to attempt this momentous task.

The first setback came before they had even left Egyptian territory. While reconnoitering the fortified town of El Arish the advance guard under Reynier was set upon by the Turkish garrison and badly mauled: they lost 20 killed and had nearly 300 wounded. When news of this reached headquarters—still at El Salhiya 110 miles back—Larrey sought, and received, the Commander-in-Chief's permission to attach himself to a troop of dromedary-mounted cavalry that had been ordered to press on to El Arish.

'We reached El Arish on the evening of the 15th, during a spell of wet, cold weather, to find the wounded laid on beds of palm leaves in the middle of Reynier's encampment. For shelter they had only damaged tents of palm branches. They were thus exposed to the rain from above and the damp from below. Their wounds were severe and almost all were in need of surgery which I at once proceeded to carry out with the help of the surgeon-major of the division. I also asked the divisional medical officers to lend a hand on this occasion and assist the surgeons of the ambulance division. Some of the operations were difficult and delicate on account of the complications that had set in; but in general they were successful.'[2]

This situation was not due to some sudden catastrophe that had afflicted the surgeons of Reynier's division. It was in fact just what Larrey had expected to find, and brings home to us with a shock the lamentable state of military surgery at the end of the

18th century. All the agony and ineptitude of past battlefields were there still. The minds and abilities of surgeons had not changed for one hundred, two hundred years. . . . Hippocrates was still a standard text in the medical schools. Even the surgeons of Larrey's ambulance divisions became mentally paralysed and reverted to type if he was absent. The views of the surgical establishment undermined their judgment when they had to act on their own initiative. In the field they were no more than competent 18th-century surgeons, though they had learnt the merits of immediate first aid and rapid evacuation. Yet in comparison with the divisional medical officers—mostly products of the Schools of Health and therefore inadequately qualified—they were paragons.

The next day, the sixteenth, Bonaparte arrived with his headquarters and the artillery—an extremely rapid march. Without delay he laid siege to the fort and in a short while the artillery had created a breach. At this the defenders gave in and after two days of negotiations were permitted to retire with the honours of war.

While Larrey was busy supervising the disinfection of the unbelievably filthy buildings and dealing with the verminous, plague-ridden wounded abandoned by the Turks, the quartermaster's department, once again, relieved him of his camels. The sight of 50 of the beasts, each with two large empty panniers, was more than any quartermaster, short of transport for stores and ammunition, could bear. For the second time in Egypt Larrey was made keenly aware of his lack of military rank. The unhappy state in which he now found himself—and it was one that grew progressively more acute as the weeks passed—suddenly illuminates the whole situation regarding Larrey and his transport in Egypt. All he had had room to bring with him from France was a large number of collapsible stretchers; for everything else he was supposed to rely on local resources but with no Villemanzy to help him.

The fort at El Arish was badly provisioned and after only a day or two the French were compelled to move on into the desert heading north for Gaza. This town soon surrendered, but during the assault a cannon-ball struck an aquaduct close by the Commander-in-Chief. Stones rained down about his head. When he returned to camp he sought out Desgenettes who recommended he should consult Larrey.

'No,' replied Bonaparte, 'it's your advice I'm asking for; I don't want someone to start trepanning to find out what's the matter'[3] —thus demonstrating his strong aversion to the scalpel. Throughout his life he was always careful whom he consulted when he required a surgical opinion.

With the fall of Gaza, Larrey was at last able to find suitable shelter for the sick and wounded who until then had had to move with the army. After two or three days' halt Bonaparte continued his march north and arrived before Jaffa (Tel Aviv) on the evening of March 3.

Larrey was, as he put it, 'a mournful witness to the horrors that attended the assault and sacking of Jaffa'.[4] He set up his advance dressing station in a farmhouse close to the siege trenches but on the reverse slope of a hill and so sheltered from enemy fire. Field dressing stations were sited at intervals throughout the trenches and, three miles away, Larrey found a building that served admirably as a hospital. In the final bloody assault on March 7 100 were killed and 240 wounded. Larrey, following close behind, performed several major operations almost in the breach. As soon as the town was taken he had the wounded transported to a huge mosque.

Among the walking wounded who came every day to this improvised hospital was an Egyptian entertainer who had decided that the French were more appreciative of his act than the Turks. He had been caught in a minor skirmish and nearly deprived of his livelihood—his pet monkey had received a sabre cut on its head. While Larrey was dressing the man's wounds he noticed that the animal seemed to be suffering and offered to dress it too. The Egyptian, already impressed by the surgeon's care and gentleness, could scarcely contain his thanks. Talking incessantly and with tears streaming down his cheeks, he held his little friend while Larrey tidied up the wound and dressed it. The monkey quietly accepted the treatment, and came back regularly and willingly for the dressings to be changed. The wound healed without trouble and thereafter whenever the animal saw Larrey it ran to him and jumped into his arms.[5] In later years, Larrey drew a comparison between the gratitude shown by the little animal and the indifference of the many great men whose wounds he had dressed and whose lives he had saved.

The only enemy that Larrey treated at Jaffa were 20 women who had been wounded in the defence of their town. They attended the hospital daily. The other prisoners of war were shot by order of Bonaparte, an action that Larrey defended on four main counts. One, the garrison at Jaffa included the Turks who had been freed at El Arish on condition that they did not bear arms again. Two, to keep them as prisoners would reduce further the already inadequate rations of the French. Three, to send them back to Egypt would call for a large escort that would drastically weaken the army. And four, to let them go would simply be to reinforce the garrison at St Jean d'Acre.[6]

But of far greater concern than what to do with prisoners of war or the number of French wounded, was the steady trickle, fast becoming a flow, of sick. Many died very suddenly. Citizen St Ours, surgeon-major of the thirty-second demi-brigade, showed Larrey his dead and pointed to the bluish swellings in the groins of several and the gangrenous blotches on the skin of others. The dance of death was not to be stilled by ignoring it, and Larrey reported the matter to the Commander-in-Chief.

As no one knew where plague came from, ideas about prevention and treatment could neither be proved nor disproved and conseqently everything had to be geared to the needs of the military machine. And this machine was in serious danger of coming to a grinding halt from plague alone. Larrey believed the disease to be contagious, but could go no further than warn his senior surgeons to assume that this was so and to act accordingly. Morale had to be sustained. What the men had to believe they were suffering from, said Bonaparte, was a well-recognized but non-contagious disease: 'fever of the buboes', a disease that in some strange way affected those who lacked courage or whose spirit was weak. Larrey agreed with this at first, but gradually became vigorously opposed to the idea. Desgenettes, by all accounts, also believed in the contagiousness of plague but proclaimed the opposite.[7] He squared his conscience by having the troops live in bivouacs outside the town, ordering them not to wear Turkish clothes, and burning everything, including uniforms, he judged to be contaminated—a move that infuriated the mercenary-minded quartermasters.

Yet still the number of cases increased, particularly among the wounded. On March 11 Bonaparte acted according to his lights. He visited the mosque that Desgenettes had converted into a plague hospital and spent an hour and a half chatting with the sick and their attendants. At one stage he helped to move a corpse whose tattered clothing was soaked with pus from the buboes, and he may even have squeezed the bubo of a patient. Desgenettes was on tenterhooks and tried to get the General to leave. 'But I only do my duty,' Bonaparte replied. 'Am I not the General-in-Chief?'[8] When he visited the hospital for the wounded, where plague was also rife, he was quickly hustled through by a more determined Larrey. But though these visits caused his doctors much anxiety they served their purpose and raised the tottering morale of his men.

After a week's stay in Jaffa the army set out for St Jean d'Acre which was reached five days later and promptly besieged. 'Desgenettes and I had the task of finding buildings for our hospitals. The difficulty of this is evident from the fact that we had to site the principal one in the stables of Pasha Ahmed Djezzar, the Turkish commander. This was the only place in the neighbourhood of Acre where we could protect the sick and wounded from the weather. Its only other advantages were a deep brook, which ran alongside, and an arm of the sea, which separated it from the town, thus making it safe from the sorties of the besieged. The wounded were mostly without covering or bedding of any sort, and had to lie on rushes which could not be changed frequently. In addition we lacked wine, vinegar, and medicines.'[9]

Just how short the expedition was of every kind of medical supply became patently evident at Acre. It was not, as might be expected, due to incompetence or misfortune but to the appalling corruption of the pharmacist-in-chief, by name, Claude Royer. Back in Cairo, he had been given the job of bringing lint, linen, and medical necessities, but instead had loaded his camels with wines, liquors, and other luxuries which he had sold en route. Bonaparte was informed and the man was court-martialled and sentenced to be shot. Yet despite the terrible situation Royer had caused, Larrey interceded on his behalf.

'So be it!' said Bonaparte. 'I give him to you, Larrey; do with him as you wish. But I never want to set eyes on the man again. Is that understood?' And besides giving him Royer, he also gave him his own wine for the wounded.[10]

Larrey had much else to worry him. Plague had by now become a very serious problem indeed and was being treated in a variety of ways by the army surgeons. The time had come for some plain speaking. There was also trouble in finding enough surgeons to man the field dressing station—not surprisingly, since it was only 60 yards from the walls of Acre. So on March 22, two days after the start of the siege, Larrey sent a circular to the surgeons of the army:

'Citizens, I beg you to report, every fifth day, the number of sick in your respective units; the character of the prevalent disease, its progress, and the nature of its termination. This information is necessary to enable the chief officers of the surgical staff to make out such reports as are required by General Bonaparte.'[11]

He then gave details of medical and surgical management before continuing: 'When this disease has reached a certain stage it is contagious. Therefore it is necessary to take proper precautions for guarding against it; the soldiers, whose health is in your hands, must observe these precautions—without, however, your telling them of the reason. The most important are cleanliness, frequent washing of the body in cold water and in vinegar, the wearing of clean linen and other clothes, and regular exercise. It is also proper to prohibit the wearing of Turkish pelisses. But above all the soldiers must be convinced that sleeping in holes dug in the sand is most pernicious.

'You will all realize, Citizens, the necessity of arresting the spread of this disease which has already carried off so many of our brave companions. I hope you will neglect nothing that can further my efforts towards achieving so desirable an objective.

'After an engagement, I ask you to assist the surgeons of the ambulances, with the same zeal that you displayed at the capture of Jaffa, in dressing those who may be wounded during the siege or capture of Acre.'[12]

Evidently his plea for assistance had little effect among the medical officers since daily orders for April 11, signed by Alexandre Berthier, the Chief-of-Staff, contained the following two items:

'I. All the medical officers of the different units shall, when an attack begins, report to the central ambulances there to be at the disposal of the Surgeon-in-Chief.

'II. The Surgeon-in-Chief of the army shall see that this order is obeyed, and shall inform the Chief-of-Staff if any surgeon fails to do so.'[13]

Desgenettes was less worried about casualties; his major concern was plague. Whatever his real beliefs about its contagiousness, he laid great stress on maintaining morale as the best means of prevention. The story goes that one day he outdid Bonaparte's gesture at Jaffa by dramatically pricking himself in groin and armpit with the point of a lancet dipped in bubonic pus to demonstrate that the disease was not contagious. At the first opportunity afterwards he washed carefully with soapy water!

The truth of what really happened will probably never be known. In one of his notes[14] Larrey said that Desgenettes only went through the motions of inoculating himself without actually doing so. The tale may have been put around by high-ranking officers to raise morale—or even to try to curry favour with the Physican-in-Chief whose signature was required for postings back to France on medical grounds. Desgenettes himself, later in life, denied ever having done anything at all.

The opening assault on Acre began well but ended in disaster. The French had carried their siege trenches up to a large tower which they breached and then assaulted after an artillery bombardment. Unfortunately the first grenadiers into the breach found their further progress blocked and were all killed in a hail of stones and balls. A second assault went the same way. Whether it would have made any difference had Bonaparte possessed his heavy siege artillery is problematical. The fact remains that on its way by sea from Jaffa, together with desperately needed stores and ammunition, it was captured by the British naval captain, and backbone of the Acre defence, Sidney Smith. The sour breath of failure was on the air.

Meanwhile, some 20 miles away to the south-east, Kléber's division was defending the mountain passes which were the main route from the north to the plain of Acre. Ibrahim Bey attacked with vastly superior forces and Kléber was saved from disaster only by the timely arrival of Bonaparte.

'This battle cost us about 100 wounded whom we sent to Nazareth to the convent of the Holy Land which had been converted into a hospital. The troops returned to St Jean d'Acre, although the Commander-in-Chief stayed behind to climb Mt Tabor—at the foot of which the battle had taken place—and to visit Nazareth, where he was regarded as a second Messiah and received with the most extravagant enthusiasm.'[15]

That evening Bonaparte and his senior staff were invited to dine at the quarters of the commandant, General Jean Verdier, one of the few officers to have taken his wife on the expedition. All except Larrey were assembled and so Madame Verdier gave the signal to go into dinner—it was impolitic to keep the Commander-in-Chief waiting. But Bonaparte noticed that Larrey was missing and refused to follow, saying that he would not sit down without his Surgeon-in-Chief. Madame Verdier explained that Larrey was at the hospital and as no one knew when he would finish his work, instructions had been given to keep his dinner for him.

'No, Madame,' said Bonaparte, 'we will wait.' And wait they did. When Larrey arrived an hour later, Bonaparte sat him on his right and Madame Verdier on his left. 'It was fresh proof', wrote Larrey, 'of the particular esteem and friendship with which this great man honoured me.'[16]

On his return to Acre Larrey was kept fully occupied by the renewed assaults on the town. 'I was continually at the field dressing station or running from the camp to the trenches, from the trenches to the hospital, or busy visiting the divisions where there were almost as many sick and wounded as in the front line itself. We had 2,000 wounded during the siege; in general, the wounds were severe and sometimes multiple. Seventy amputations were performed, six of which were disarticulations at the shoulder joint (four were perfectly successful) and two of which were disarticulations at the hip joint.'[17]

These latter disarticulations were memorable feats, though in both cases the patients died when seemingly well on the way to recovery: one from plague and the other from the effects of being evacuated immediately after surgery. Larrey had once before—on the Rhine—carried out the procedure but like the rare attempts by other surgeons, it had been unsuccessful. The prevailing opinion about disarticulation at the hip was highly unfavourable.[18] Yet in Larrey's view, 'the frightful appearance of the wound, the difficulty of detaching the thigh-bone from its socket, and the dangers of the retraction of the flexor muscles and of sudden loss of blood have, without doubt, prevented army surgeons from performing this operation'.[19] The technique in use at the time did nothing to ease these difficulties, apart from which it was exquisitely painful. But before he had even joined the army, Larrey had worked out, on dead bodies and animals, a new method that was quick, easy, and avoided the previous hazards.

Among the wounded senior officers was Duroc, Bonaparte's first aide-de-camp and a particular friend of Larrey's, who very nearly died from the effects of a terrible injury of his right thigh caused by the bursting of a bomb. Fortunately the destruction was confined to the soft tissues, and although the main nerves and blood vessels were exposed they were intact. Larrey carefully débrided the wound and with 'gentle dressings and the most assiduous care prevented the fatal result, which appeared likely, and brought about the officer's recovery'.[20]

General Bon, another casualty, was, as Larrey put it, a victim to the 'sort of faint-heartedness that makes a man dread pain'.[21] At the seventh assault a ball entered his right groin and passed through his bladder and pelvis to emerge at the buttock on the other side. Regrettably Bon refused treatment. Larrey gave him into the care of a colleague, who was no happier about the case than his chief. Urine diffused into the pelvic tissues where it soon produced a gangrene that was 'promoted by the corpulency of the general'. He was the only man to die in Syria from a wound of this nature.

But perhaps the most dramatic surgical episode concerned Toussaint Arrighi, aide-de-camp to General Berthier and Bonaparte's cousin. He had just arrived at the forward gun battery with an order for the officer in charge when a ball passed through his neck from left to right cutting the right external carotid artery. He fell to the ground with blood spurting in jets from the wound. One of the gunners, who must have had remarkable presence of mind, quickly put an index finger into each end of the wound and stopped the bleeding. Larrey was immediately sent for and, to his great astonishment, found that a compressive bandage carefully applied saved Arrighi from what seemed certain death. While the dressing was in progress a grape-shot shell burst directly above the heads of those gathered round the wounded man. Incredibly, no one was hit, though Larrey's hat, at his side, was riddled with shot. He himself did not even glance up but continued his work completely unperturbed.[22] News of the incident became broadcast throughout the army and Larrey's stock, already good, reached new heights.[23]

By the middle of May Bonaparte had to concede that his great plan had aborted. The siege was deadlocked and any attempt to prolong it would court disaster from the plague. Rumours of threatened rebellion in Egypt, of a British or Turkish fleet off Alexandria, and of an English army menacing Suez, all helped him to make up his mind. He would have to swallow his pride and return.

Although the disabled had been returned to Egypt throughout the siege whenever circumstances permitted, the evacuation of the remaining wounded was a major organizational task which Larrey began several days before the army itself pulled out. He began by sending 500 men to Jaffa, from where Rear-Admiral Honoré Ganteaume shipped them to Alexandria and Damietta. The others, approximately the same number, would have to cross the desert and that meant transport. But he had none and could obtain none; so by threatening to leave the wounded behind at Acre, he persuaded Jean Pierre Daure, the quartermaster-general, to find him horses and donkeys. These were still not enough, but by this time Bonaparte had heard of his troubles.

'General Bonaparte ordered that all horses belonging to the headquarters staff—his own included—were to be used for transporting the wounded who would otherwise have been left to die of hunger and thirst or at the hands of the Arabs. Each demi-brigade was held responsible for the care of its own wounded and I had the immense satisfaction of seeing every wounded man brought safely out of Syria into Egypt.

'Considering that these men were rationed to a few hard biscuits and a little sweet water; that they had only brackish water for their dressings; and that the great majority had severe wounds of head, chest, or abdomen, or were missing a limb, it will no doubt seem surprising that they crossed 180 miles of desert without accident. Indeed, the journey may well have been advantageous since most were healed when they reached Egypt. The change of climate; exercise; the dry, warm air of the desert; and the joy felt by everyone at leaving behind the privations of the siege, seem to me to be the reasons for this happy result.'[24]

The army broke camp on the night of May 21, 1799, and took the road to Egypt.

'If', said the Emperor Napoleon on the island of St Helena, 'if St Jean d'Acre had fallen, I would have changed the face of the world.'[25]

Just three months after entering Syria, the army that should have changed the face of the world was on its way out again. In that time it had penetrated a mere 125 miles into hostile territory and achieved nothing—except 500 men killed in action, 700 dead from plague, and about 2,500 wounded; a casualty list approaching a third of its total force. The battered remains, weakened by disease, suffering, and lack of food stumbled southwards along the coast. The wounded were led or carried on improvised stretchers so long as their comrades had the strength and humanity to aid them.[1]

When Larrey reached Jaffa he found both hospitals crammed with the wounded who had been evacuated down the coast ahead of him; those who could not get in were lying about the harbour streets. The surgeons spent three days and nights attending to these men and dressing their wounds before sending most of them on through the desert to Egypt. As Larrey said, 'It is almost impossible to imagine the strain the army surgeons were under during this period.'[2] The seriously injured were embarked on the last ships leaving for Damietta—some arrived safely but others were captured by the English.

Jaffa was the scene of another of the apocryphal episodes involving Desgenettes. Bonaparte is reputed to have ordered the physician to poison (with opium) the plague patients who could not be transported, thus saving them from almost certain torture should they fall alive into the hands of the Turks and Arabs. Desgenettes took the strongest exception to this and answered, 'My duty is to save life, not to take it.'

Desgenettes himself referred to the matter only when Napoleon was dead. Writing shortly after the campaign he merely said that in his view some of the plague patients were on the point of death and should not be moved—an opinion he passed on to higher authority.[3] Years later Larrey said the order had never been given, and anyway there was no opium or laudanum to be had.[4]

As might be expected, the story gained momentum after Napoleon's fall; nevertheless, the version told by the ex-Emperor to Dr Barry O'Meara on St Helena has the ring of truth to it. According to this, Bonaparte was told that seven or eight of the plague patients were dangerously ill and could live only another 24 or 36 hours; those who were conscious were demanding to be put to death, a task which Desgenettes refused to perform. Later, Larrey came to Bonaparte to report the situation and what Desgenettes had said. He added that perhaps Desgenettes was right. However, Larrey went on, as these men could not live much longer it would be sufficient to leave behind a rearguard of cavalry for their protection. This Bonaparte did, and between 400 and 500 horsemen were ordered not to leave the town until all the sick had died. On rejoining the retreat they reported that the order had been obeyed. But later Bonaparte heard that Smith had found one or two alive.[5]

In Napoleon's view the poisoning story arose out of a misunderstanding of something that Desgenettes must have said. Still, whatever the truth, the journey had to continue and, once back in Egypt, the sick and wounded were distributed among the hospitals along the way, as much for Bonaparte's benefit as their own. The Commander-in-Chief was determined to scour his army of every last stain of contagion for, no matter what propaganda he encouraged, he now either believed in the contagiousness of plague or was taking no chances. At Matharieh, a village 6 miles outside Cairo, the army halted for two days and Bonaparte ordered every man to wash his linen and clothes and to burn all personal items that could not be scrubbed clean. He was playing a crafty game. He wanted to march into his capital at once without running the risk that his medical advisers might insist on a demoralizing period of quarantine spent in camp outside the city. His troops were in good heart and any delay would destroy the build-up he had planned. He was not bringing back a beaten rabble. He intended to enter Cairo in triumph at the head of a victorious army. And, incredibly, he did just that.

'General Dugua left Cairo with the troops under his command to meet us. With what pleasure did we embrace our old companions in arms! We met as brothers and friends, united by the same interests and love of glory, in a foreign land that we now regarded as our adopted country.

'The Commander-in-Chief entered the city through the Bab-el Nasr gate at the head of his army. The inhabitants crowded the streets shouting with joy. Our arrival pleased them greatly, as their country was menaced on all sides by innumerable enemies, especially the Turks whom they had always dreaded. The presence of General Bonaparte was their shield, and from that time they felt perfectly secure.'[6]

The surgeons left in Cairo came looking for Larrey to welcome him back, but he was nowhere to be seen. At headquarters, however, they met a strangely magnificent personage enveloped in a bright scarlet robe held round the waist with a cashmere shawl and wearing an old-fashioned brass helmet on his head. They approached this character and asked if he had news of the Surgeon-in-Chief. Was it true that he had been killed?

'No,' said the man, 'he is not dead; go further and you will find him at the very heart of the army.'

The surgeons began to move on. 'Casabianca! Am I so changed that you don't recognize me?' Only then did his colleagues recognize a Larrey burnt black by the sun of the Syrian desert and wearing this unaccustomed garb to replace the rags and tatters of his uniform.[7]

Larrey needed but little time to recover from the expedition and was soon back at work catching up on the reports from surgeons scattered with the garrisons and divisions throughout Egypt. Then, the desk work done, he began to reorganize the hospitals which, in his absence, had become dirty and inefficient. Throughout his time in Egypt he bombarded the Commander-in-Chief, the senior officers, and the quartermasters with letters written by François Zinck, his surgeon-secretary, in an attempt to keep the army healthy. But unless he supervised everything himself, he was fighting a losing battle, and with the present task still incomplete orders came from Bonaparte to join the headquarters at the Pyramids.[8]

The Commander-in-Chief had received a dispatch from Marmont in Alexandria. Dated July 11, 1799, it arrived on the fifteenth and announced that a force of 20,000 Turks supported by an English squadron under Sidney Smith had landed on the peninsula of Aboukir where they had captured the fort and its protecting redoubts, and, for good measure had beheaded 40 French prisoners. Bonaparte wrote to General Jacques Destaing ordering him to rendezvous at El Rahmaniya; to Kléber to march on Rosetta; to Desaix to fall back on Cairo; and to Reynier, encamped on the Syrian frontier, to hold himself ready to move at a moment's notice. Then on July 16, with Lannes and Murat he marched rapidly north through the Libyan desert—though keeping close to cultivated country on the right—reaching El Rahmaniya on the nineteenth and Alexandria four days later.

Acting on instructions from Berthier, Larrey organized two large hospitals in Alexandria and ordered a great quantity of dressings to be prepared. Then before rejoining the army he sent a note to the naval surgeons asking them to report to the hospitals and be ready to help in dressing the wounded.

The army had advanced during the night along the peninsula towards Aboukir. 'At daybreak on July 25 we found ourselves but a short distance from the Turkish army. The signal to attack was given and, in spite of vigorous resistance by the Mussulmans, our men leaped the trenches and climbed the redoubts carrying them by assault. The first shock of combat was terrible and for some time the outcome was uncertain; but the presence of the General-in-Chief inspired our soldiers to renewed efforts and victory was ours. It was complete: the enemy were repulsed and their whole army routed. Those who escaped our swords fled towards the fort or tried to reach their ships anchored in the bay. Murat's cavalry under his brilliant second-in-command, General Roize, pursued them with such determination that few survived. More than 10,000 of the enemy were left dead on the field, and we took 300 prisoners among whom was their Commander-in-Chief, Mustapha Pasha, who was wounded in the hand.

'During the engagement, the field dressing stations were placed at the principal points on the line to give immediate assistance. The most severely wounded were all brought to my own station in the centre where I did the dressings and performed such operations as were necessary. More than 40 amputations were carried out and with astonishing success. Throughout, the wounded received the most prompt and effectual assistance from the surgeons of the ambulance divisions and of the line; none was left more than a quarter of an hour without being dressed. They were then carried on stretchers to our boats which were moored in a creek out of sight of the enemy squadron and transported to Alexandria without accident.'[9] Larrey's lines of evacuation were a model of impeccability.

The French had 50 killed and 800 wounded in the fight. Brigadier Henri Bertrand was caught a glancing blow on the head by a ball which removed some of his scalp. When Larrey reported the incident to Bonaparte, he commented on the courage and distinction of this engineer officer. The General asked to see the man and from that moment on attached him to his personal staff[10]—an attachment that ended with the Emperor's death in exile on St Helena.

Murat was wounded in the very moment of victory. He galloped up to the Turkish commander's tent, leapt from his horse and with drawn sword strode inside to take Mustapha prisoner. But the Turk got the wrong idea and, thinking he was about to be killed, raised his pistol. As his finger tightened on the trigger, a cavalryman with Murat fired quickly to divert his aim. The two pistols exploded simultaneously. Murat was hit in the neck; Mustapha lost an index finger.

The Turk's ball entered behind the angle of the right side of Murat's jaw, passed across the back of his throat injuring his epiglottis, and without damaging any major blood vessel emerged above the inner end of his left collar bone. Murat spat out a piece of his epiglottis—a dramatic gesture that must have appealed to him despite the unfortunate circumstances—and made his way to Larrey who débrided the wounds of entry and exit and then bandaged his neck. Murat lost the use of his voice for three weeks, and in the early days of treatment was unable to swallow. Larrey overcame this problem by feeding him with nourishing liquids through a gum-elastic stomach tube.[11]

Mustapha, meanwhile, had been taken to Bonaparte who gave

him refreshment until Larrey had finished treating Murat. Larrey continued to look after the Turk while the wound was healing and was rewarded with gifts that included a fine Damascus sword.[12] This was, in fact, the second sword Larrey received at that time. During the heat of the battle General Fugières was hit by a ball in the right shoulder which had made an appalling mess of the joint. The arm was hanging by shreds of skin and tendon and the axillary artery, which had retracted under the pectoral muscles, was pumping out blood each time the General moved. The shock of the injury and the large quantity of blood he had lost reduced him to a very critical state and he was in such agony that Larrey feared he would die at any moment. When Bonaparte heard of this he came to the dressing station to make his last farewells; he was thus a witness to the operation.

Removing the arm at the shoulder joint was easy, but Larrey had great difficulty forming covering skin flaps owing to the extensive destruction of tissue and also to the fact that he had to enlarge the wound considerably to find and tie the axillary artery. But he managed to get a fair degree of cover. After the operation Fugières raised himself from his own blood and said, prophetically: 'One day perhaps, General, you will envy me my fate. Now, with my farewells I beg you to accept this sword for which I have no further use.' And he indicated a glorious Damascus sabre exquisitely decorated with gold.

'Yes, I accept it, but only to present it in my turn to the surgeon who has saved your life.' Bonaparte then ordered Berthier to have Larrey's name engraved in golden Arabic letters on one side of the blade and on the other 'Aboukir'.[13] This gift was a great honour as swords were highly prized by French officers in Egypt and only given as a mark of great esteem. But Bonaparte's assessment and confident prognosis proved correct: Fugières recovered, though he was bothered by painful sensations in the healed socket.

Immediately after the battle the Anglo-Turkish fleet sailed away to the east, but not before Sidney Smith had laid a subtle trap for Bonaparte. He left behind English newspapers which carried news of French defeats in Europe and of the politically disastrous state of the Directory. Smith hoped that one or both of the items would induce Bonaparte to make a run for home, and once at sea he should be in the bag. Only the first part of the plan succeeded.

The victorious army returned to Cairo led by a man scheming to leave it in the lurch: Bonaparte announced that on the seventeenth he would give a grand party for all his senior officers to celebrate the victory at Aboukir. At the celebration he was in fine form, talking about his future plans in Egypt and how he relied on each and every one to serve France to the utmost of his ability. After stating publicly that he was setting out to inspect the sea coast from Lake Burullus to Alexandria he took Larrey to one side and said that he counted on his surgeon coming with him.

'Be ready tonight in four hours.' Larrey had guessed what was in the wind and, although desperately anxious to return to France, he replied, 'I can be ready in *two* hours if that is your wish, General; but if my presence is not indispensable, it is more important that I stay with my wounded.' Bonaparte was amazed. He was silent for a moment. His right shoulder jerked up and the right corner of his mouth twitched down. Then he took Larrey by the hand, 'You are right, my dear Larrey, you shall stay.'[14]

Larrey had put the men before their Commander-in-Chief and it was a mistake. Napoleon Bonaparte had a long memory, and although he showed it only in apparently petty ways he never forgave his Surgeon-in-Chief.

Bonaparte left early in the morning. Among those he took with him were Berthier and Marmont, and on the coast he was joined by Lannes and Murat. Kléber was told to leave Egypt as soon as conditions permitted and Desaix as soon as he could hand over the command of his division. Outside Alexandria the departing Commander-in-Chief dictated a letter of farewell to the Army of the Orient in which he appointed Kléber to his place. Menou was instructed to wait 48 hours before returning to Cairo with the letter.

Not for the last time Bonaparte's speed of decision and action had caught his opponent unawares. The English fleet was taking on water at Cyprus. On August 23, in the darkness of night, Ganteaume set an untroubled course for home. Bonaparte did not look back.

10. *Homeward Bound*

Menou arrived in Cairo on August 30 with the news of Bonaparte's desertion. The army was shaken to its core and uncertain whether it was standing on its head or its heels, but thankfully Kléber was popular and rapidly proved himself an able administrator as well as an outstanding commander in the field. He pursued with success the policies laid down by Bonaparte for the government of the country, and adopted the public health measures proposed by the commission of public safety. Nevertheless, he intended to evacuate Egypt at the earliest opportunity and to pave the way at home he wrote to the Directory painting a grossly exaggerated picture of the miserable state of the troops and their lack of supplies and equipment. The letter fell into English hands with unfortunate consequences.[1]

After the battle of Aboukir the French thought they would be left in peace. Their hopes were shattered when, in the opening days of the new year, they learnt that a large army had marched across the Syrian border, surrounded the fort at El Arish and forced the garrison to surrender. Terms were proposed and accepted, but immediately violated. Most of the French were beheaded and, to Larrey's utter disgust, 'the barbarians did not even respect the surgeon, but cut off his head while he was dressing one of the wounded'.[2]

On January 8, 1800, Kléber set out from Cairo with all the troops he could spare and camped at El Salhiya where, through Desaix and Citizen Pousielgou, he opened negotiations with the enemy. And this is where the trouble began. The self-appointed chief negotiator on the other side was Sidney Smith who fancied himself as an exponent of high diplomacy. He completely ignored definite orders from London that any terms made with the French must include their unconditional surrender, and on January 24 he took it upon himself to conclude the treaty of El Arish which provided for the French soldiers, their arms, baggage, and effects to be transported to France by the Turks and their allies.

While the negotiations were in progress the French learnt, through newspapers given them by the English, of Bonaparte's safe arrival in France, of his achievement in being made First Consul, and of his renewed military success. This nearly upset the apple-cart as it filled French hearts with enthusiasm for continuing the fight in Egypt, but Kléber was able to persuade them of the wisdom of leaving the country to rejoin their old commander whose misdemeanours had now conveniently been forgotten.

'We prepared without delay to evacuate Egypt, but as we were about to hand over to the enemy the General [Kléber] received a letter from Admiral Lord Keith. By an order from his government, Lord Keith declared, the French army could not be allowed to pass except as prisoners-of-war. This news was published in the orders of the following day and aroused the indignation of the whole army, which determined to avenge the affront.'[3]

It is conceivable that Keith, the English commander in the Mediterranean, might have permitted the treaty to stand had he not believed that Kléber's letter revealed the true state of affairs. The French, he thought, were in no condition to lay down any terms. His error prolonged the conflict by 18 months,[4] though events might have turned out differently had Kléber not been assassinated.[5]

June 14, 1800, the day of the assassination, proved in retrospect to be a particularly sad one for Larrey who later learnt that at the very hour of Kléber's death, his great friend, Desaix, had been killed beating the Austrians at Marengo: 'The battle is lost,' the First Consul had said. Desaix looked at his watch. It was four o'clock in the afternoon. 'Yes,' he had answered, 'this battle is lost, but by God there is time to win another.' In later years Napoleon said that had Desaix lived he would have made him a king.

If the death of Desaix was a tragedy, that of Kléber was an outright disaster for France. During his short spell as Commander-in-Chief he had brought stability and prosperity to Egypt. Cairo had become a cultural and industrial centre; arms and munitions were manufactured, as well as some of the luxuries and necessities of life. The army had been refitted and brought up to strength with locally recruited auxiliaries. The men had learned to live with the climate; they were happy and in fine fettle.

Menou succeeded Kléber and this whole edifice, so painstakingly built up, began to crumble. Menou was hopelessly incompetent, vain, and ambitious. He shut his ears to reason and his eyes to the evidence of disintegration around him. He removed all the best officers from their jobs because they had served Kléber. The morale of the army and the administration of the country fell apart.

Larrey, who could not abide incompetence, was well disposed towards the new Commander-in-Chief—an anomaly that had a simple explanation. Throughout the campaign in Egypt and Syria the medical and surgical services had enjoyed a fair degree of autonomy so long as they conformed to relevant daily orders, but their officers lacked military authority. When Menou assumed command the members of the medical and surgical staffs, according to grade, became entitled to the honours and privileges of military officers. This was the first time in history such a thing had happened—and it was not repeated until the end of the century. Larrey was so impressed and grateful that he did not inquire too closely into Menou's motives which probably were simply to snub the other officers.

According to Larrey, Menou 'soon adopted many useful regulations.[6] He reformed the executive department; he gave orders for the organization of the hospitals and flying ambulances; he rewarded the courage and enthusiasm of all the medical officers by an increase in pay; and he established a privy council which included the physician- and surgeon-generals.'[7]

But Larrey was desperately unhappy—although letters from France had got through to some of his friends, he had heard nothing from home all the time he had been in Egypt.

'What torment,' he wrote on August 3, 1800,[8] 'to spend two whole years without knowing what has become of the object most dear to my heart, a wife whom I adore and whom I have scarcely possessed; and a child whom I have never seen and for whom I would give my blood and my life, and be sure that I have never been more worthy of your love and trust. Since I have been in this ancient land I have thought of no other woman than my Laville.'

Then, to his delight, at the end of October he received the one and only letter from Charlotte to reach him throughout the entire campaign.

'For the first time since I saw the rivers of Africa,' he wrote in a turmoil of emotion on November 1,[9] 'I have received your news, my beloved; your letter of November 5, 1799, has arrived. What a surprise, what pleasure, or, rather, what state of confusion am I in all at once. I skimmed through the letter quickly with a secret uneasiness constantly at the back of my mind. I first caught a glimpse of the name of our new little one, and, scattered throughout, several words of tenderness and love. I read that mama was doing well. My fears were set at rest, and I collected myself for a moment to relish the most joyous sensations. At last I knew you were perfectly happy. After a few minutes, my heart was calm and I began to read your letter again.

'You can be sure, my love, that there are still some husbands faithful to their wives, and I am assuredly of that number.'

The 'new little one', already more than a year old when Charlotte wrote the letter, was named Isaure after a legendary heroine of Toulouse.

Later, when news reached Egypt that Berthier had been appointed Minister of War, Larrey decided that here was an excellent opportunity to put in a word for the medical service. On January 29, 1801, he wrote to the Minister:

'The honour of surgery, the interests of humanity, and the progress of our work require that a special corps should be formed like the other special corps of the army, such as the artillery and the engineers. How can we act responsibly and count on our labours being successful if we are under the surveillance of incompetent men and if we are not free to follow the impetus given by the love of glory and the cause of humanity which guide us?

'Such is the main cause of the troubles which persistently afflict us and which can only be overcome with the greatest difficulty. You yourself have seen that, in the absence of the necessary authority, we have often been unable to attend to the wounded.

'If you have need of a plan, I recommend to you the Surgeon-in-Chief of the army, Percy, a true and worthy upholder of military surgery. His talents, his profound knowledge, and his principles are well known to you.'[10]

Confident that Berthier would fall in with his ideas, Larrey began to take matters into his own hands in Egypt. Unfortunately for future relationships he did not know where to stop and wrote to the local quartermaster telling him in no uncertain terms to mind his own business as the medical officers now came under his (Larrey's) orders, as did the administration of the military hospitals—and if the quartermaster wanted confirmation of this, Menou would gladly oblige.

What Larrey did not know was that the Administration was more firmly than ever entrenched in France. It believed that Marengo had brought peace and was hard at work running down everything connected with the medical services—hospitals, schools, and staff. Percy had tried to resign in protest. In his ignorance, Larrey was happily studying the medical practices of Egypt, both ancient and modern. 'But in the midst of our pleasures[11] we were threatened by a sudden invasion of several hostile armies. In the south was an Indian army advancing from the Red Sea [this was Brigadier-General Sir David Baird's force from Bombay whose object was to prevent any possibility of the French invading the East India Company's territories in India]; in the east, on the frontier with Syria, was a considerable army of Turks; in the north was an English and Turkish fleet blockading Alexandria and threatening to make a landing; and in the west were the Mamelukes and Arabs, prepared to join the strongest side and plunder the vanquished.'[12]

It was a terrible predicament for any commander to find himself in and Menou had no satisfactory answer. He sent Reynier, his best general, to Bilbeis, Charles Morand to Damietta, and François Lanusse to Alexandria. He himself stayed in Cairo. By splitting his forces he had sealed his fate.

On March 8, 1801, the English landed 20,000 men at Aboukir. General Louis Friant with the totally inadequate Alexandrian garrison—Lanusse was still two days' march away—made an attempt to stop them but was repulsed. News of the landing reached Menou and on the twelfth he set out for Alexandria accompanied by Larrey with five ambulance divisions equipped with camel-borne panniers. Reynier was ordered to join them with all speed.

The British siege of Alexandria dragged on throughout the summer with the conditions inside the city slowly worsening. Nevertheless, on May 20 Larrey was able to report to Menou that more than 1,000 of the wounded had rejoined their units and that the 600 remaining in hospital were on their way to recovery. Yet disease inevitably proved a far greater problem than wounds: in June a serious outbreak of ophthalmia put 3,000 men in hospital. And no sooner had this been brought under control than scurvy appeared and rapidly assumed epidemic proportions—it was, in some quarters, believed to be contagious. By mid-August the 20 or so hospitals were full and Larrey had to order the building of a large shed to cope with the steady stream of casualties.

Cairo and the rest of Egypt had by now been lost, and when the British worked their way round to the west of Alexandria, captured Port Marabout, and under cover of a naval bombardment advanced on the old city, there seemed little point in holding out. Menou opened negotiations. Larrey attended the meeting to report on matters of health and nutrition, but he made his presence felt in quite another way. The French generals put on a great show of their consideration for the sick and wounded. They should be left behind, they said, until they were fully restored to health. Larrey stormed to his feet.

'What you really want,' his anger was scarcely controlled, 'is to avoid a long quarantine at Toulon and arrive with a fine-looking army in good shape. You raised the problem of scurvy: well, your fears are groundless, the disease is not contagious. The sick will embark apart from the rest of the army, and I shall indicate those who cannot be moved. Furthermore I insist that the best ships shall be made available for the sick and wounded and that these shall sail first.'[13]

The French sat in stunned silence while Lord Keith accepted the proposal. The capitulation, signed on August 31, provided that the French troops should return to France with all the honours of war.

During the preparations for departure Larrey visited the British camp where he was taken round by Mr Thomas Young, the Inspector-General of hospitals. 'His hospitals were well kept and provided with every necessity. Yet I was astonished to find but three successful cases of amputation out of a great number of soldiers on whom this operation had been performed. This proves the superiority of French surgery over that of the most civilized nations.'[14]

The army began to embark on September 23 and on October 17 Larrey sailed with Menou in the last ship to leave. Thirty days later he saw his beloved France again, but before he could step ashore he had to endure the customary period of quarantine.

'What joy to embrace you, my love!' he wrote from the Toulon roads. 'My cup will then be full and my wishes come true. If I were to end my life on such a glorious day, I would die in blissful happiness.' But Charlotte had told him of trouble at home, where certain so-called friends had been spreading malicious gossip about him and, in this letter of November 24,[15] he asked her to do what she could to put an end to it.

'My heart is generous, it can forget the past, but it will not be deceived. It now needs peace and quiet, having had enough of frustration and annoyance. Assure those who seem to you to be honest and trustworthy that I shall reciprocate fully all their kindnesses.

'But do not pursue Dubois too hard, as I do not wish to make an enemy of him. [Larrey had invalided Dubois home from Egypt with dysentery; but he knew, and Dubois knew, that the real reason was lack of guts.] I wish to enjoy the pleasures that your society and that of my true friends will give me and to make the most of the advantages of such a position. It would give me the greatest pain to incur anyone's hatred. I know that my defects and my extreme self-assurance invite criticism from those who wish me ill; but if they understood my feelings and my generosity they would be aware of my goodwill and of my esteem.'

When the quarantine period had ended, Larrey went to Marseilles where the army was reassembling. Here his duties as

Surgeon-in-Chief of the Army of the Orient came to an end and he set out for Paris. But unfortunately, by hurrying back to Charlotte, Larrey was guilty of a diplomatic error as great as his decision to stay in Egypt. The First Consul was coming to Lyons to review the Army of the Orient, which was under orders to proceed there, and had sent a message to Larrey asking him to await his arrival. Although Larrey never received the message, he knew that Bonaparte would wish to see him. He had now shown that he put his wife, as well as the men, before the ruler of France.

There were three things Napoleon Bonaparte never really understood: the English, the sea, and the human element in warfare. The English refused to behave as his logical mind thought they should; the sea would not allow him to move ships as he could his armies on land; and men were men, not machines. The disregard for human life during the Revolutionary wars had led him to believe that a nation at arms implied unlimited manpower— he could not grasp the need for husbanding his troops. Yet even had his belief been correct in principle it would still have been wrong in practice, since a steadily increasing number of conscripts failed to report for duty (by 1806, as many as 25 per cent). He was also impatient. Like unseen flaws in a foundation, these crucial defects determined the fate of the edifice he was building around him. But when Larrey's coach slithered home through the mire of that January in 1802, the First Consul had Europe in his pocket and, in his own inimitable style, was fast turning the defeat in Egypt into a victory at the conference table at Amiens.

On his return Larrey was received by Bonaparte in the dazzling splendour of the Tuileries. It was as if the ancient régime had been reborn, but more vulgar and coarsened by its bitter sleep. Bonaparte welcomed him with kindness, affection even, yet the innocent mistake of not accompanying his master from Egypt had cost Larrey dear. When the First Consul made his appointments his sense of occasion demanded that the men should be there to receive them, not languishing in some foreign clime. So Pierre François Percy became Surgeon-in-Chief of the army. Likewise, no absent surgeon was attached to the First Consul's personal staff. In an order dated November 1, 1800, Larrey had been appointed first surgeon to the Consular Guard and to the Hospital of the Guard (the Hospital of Gros Caillou, a short distance west of the Hôtel des Invalides). Although the salary of 4,800 francs—brought up to the equivalent of more than 9,000 on active service, since fodder for his horses, their shoeing, and remounts were supposed to be taken care of—was quite respectable, one is left with the inescapable impression that this was merely a sop to the Surgeon-in-Chief of the Army of the Orient.[1]

But in the end it was Napoleon and France who paid the greater price. For Larrey understood the human element in warfare and the men loved him for it. While Bonaparte listened to his surgeon's report his mind was clearly elsewhere, driven on by his boundless ambition: Percy had the surgical services in hand; a gesture here, a gesture there, was all that was required of the First Consul. Now Amiens, he could shape the future there, but would the English see through the wool he was pulling over their eyes? If they would put up with the deception and double-dealing of his representatives, they would put up with anything. They wanted peace as much as he did, though for a vastly different reason. They wanted to develop their trade, while he sought to extend his dominion. . . .

The First Consul's energy was inexhaustible. Besides directing the fortune of France abroad, he completely reorganized the internal running of the country. The system amounted to the centralization of government, with himself holding tightly to the reins. In two years he transformed France from a rent and ragged catastrophe to a well-regulated victorious power. The country was a military state ruled by a dictator, but this did not worry the people. It was what they needed, what they wanted, and they gloried in their First Consul for all his ungovernable outbursts of rage.

Larrey was scarcely any less idle. His first task was to have something done about the returned medical officers of the Army of the Orient who had been shabbily treated, since the Administration was energetically running down the medical services. It even argued that the commissions for the Egyptian campaign had been temporary and so there really had been no medical services with the army; thus there could be no gratuities—and, what is more, it must be right as it had passed decrees that said so. Larrey was outraged. Many of his colleagues would lie for ever in Egyptian soil, but of those who had returned the greater part were in poor physical shape and reduced to begging for a living. He wrote to the First Consul, he wrote to the Minister of War, he wrote to many others, not once but time and time again, and all to no avail.

So Larrey concocted a plan which somehow or other he induced the First Consul to sign on March 16, 1802. This gave him the authority to appoint his own nominees to vacancies in the Hospital of the Guard and in the medical service of the Guard. For once he had succeeded in putting the Administration's nose out of joint. But while looking after others, Larrey neglected his own interests. He had lost his house and a valuable collection of antiquities in Cairo,[2] yet he contented himself with writing in a letter to the First Consul: 'I rely confidently on your kindness, of which you have already given me many tokens that I prize.'[3] Compared with what others received, tokens were the most he ever saw.

Larrey threw himself into his academic life with all the enthusiasm and vitality that he displayed on active service. He resumed his duties at Val-de-Grâce and by popular request began a public course in experimental military surgery. He took an energetic part in discussions on surgical education. In between whiles he found time to sit for Girodet whose recent painting 'The Shades of French Warriors . . .' now hung on a wall in Malmaison. And in the evenings he settled down to write his *Relation Historique et Chirurgicale de l'Expédition de l'Armée d'Orient, en Egypte et en Syrie.*[4] This, with permission, was dedicated to the First Consul and published in 1803. Bonaparte graciously accepted the first copy and in return presented Larrey with a gold box decorated with his (Bonaparte's) portrait and containing 6,000 livres. When the Prussian envoy saw the book he suggested that his king, too, might like a copy. Larrey took the hint and was rewarded with a personal letter from Frederick William III and a gold medal.

In March 1803 the First Consul restored the medical faculties—abolished at the beginning of the Revolution—and Larrey found that he had to defend a thesis as his existing qualifications failed to satisfy the new regulations. For his subject he chose amputations

G

and, not surprisingly, he was the first to have the new degree of Doctor of Surgery conferred upon him.[5]

Later in the year the Larrey family moved into 3 cul-de-sac Conti at Monnaie on the south bank of the Seine, the house that was to be their home for the next 29 years despite Charlotte's yearning for somewhere in the country. With her husband on active service for 12 of the first 21 years of their marriage Charlotte had to rely heavily on her artistic interests to ease her loneliness. She and Émilie were extremely fond of one another and the two sisters were rarely without the company of artists or writers. The poet Charles Demoustier worshipped Émilie and carried the torch for her for ten years but he never proposed and she eventually married Pierre Vincent Benoist, a chief of bureau in the Ministry of the Interior.

Charlotte was popular in the salons and was received at the Tuileries and Malmaison by Josephine and her daughter, Hortense Beauharnais, with a special kindness in gratitude for Larrey's treatment of Eugène when he had been slightly wounded in Egypt.[6] The First Consul, too, behaved courteously towards her—something not necessarily to be expected—and she was able to induce him to grant Larrey's mother a pension.[7]

At the beginning of 1804 Joseph Fouché, the unsavoury Minister of Police, uncovered a tangled plot to murder Bonaparte. The First Consul was vulnerable and his death would throw the country back into the cauldron of revolution. The solution therefore was to make the office hereditary—which suited Bonaparte most admirably. A month later, on May 18, 1804, the First Consul was elected Emperor of the French, and there was no doubt in his mind that he was founding a mighty dynasty to rival the greatest the world had ever known.

One of the hitherto First Consul's acts had been to institute the Legion of Honour—if he had any qualms about betraying such revolutionary principles as he may still have had, he doubtless recalled the words of the good republican, John Milton, 'Orders and Degrees Jarr not with liberty, but well consist'[8]— and Larrey had been among those created an Officer. At the ceremony in the church of the Invalides on July 15, 1804, when the insignia were distributed by the Emperor, Larrey was pleased to be told, 'It is a well-deserved award.' A few days later he was appointed an Inspector-General of the Medical Services of the Armies, together with Percy, Desgenettes, Nicolas Heurteloup, Jean François Coste (medical inspector of military hospitals), and Antoine Augustin Parmentier (the Pharmacist-in-Chief of the home forces).

At this time, too, the official appointment of First Surgeon to His Majesty had to be made. (Alexandre Yvan was Napoleon's personal surgeon—a different matter entirely. He had held the post since 1796 and continued to do so until 1814.) Larrey felt sure that the honour would be his, but he reckoned without the influence of Jean Nicolas Corvisart who had had the First Consul's ear since a fortunate consultation in 1801.[9] Corvisart, now First Physician, scented unwelcome competition for the Emperor's favours if Larrey was appointed and so proposed Alexis Boyer, a former chief assistant to Desault, instead. Boyer got the job, and Larrey once again limped home for Charlotte to soothe a wounded ego.

The year ended with the grandest display of ceremony the French had seen for many a long year and one that served to distract their thoughts from the military stagnation on their northern coasts, where Napoleon's scheme to invade England met only with frustration, and the all-too-successful blockade of their major ports by the British fleet. On December 2 the attention of the world was focused on the coronation in Notre Dame Cathedral. Charlemagne had been crowned by a pope and nothing less would do for Napoleon. But while Pope Pius VII remained seated the Emperor took the crown from the altar and himself set it upon his own head: let it be plain for all to see that Napoleon is answerable to no man.

After the coronation Larrey was worried. Like Milton he was a good republican and had regarded the recent wars of the Revolution and Consulate as battles for liberty and the defence of freedom. But now events were taking a dangerous turn.

'I had deep misgivings,' he said to Charlotte, 'when I saw this illustrious soldier take up the sceptre of kings. Everything tells me that this instrument of tyranny will bring about his downfall and the ruin of France. Had he only kept his modest title of First

Consul of the Republic, he would be respected by the whole world and would remain the idol of all the French people.'[10]

But Napoleon himself had no misgivings. With his coronation out of the way he continued his relentless drive forward. At the end of March 1805, his plan to lure the English fleet away from the Channel and out across the Atlantic to the West Indies began with Admiral Pierre Villeneuve's escape from Toulon.

On the orders of the Emperor, Larrey reported to the imperial headquarters at Boulogne. 'The troops had already embarked and were awaiting the arrival of the French and Spanish fleets to cover the crossing. I had arranged to be with the Imperial Guard during the voyage and on landing. The ships resounded with the cheers of our soldiers who could scarce contain their impatience to reach the enemy's shore. And to judge from their behaviour, the English were already struck with terror and seemed unable to avert the threatened invasion.

'But in the midst of these immense preparations a new continental coalition was formed, and France in her turn was threatened by the preparations of Austria.'[11]

Bedevilled by ill-found ships, disease, and desertion, Villeneuve decided to leave the West Indies and return to France, without waiting for Ganteaume, as soon as he learnt that Nelson was on his tail. At Ferrol, on the north-west corner of Spain, he received orders from Napoleon to sail for Brest and, at any cost, lift the British blockade long enough for Ganteaume to break out. But Villeneuve had had enough; on his own initiative he abandoned the plan and sailed south for Cadiz.

When news of this reached Napoleon at Boulogne on August 23, he became furious. Larrey had never seen his Emperor in such a state. He turned purple, the veins of his forehead swelled as if they would burst, and clenching his fists he fumed against Villeneuve, his cowardice, and his incompetence. Two years of preparation brought to naught because the admirals would not do as they were told—money, time, effort wasted, all wasted. Larrey tried to say something but was brusquely told to get out.

'Several evenings previously,' Larrey noted that night, 'the Emperor had left his quarters and, hearing military music, walked towards the sound to find a band of musicians in front of my billet. He was told that some veterans of the Egyptian campaign had persuaded their comrades to give me a concert. The Emperor took it well and congratulated these soldiers on the attachment they had kept for their surgeon. But in his foul humour, this came back to him and he told me to go to my Egyptians, much as he might tell me to go to the Devil.'[12]

Yet as quickly as it came, Napoleon's rage subsided and his mind cleared. He could no longer strike at the new coalition through England; the wedge had to be driven home in Europe and the Austrian and Russian armies kept from uniting.

'In a moment everything was changed and a new campaign resolved on. The troops disembarked and formed into columns. They marched rapidly through France and had crossed the Rhine into Germany before the enemy was aware that they had moved.'[13]

12. *Austerlitz*

With his army sped on its way, the Emperor returned to Paris. Larrey followed a day or two later to receive his orders from Marshal Bessières, Commander of the Imperial Guard, who promptly sent him on to Strasbourg. If he had had even the faintest hope that some miracle might have overtaken the Administration with the arrival of the new French empire, Larrey was soon to be disillusioned. Matters medico-military were still run in the traditional mixture of inefficiency, incompetence, obstruction, and corruption. Napoleon might have rectified the situation had he really wished, but he was content with his occasional gesture; and in the absence of any further action or inquiry, these gestures were treated for what they were by the Administration.

Percy, the army's Surgeon-in-Chief, had fought unceasingly throughout his career against the injustices of the Administration but with no success. Although recognizing Larrey's achievements on behalf of the Guard, he was not a little envious and, at this stage, was beginning to lose heart in the unequal struggle.

After a brilliant student career, Percy had followed in his father's footsteps and joined the army in 1776. He was a skilful surgeon and, like Larrey, physically courageous. In June 1792 he had replaced Sabatier as consultant surgeon to the Army of the North and by the next year had realized—again like Larrey—that something had to be done about the wounded. His solution was to send three surgeons and an orderly on horseback into the battle to do what they could to help. Admittedly they did not confuse the military situation but neither did they give effective aid. So, during the campaign on the Rhine in 1799 Percy introduced his 'wurst'. This was a long, four-wheeled, trunk-like box drawn by six horses and containing instruments and dressings sufficient to deal with 1,200 casualties. It had a rounded lid astride which sat eight surgeons one behind the other. Eight orderlies, riding the horses or sitting at the front and back ends, accompanied the surgeons. The vehicle could manœuvre fairly rapidly and was designed to approach close to the rear of the action where it would be easily accessible to the walking wounded. Stretcher bearers—stretchers were stored underneath the vehicle—were sent into the battle to collect casualties unable to walk. The wurst, however, never succeeded as it could not compare in manœuvrability or efficiency with Larrey's flying ambulances and, besides, Percy's ideas lacked the whole broad concept of casualty evacuation.

So, despite Percy's efforts the plight of casualties in the regiments of the line was deplorable. In fact a decree of September 1, 1805, had reduced the surgical allocation to a single ponderous fourgon for each regiment. Added to this the War Ministry was unable to recruit a sufficiency of medical officers, so it posted the poorly-trained surgeons from the military hospitals to active service and left the hospitals to be staffed by local civilian doctors. In consequence, Percy was still busy in Paris organizing as much as he could when the campaign began. Larrey was horrified, but as there was nothing he was able to do officially, he wrote to Bessières pointing out the situation and saying he would have to help the line regiments as best he could when they went into action.[1] His own ambulance division for the Imperial Guard was organized and awaiting inspection when Napoleon arrived in Strasbourg towards the end of September.

'Larrey,' said the Emperor, 'you were all but ready before me!'[2] This was just the sort of remark that pleased Larrey, but provoked jealousy among the attending administrative officers.

The army corps of Nicolas Soult, Michel Ney, Louis Davout, and Lannes from the Boulogne area were joined by those of Bernadotte from Hanover and of Marmont from Texel in north Holland. Then, with Murat's cavalry and the reserve corps of Pierre Augereau, the Grand Army—so named by the Emperor himself—crossed the Rhine and marched swiftly towards the Danube in a great sweep behind the Austrian position. After some skirmishing on the banks of the river, the advance guard forced a crossing at Donauwörth on October 7. Larrey's ambulance, in close attendance, was able to give immediate aid to the wounded.

The Austrian army had tried to adapt itself to the French method of warfare, but with conspicuous lack of success. Both structurally and temperamentally it was incapable of rapid movement over long distances; the Austrians preferred to fight the prepared defensive battle. Unaware that Napoleon had left Boulogne, their Chief-of-Staff, General Karl Mack von Leiberich, had crossed the Inn without waiting for his Russian allies (an uncouth lot whose proper place was deep inside their own country) and had marched leisurely westwards to Ulm where, on September 14, he had made himself comfortable and prepared his defence. Unfortunately, he omitted to cover his rear to the north-east—and Donauwörth lies 45 miles away in that direction. Once the French were across the Danube, the Austrian outposts retired rapidly on Ulm. Napoleon, however, continued his encircling movement southwards and established his headquarters at Augsburg in anticipation of Mack's escape. Incredibly Mack sat tight. Yet his inactivity almost proved the undoing of the French whose lines of communication had become unhealthily long. On October 11 Mack realized his danger and decided to strike along the north bank of the river at those attenuated lines. In really appalling weather that practically immobilized him he got as far as Elchingen where, on the fourteenth, he met Ney. The French crossed the river at their first charge, but the Austrians holed up in the abbey of Elchingen and made Ney fight hard to dislodge them.

Larrey had the wounded of both sides collected in what remained of the abbey and attended them in order of medical priority, regardless of nationality—a move that greatly displeased the French officers, particularly as conditions were bad and dressings in short supply. Nevertheless, they were fortunate to have any attention at all: the French wounded were entirely from line regiments; none of the Imperial Guard was hurt.

'What suffering we had to endure, my beloved,' Larrey wrote to his wife,[3] 'for three or four days we marched in the wet and the mud which was sometimes up to our middles. Some of the horses were swept away, and the sleet did not stop from the time we left Augsburg.

'The poor wounded were in a very sorry state, for hardly had the main body of the army crossed the river than the bridges were washed away by flood waters overflowing the banks far and wide. All our communications were severed. The carriages were still on the far bank and had to be driven away to avoid being submerged; as a result we had nothing. We had no rations, no equipment, and no linen for dressings except the small quantity we carry in our portmanteaux. However, I dressed the wounded as well as I could, gave them comfort, and by perseverance and hard work managed to have them carried eventually to the distant ambulances. I shall not tell you of all we suffered; physically, I am only a little weary, but my confidence has been badly shaken.'

Mack squelched back to Ulm and the French fist closed. As it tightened the Austrians found their stores and magazines to be almost empty and, when the French artillery opened fire from the surrounding heights, they capitulated. The surrender made a great impression on Larrey:

'I much regret, my dear friend,' he wrote to Girodet,[4] 'that you were not with me on several occasions during our campaign, but above all at Ulm when the Emperor made the whole Austrian army—30,000 prisoners who had foolishly shut themselves up in a town we were about to take by assault—march past before him. Six generals, including the Chief-of-Staff, were at their head. Never was a spectacle more worthy of a great painter. The scene surpassed all that history, ancient or modern, could offer.

'Picture, will you, an army of about 100,000 men in full battle array massed on the slopes of a regular, semi-circular hill which enclosed the left bank of the Danube and the town of Ulm.

'The Emperor, with his staff, stood facing the town on a rocky outcrop overlooking the road where the prisoners were passing. He was so in command, it seemed that nature had put the rock there specially for the purpose. The column of prisoners laid their weapons and equipment on the ground and then filed back into the town to await departure for France. Our foot dragoons stood beside the dump to take the enemy's cavalry horses which he was compelled to give up.

'Judge for yourself the humiliation on the one side and the jubilation on the other. The glacis in front of the town was covered with arms of every description. Many of the enemy seemed not to comprehend the fact of their surrender; others tore their equipment or smashed their arms in anger and despair; others could be seen, under their helmets, to be silently weeping.

'Near the Emperor in his grey redingote and his dilapidated hat, were his generals; behind him was his white horse. He gave the impression that the Austrian generals were a great distance from him. His look shrivelled them into insignificance and he acknowledged not a single one. No one approached him except with the greatest respect. Truly, he was in his glory that day.'

The campaign so far had resulted in the capture of 67,000 Austrian prisoners-of-war, 150 pieces of cannon, 80 standards, and 26 generals as prisoners-of-war on parole including a prince and the General-in-Chief, Mack. 'I have seen nearly all these prisoners,' he wrote in his letter to Charlotte,[3] 'and I guarantee the truth of these facts. Happily our own casualties are not very numerous, bearing in mind the major success we have achieved— at the most 600 wounded and 100 killed.'

Despite its heavy losses the Austrian force was still an army. It retreated rapidly to Vienna and then marched north into Moravia to join the Russians. In the second week of November Napoleon left his headquarters at Schönbrunn, and his advance guard under Lannes soon had a vicious tussle with Peter Bagration's Russians at Hollabrünn. The town was taken and retaken several times before it was finally burned by the Russians.

The casualties were sent back to Vienna where they were received by Percy, who had at last managed to put in an appearance, while Larrey continued north to join the headquarters at Znaim (Znojmo in today's Czech Republic). Here the Russians made overtures for peace which were unacceptable; in fact Larrey felt they were simply stalling for time while their army continued its flight towards Brünn (Brno). However, despite the town's defensive advantages, the Russians did not stop there and Murat entered unopposed.

'Eight or ten days were spent in reconnaissance and conferences. Eventually, on December 1, arrangements were completed for the reception of the wounded of a great battle, which was now regarded as inevitable. The convents and civil hospitals were well ordered and I had already commandeered them; the almshouses were reserved for the Imperial Guard. The Guard's ambulance was also ready'[5]—one of Larrey's skills was a genius for accurately estimating the number of casualties he could expect from a battle.

In the absence of Percy, who was still in Vienna organizing the hospitals, Larrey was ordered by Napoleon to take medical charge. After making an inspection he wrote to the hospital quartermaster at Brünn:

'His Majesty has made me responsible for the medical services of the army and, acting on his verbal orders, I pray you send me tomorrow morning a sufficient number of carriages for the transport of the wounded; meat and brandy for each ambulance; and all the stretchers you have available.

'Will you also instruct the divisional quartermasters to report tomorrow morning to the three main field dressing stations (the mill [at Paleny] for the third line of the army, the farm for the second line, and the position chosen for the front line). From there we will be able to dispatch as many subdivisions as will be needed to follow the advancing columns even if they pursue the enemy far and wide.

'Today, I inspected the ambulance divisions and the medical officers of the army corps. I told them where to find instruments and dressings on the field of battle and entrusted their care to the senior surgeons. I shall repeat my inspection tonight.

'I think these measures and my own over-all supervision will give the wounded all the help they have a right to expect of us. I only urge you to act most speedily in supplying my needs.'[6]

The quartermaster, one Joinville, was furious at being told what to do by a mere surgeon even though the orders emanated from the Emperor. Whether deliberately delayed or held up by the state of the roads, the requested items did not arrive until midnight after the battle.

As darkness descended on December 1, the freezing rain and hail, that had made the last day of waiting one of sheer misery, gave way to clear starry skies and the promise of fine weather. Close on 100,000 men of the Grand Army in bivouac on the hillsides forgot their discomfort and cursing in an ecstasy of enthusiasm as Napoleon passed through their ranks.

'Comrades! Tomorrow the great question will be resolved: who is the best infantry in the world, you or the Russians?'

'We will conquer,' roared the heart of France. 'Vive l'Empereur! Vive l'Empereur!'

'Tomorrow is the anniversary of our coronation,' said the Emperor, pausing in reminiscence.

'So much the better,' replied a grenadier, 'you shall have the Russians to dance at your celebration.' Saying which the man set fire to a handful of straw from his bivouac and held it high above his head. In a moment the hillsides were aflame as soldier after soldier honoured his Emperor.[7]

'Convinced that he was to be attacked on the morrow,' Larrey wrote to his Uncle Alexis,[8] 'the Emperor called his generals together during the night and gave them their orders. In particular, he told me to have everything ready for treating the wounded. You can well imagine that I did not close my eyes for the rest of the night; already I could see the wounded on the field of battle calling for my help.'

The Emperor was on horseback long before dawn on the day of Austerlitz. The first hint of what that day was to bring came when the stillness was broken by a distant cannonade. But in their desire to turn the French right (the cause of the gun-fire) the allied armies of Russia and Austria had abandoned the key to their position. When the sun broke through the morning mist the commanding heights of Pratzen were bare; the conspicuous bayonets and artillery of the previous day had gone.

'On a signal,' Larrey continued in his letter, 'the Muscovite hordes threw themselves with blood-curdling yells on our advance guard. They believed themselves certain of victory for they had left their packs and greatcoats at their bivouacs. Their attack was spirited, but they did not realize that courage alone never won a war; tactics were essential.

'It was amazing how the course of the action seemed to follow the plans of the Emperor. He commanded in person and seemed to be wherever the action was thickest. He moved so quickly that I often saw him alone on his arab horse in the midst of the combatants. The Emperors of Russia and Austria were also at the battle and in command of their armies which truly gave proof of their valour; the Russians, particularly, fought to the last man and their fearlessness was such that they were shot to pieces at the very mouths of our cannon. Never, my dear uncle, have I seen so bloody a battle; it lasted from six in the morning until eight at night.'

Percy turned up early in the day and so, at the height of the battle, Larrey returned to his duties with the Imperial Guard, some of whom had been wounded in a furious charge by their Russian opposite number. 'Every operation and dressing was performed on the field and the wounded were conveyed by the carriages of our flying ambulance to the main field dressing station in the barns of the mill.

'The speed of these carriages allowed me to use them for evacuating the wounded of the line. I stayed with the Guard, although I halted my ambulance wherever my presence could be of use. We returned to the mill at about four in the morning [after working all night on the field] to dress those who had not received immediate attention. I ordered them all to be removed to Brünn on the next day, in charge of Surgeon-Major Paulet, and to be admitted to the building that I had previously prepared for the purpose.'[9]

Among the French wounded was Brigadier-General Paul Charles François Adrien Henri Dieudonné Thiébault, a writer and a man with a great fondness for himself whose sorry tale[10] gives a glimpse into the difficulties Larrey had to face and shows that the 18th-century, feudal even, attitude to war was still very much in evidence.

General Marc Antoine Geoffroy Saint-Hilaire's division, which included Thiébault, was on the heights of Pratzen courageously repelling all attempts to dislodge them. Towards the end of the day, while leading a charge on a Russian battery, Thiébault was hit in the left shoulder by a ball that smashed through the middle of the collar bone in front and emerged at the top of the shoulder blade behind. He was given first-aid by a regimental surgeon before being carried to Brünn in an immense old four-wheeled coach that had been found in a nearby village and was large enough to hold a bed. Inside with him rode his servant and the surgeon whom he had grabbed for his own exclusive use.

The next morning, the senior army surgeons—Percy, Larrey, Yvan, and two others—gathered round his bed. By general consent, Larrey was given the job of débriding the wound—an unpleasant injury but nothing like as serious as Thiébault made out.[11] After the operation, Larrey insisted that the surgeon appropriated by the patient should be released, or at least replaced by an orderly; Thiébault was a picture of indignation and, as Percy sided with the General, the surgeon stayed.

(This appropriation of surgeons was nothing new and Larrey had already tried to have the practice stopped. On November 25 he had written to the Chief-of-Staff from Brünn:

'With reluctance I have to report that the generals, believing the best surgeons to be entirely at their disposal, sometimes attach them to their persons so as to have immediate attention when wounded. This seems to me to be a waste when the surgeon's time could be more profitably occupied.')[12]

Yet, this apart, Larrey did not endear himself to Thiébault as he could spare him only a few moments each day. Percy, on the other hand, visited the patient night and morning to spend an hour or two in pleasant conversation. Thiébault remained at Brünn for several weeks before setting out for Vienna en route to Paris in a comfortable carriage with two aides-de-camp and his surgeon. Passing through Bavaria he met Berthier who ordered him to leave the surgeon at Munich where the hospitals had dire need of staff, but Thiébault simply laughed and went on his way with his entourage intact.

From Brünn, on December 8, Larrey wrote to his wife airing his personal problems:[13] 'The Emperor will be in Paris for the New Year, but, my beloved, I cannot see myself being able to follow for about two months because of my duty to the Imperial Guard. I have also been ordered by His Majesty to embalm the body of the colonel of the light cavalry of the Guard who was killed in the fight.[14]

'Just at present I have had no chance of raising our own interests with the Emperor, and his imminent departure makes me fear that I shall be unable to speak to him again before Paris. But you, my fascinating Laville, can do something: finish your portrait of him so that you can present it on his arrival. This will also give you the opportunity to ask for news of me. Make a point of seeing him, beloved, and ask for a country house—assuredly, if he grants it, no one will be happier than I.'

Yet this was only a minor part of his—and the medical service's—troubles. With the rise of the new empire, military surgeons were once again regarded as confounded nuisances, probably with a fair amount of justification since many of them were merely half-trained medical officers more likely to do harm than good. The Administration took its cue from the Commander-in-Chief: if the supply of manpower was inexhaustible what need was there to slow the military machine by carrying out running repairs? Consequently, the Administration seemed bent on degrading, if not destroying, the military surgeons both morally and materially. Whenever it could, it disputed a surgeon's pay, his travelling expenses, and his allowances for horses killed or equipment lost or captured by the enemy. It would not permit surgeons of the line to wear the aiguillette (shoulder knot and lanyard), a right enjoyed by surgeons of the Imperial Guard. (Half a century later, Larrey's son, the Surgeon-in-Chief of the French army and denied a semblance of authority, was compelled to stand a helpless spectator of the carnage at Solferino.) It was this knife continually twisted in his back that eventually wore Larrey down into defeat, but it never broke his indomitable spirit.

However, personal matters were soon thrust into the background. Almost immediately the wounded had been collected in Brünn an epidemic of typhus broke out and, to add to the troubles, hospital gangrene became rife. The wounded did not stand a chance and as often as not were affected by both diseases. The hospitals of the line lost a quarter of their patients in this way.

'The epidemic also broke out among the Russian prisoners who had necessarily been crowded in great numbers into the churches and other large buildings. It soon spread among the local inhabitants and finally extended along the whole line of evacuation, even to France, due to the movement of the prisoners and of the sick of both nations.'[15]

On the periphery of all the foetid horror, the wounded of the Imperial Guard remained almost free of disease. The almshouses that Larrey had reserved for them were 'distant from the other hospitals and from the populous parts of the city. They were well lit, well aired, and kept perfectly clean. The sick owed their security to the benefits of prompt medical and surgical assistance and to their early evacuation to another hospital prepared for them in Vienna.'[16]

Here Larrey spent Christmas and, like a dog worrying at a bone, wrote again to Charlotte:[17]

'The Emperor is setting out for Paris and we shall follow shortly. Would you, my lovely Laville, think seriously about offering him the portrait. You could profit from the occasion to ask for a little farm, for I have certainly earned it. Give my compliments to General Rapp[18] who will present you to the Emperor. Don't lose this most favourable opportunity. Since we shall not be together for the New Year, we shall instead celebrate our wedding anniversary and have our marriage blessed in church if you agree.'

A dutiful wife, Madame Larrey did as she was told. Napoleon charmingly complimented her on the portrait and gave her a sum of money, but the request for a house or a farm in the country was quietly ignored.

When the Imperial Guard was ready to leave, Larrey went ahead to see that all was ready for the wounded along the route. But from Strasbourg he had to complete the journey to Paris in short stages, lacking as he did the money to travel by post-chaise. In another letter to his wife,[19] he made caustic reference to the senior assistant surgeon of the Guard, Paulet,[20] who early on had posted back to Paris from Vienna: 'Probably he feared the sickness which reigned there as it did in all the hospitals. I sometimes wish that I could follow the example of all these selfish people and do things in the easiest way—particularly as it seems to be the way to gain the highest rewards. But no matter, I shall carry on and complete the campaign with all the enthusiasm I can muster. Too bad if it is disagreeable; I shall do my best and so find the greatest satisfaction.'

13. *Jena*

The spring and summer of 1806 passed peacefully enough in Paris where Larrey resumed his duties at Val-de-Grâce and at the Hospital of the Guard. Charlotte was as pleased to have her husband at home as he was to be there, and never more so than one morning when their daughter, now eight years old, had an accident that in those days could have had tragic consequences. Isaure was in the kitchen cutting the bread for breakfast when a fragment of crust shot into her right eye. Instinctively she put up her hand to rub it away; but, instead, she plunged the point of the newly sharpened blade into the centre of the cornea. Through the quarter-inch wound aqueous humour gushed from inside the eye to join her tears, and, bulging like a brown pea, was a hernia of the iris. The eye rapidly became sunken and blind. Charlotte called desperately for her husband who took in the situation at a glance and with incredible sangfroid set about repairing the damage. He sat his daughter on her mother's lap and, using a blunt-ended golden style, gently returned the herniated iris through the wound. He then closed the eye and bandaged it with compresses soaked in a solution of lead acetate containing a few drops of spirits of camphor. 'A light diet and absolute rest in a dark room produced a perfect cure within a very few days. The sight of the eye is unimpaired and the scar on the cornea is imperceptible.'[1] He was justifiably proud of his success.

Larrey's purely military responsibilities, however, were gradually increasing as Napoleon continued to transform the Guard into what amounted virtually to an army in its own right. At its creation (as the Consular Guard) in January 1800, the Guard had consisted of 2,000 men; two years later, of 5,000; two years later still, of nearly 7,500; and in March 1806 the Emperor added the only regiment of dragoons. Besides the dragoons, there were

H

foot grenadiers, fusiliers, light infantry, horse grenadiers, light cavalry, Mamelukes, engineers, artillery, military police, and even a batallion of sailors. They were the elite of the French army, and every man a veteran of at least three campaigns.[2]

But if France seemed to be resting peacefully on the laurels of Austerlitz, her Emperor most certainly was not. The memory of Trafalgar was a constant irritation, for that defeat had put paid to his dreams of conquest overseas. The master of Europe was locked tightly within his estate. Perhaps he could extricate himself by guile. Napoleon had given Hanover to the King of Prussia as a reward for his co-operation. Now, without telling the King, he offered Hanover to England in return for Sicily (brother Joseph's Kingdom of Naples was incomplete without it) and other lost bases beyond the ocean. For one reason or another England did not swallow the bait. So the answer, he decided, must be to hit the trade the British were so fond of, by excluding them from their continental markets.

Yet before he could do anything about this, Napoleon ran into trouble with Prussia. When King Frederick William heard about the manœuvrings over Hanover he was justifiably incensed and on September 26 sent an ultimatum to Paris demanding the withdrawal of French troops from Prussian soil—which was as far as they had retired after Austerlitz.

Such impertinence was not to be tolerated; Frederick William would have to be taught a lesson. So Napoleon left Paris for Mainz which he reached on October 1, and then in a southerly sweep set out to catch the hurriedly mobilized Prussian army. At Bayreuth the movement took a sharp turn north for Schleiz where the advance guard had its first encounter with some detachments of Prussian cavalry. More to the point, though, the Prussians had their first glimpse of the mighty Grand Army advancing in three columns with the Emperor and the infantry of his Guard at the head of the centre. The army swung westwards, south of Gera, towards Jena and the second great victory for imperial France.[3]

The Imperial Guard was not committed at the battle of Jena. The infantry of the Guard, who had had the benefit of relays of carts and carriages to bring them from Paris, had been left at Gera to await the imminent arrival of the cavalry after its long forced march. Larrey and his ambulance division were with the cavalry.

'Marshal Bessières' orders were to keep a watchful eye on the enemy's movements and he refused me permission to leave Gera and assist my colleagues on the field of battle. Nevertheless, we did receive a large number of wounded who made their way back to the town. I had them collected in the castle where, assisted by the surgeons of my ambulance division, I operated on them and dressed their wounds. Some severe injuries required major surgery which was generally successful as it was performed within 24 hours.'[4]

Larrey was disgusted with the lack of organization for evacuating the casualties—admittedly Percy had a terrible job in getting supplies and dressings, but that was no excuse. Without Larrey the whole system fell apart at the seams. 'Those with the most serious wounds could not be dressed until some time after the battle, either because the field dressing stations were too far away or because the lightly wounded, who were able to walk, had taken up the whole of the surgeon's time during the first 24 hours.'[5]

His presence was sorely missed and he probably did not exaggerate too grossly when he wrote to Charlotte on October 20 that 'the Emperor and all the wounded did not cease calling my name on that brilliant but ghastly day'.[6] Undoubtedly he could have saved many of those who died—and the fact that Yvan and two surgeons of the imperial household (François Ribes, a very dear family friend and contemporary from Bagnères de Bigorre, and Jouan) found themselves without instruments did not help matters.

That the French were victorious at Jena is scarcely surprising. They outnumbered the Prussians by roughly 96,000 to 54,000. But more significantly the morale of the French army had never been higher; under their Commander-in-Chief they had mastered the art of warfare and were hell-bent for glory—all who had missed Austerlitz wanted a fight before they returned to France. In contrast, the Prussians were living on the reputation won for them by Frederick the Great, and their generals, almost without exception, were mentally and physically incompetent dodderers.

Yet one Prussian at least saw in the seeming strength of France her future weakness. Christian Massenbach, Chief-of-Staff to Friedrich Ludwig, Prince of Hohenlohe Ingelfingen, was visiting Murat to discuss the terms of surrender when he met Larrey whom he had known 13 years before on the Rhine.

'You have come a long way since 1793,' said Massenbach. 'Remember Mainz and Wissembourg?' He smiled sadly. 'You French then had need of a man, and now that you have found him you are capable of extraordinary deeds. But take care, if this man disappears, your power will fly away. As for us, no matter how low we are today, we shall recover from the tragedy and humiliation of the present hour—of that I am certain.'[7]

On the third day after the battle, the French army marched north for Berlin. Its headquarters were just over the border into Saxony when a violent storm blew up. Usually Napoleon was utterly indifferent to whatever the weather had to offer—a trait not always appreciated by his staff—but on this occasion he was practically on the doorstep of a lodge and decided to take shelter. The entourage was admitted by two young women and as Napoleon entered, the elder clasped her hands and cried out: 'Heavens! General Bonaparte!' The Emperor looked at her in displeased amazement, seeking an explanation for the sudden outburst. But then Larrey came through the door and the poor woman seemed to go berserk. She shot forward, seized both of his hands, and sobbed: 'Monsieur Larrey, you remember me? You remember Madame Cérésole?'

For a moment Larrey was back in a hospital in Alexandria, standing at a bedside while one of his favourite young surgeons died of plague. Watching him, her swollen eyes beseeching him to perform a miracle, was the woman who now held his hands. But there had been no miracle for Surgeon-Major Cérésole.

Larrey, deeply moved, presented Madame Cérésole to the Emperor and told of her husband's honourable death in Egypt. She then explained how, with Larrey's help, she had been re-patriated and, because she had a son to educate, had taken a job as governess to a Saxon family. Recollections of Egypt always had an emotional effect on Napoleon and he awarded the widow 1,200 francs and promised to see that her son's education would be taken care of. 'I am only paying a debt of gratitude,' he said. And when he arrived in Berlin he was as good as his word.[8]

But Larrey unfortunately fared not so well. From Potsdam, on October 25, he wrote to his wife:[9] 'I don't know what the future holds for me. I fear I shall have no appointments other than those I have in Paris. I am already deprived of travelling expenses by a decree of the Emperor which abolished them indiscriminately for all the officers of his Guard. I must make the war pay for them. I have bought a horse and now have to borrow 25 louis to continue the campaign.'

On October 27, a golden autumn day, the Emperor entered Berlin in triumph with his staff and his Imperial Guard. 'Without a doubt this was one of the Emperor Napoleon's most glorious days.

'While His Majesty was occupied in reorganizing the administration of the Prussian government and in reinforcing the army, the marshals of his empire pursued the enemy and attacked their last defences on the Oder. Once these places were taken, and a part of Prussian Poland invaded, the King of Prussia sued for peace and requested an armistice. The Emperor agreed.'[10]

Yet in the midst of this triumph, Larrey was thrown into the deepest despair by the behaviour of the Administration.

'Poor love, why does fate separate us so cruelly?' he wrote to Charlotte on November 1.[11] 'My God, how my soul is oppressed. How I hate this existence. How unhappy I am. Already smothered by arbitrary authority, paralysed by their whims, deprived of honours and of the pleasure of doing my best, I am involved in enormous expenses which are *not* reimbursed. I am subject to a thousand annoyances and humiliations.

'But have patience, my beloved. I hope when peace comes there will be no more of my enemies stirring up trouble incessantly for you. It is on your account that I have not taken vigorous measures towards certain persons who are jealous of me and intrigue against me. But I must stop, my lovely Charlotte,[12] or I fear I shall lose my reason.'

Then again on November 6:[13] 'The quartermasters persecute us without ceasing. They make false reports and are continually slandering me and my ambulances. They have succeeded in

removing the aiguillettes of my comrades, and because I pro-
tested they subjected me to harsh and unjust treatment. If I had
been able to speak with you I might have cleared my mind, but I
am keeping silent until I have a favourable opportunity for
putting the case to His Majesty.

'You are more dear to me than all I have in the world, and
without you, my love, Larrey does not exist.'

Unfortunately, His Majesty was too busy to allow any favourable
opportunities to arise. Besides ordering the affairs of Prussia, he
put into effect his plan of a continental blockade of Britain by
the issue on November 21 of the Berlin Decree. The idea that
no country under the thumb of France should have any commerce
whatsoever with Britain looked marvellous on paper. Indeed,
it took the island's breath away for one brief moment. But in a
very short space of time England bounced back by developing
her markets on the far sides of the seas, and by sitting hard on
French maritime trade. An important implication of the continental
blockade was that there should be no gaps and this led directly
to Napoleon's attempts first to extend the frontiers of Europe into
Russia and then to seal the shores of Portugal.

But while the Emperor's thoughts were directed to the east,
Larrey's were constantly turning back towards the west.

'For several days,' he wrote to Charlotte on November 25,[14]
'I have lived in the deluded hope of accompanying His Majesty
to Paris, and of spending there the month when my presence could
be of most use.' (Charlotte had told him that she was again pregnant.) 'I had even obtained Marshal Berthier's promise to let
me make this short journey. But today we received orders to set
out at once for Poland.'

14. *The Frozen Waste of Eylau*

The campaign in Poland opened in the middle of November 1806. King Frederick William had entered into a coalition with Czar Alexander, and Russian troops were marching towards Warsaw. If Napoleon needed an excuse to extend his dominion eastwards, this was it; but unwisely his plans failed to allow for the Polish winter, the abject poverty of the people, and the stark inhospitality of the countryside.

The Emperor set out from Berlin on November 25 and on the 27th reached Posen (Poznan) where he was welcomed as a God-sent liberator by the wretched Poles who had been continually squabbled over by Austria, Prussia, and Russia and partitioned three times between 1792 and 1795. The weather was atrocious and continued so throughout December; torrential rain reduced the roads to a terrible state. 'We were marching through thick clay that reached the girths of the horses. The artillery was constantly in difficulties and many baggage-wagons became stuck fast. Under these circumstances the advantages of our small ambulance carriages were evident. They had only two wheels and, by virtue of their height and lightness, travelled more easily than four-wheeled vehicles.'[1]

The speed of the Russian about turn and retreat northwards on Pultusk was so rapid that the French cut their losses and fell back on Warsaw. 'I arrived here during the night,' Larrey wrote to Charlotte on January 3,[2] 'and, as in all the big towns—thanks to our billeting officers—I am very poorly lodged in the outskirts of a suburb about three miles from the town. Things are very bad and we survive only by virtue of money. I am already at the end of my resources.'[3]

But survive he did, even though 'it was so cold that it froze the urine in my chamber pot'. He continued this theme in his letter of January 28,[4] 'As I have been unable to warm myself in my billet, I shall be less susceptible to the cold when in bivouac on the snow- and ice-covered plains. All is for the best in this world if one views it with a philosophical eye.

'His Majesty enjoys good health as always. I have proof that he still retains the same regard and friendship for me, but I see him rarely. The Pultusk campaign changed him a little and made him very tired, though several days' rest sufficed to restore his embonpoint. If I had had food and lodging like his, I believe I would be as fit and would have put on weight as I did in Paris.'

Yet there was to be no respite. In much the same way that the armies of Revolutionary France had not played the game, so the Russians, under General August Bennigsen, broke the rules. Hitherto no one in their right mind would campaign in the depth of a central European winter; but Bennigsen reckoned that his troops' experience of the climate was a strong point in their favour. So, on January 25 he took the offensive and launched a series of surprise attacks on the cantonments of Ney and Bernadotte along the Vistula.

'The snow was about three feet deep and the thermometer registered 14 or 15 degrees (Fahrenheit) of frost when we left Warsaw. [Larrey usually carried a thermometer with him which he pinned to a lapel when he wanted to take a reading.] Ice had carried away the bridges and we had difficulty crossing the Vistula. However, once across, the imperial headquarters marched towards Wittemburg where Murat had already met the Russian advance guard and forced them to retire. Despite the severe weather we remorselessly pursued the enemy. The Imperial Guard marched immediately behind Murat's troops with headquarters a short distance further back.'[5]

On February 6, at Hoff, Murat came to grief when one of his dramatic light cavalry charges failed to impress the Russians and he was driven off in disorder. The French wounded were promptly sabred by the Russians who, as they did so, took a sadistic delight in yelling in good French: 'Cry then, "Vive l'Empereur!"'[6] But before serious harm was done to French morale, General Jean d'Hautpoul threw in the heavy cavalry to such brilliant effect that Larrey commented: 'The success of this affair seemed to promise the entire defeat of the enemy's army when it should halt and we meet in pitched battle.'[7]

Hautpoul returned at the head of his cuirassiers, his breast-plate dented and blackened with powder, his helmet battered, and his uniform smothered in Russian blood; as he dismounted he was warmly embraced by the Emperor.

'Sire,' he said, 'for showing me so great an honour, I needs must die for Your Majesty.'[8] And that, alas, was tempting fate too much.

The Russians, in fact, halted at Preuss-Eylau, 'an advantageous position fortified with redoubts and batteries of heavy cannon. Their rear-guard stopped a mile or so short of the town behind a village that straddled the road. We immediately reconnoitred this position and, before noon, launched an attack that continued until nightfall. The Imperial Guard took no part in this fight. However, since I was the only Inspector-General of the Medical Services of the Armies present, I was directed by Marshal Berthier to have all the wounded carried to the village and to supervise their dressings. I had them collected in the largest house, which was hastily prepared to receive them, and we spent the rest of that day and all night attending to their needs. Several major amputations were required; they were mostly successful.'[9]

Shortly after Larrey had begun admitting the wounded, General Louis Caulaincourt, Master of the Horse, arrived to commandeer the house for Napoleon. Larrey showed him the word 'Hospital' chalked on the door and said that it was impossible to move the wounded but that the General should have no difficulty in finding somewhere else for the Emperor. At this Caulaincourt flared up and threatened to report the surgeon.

'As you please,' Larrey replied, 'but you may be sure that His Majesty will decide in my favour.' And he did.

'Larrey has done well to keep a large house for the wounded,' Napoleon told the Master of the Horse. 'It is up to you to find me another lodging.'[10]

In the palmy days of the Empire, Larrey always had a right to the first billets for the wounded, before even the generals and the headquarters staff. Napoleon gave the arrangement his blessing and it was sufficient to have the words 'Ambulance of the Guard' or 'Larrey's Ambulance' scribbled in chalk or charcoal for that building to remain inviolable.[11] This gave Larrey a certain moral ascendancy over the administrative officers who, like Caulaincourt, did not take it kindly. Nevertheless, at such moments Napoleon may perhaps have experienced the occasional twinge of conscience over his treatment of Larrey and was in some way—not too demanding, though—trying to make amends to him personally and to the army generally.

By the evening of February 7 the Russians were in position on the hill commanding Eylau; the French passed the night in bivouac with the temperature falling to about zero Fahrenheit. In the small hours Larrey was called to a despairing General Louis Lepic, Colonel of the horse grenadiers of the Imperial Guard. The previous day the General had had an attack of gouty rheumatism in his knees and was fuming at his inability to lead his men into action.[12] Despite the hour, Larrey happily set to work and at dawn a delighted Lepic was back in the saddle as French troops 'descended through a narrow defile into the basin of Eylau which in summer is an attractive lakeland area but now frozen over and deep in snow. The advance guard moved towards the enemy while the Imperial Guard, with several other divisions of the army, deployed in the basin.

'The Russians, believing themselves strong and in a favourable position, prepared for a general attack. A brisk cannonade soon started on both sides; the two armies approached; and a bloody battle began. The issue was in doubt until a vigorous charge by the Imperial Cavalry [under Lepic] decided the fate of the day in our favour. Although the infantry of the Guard was not engaged, it suffered heavily from artillery fire.'[13]

Larrey later described the scene for Girodet:[14] 'The barns where the wounded found shelter [and where Larrey established his casualty clearing station] were at the entrance to Preuss-Eylau, close to the gate of the town and to the left of the plateau where the infantry of the Guard was stationed. We were at a very short distance from the church, in the angle of which the Emperor and his staff set up headquarters during the horrifying combat. The main action took place to the right of the town, several yards in front, and on the hill where the enemy had concentrated his forces.

'The barns were open on all sides (the straw having been removed for the horses), the roofing was part missing, part damaged and the wind and snow penetrated everywhere. We had scarcely any shelter from the bullets. The unhappy wounded were huddled together on such poor straw as we could find; their only covering was their clothes. All arms were there: infantry, cavalry of the different corps, artillerymen, and a few Mamelukes. Officers were mingled with the soldiers, and the wounds were terrible since nearly all had been caused by artillery. They called my name, and the air was full of their anguished cries for help.

'Despite their size, the barns soon were filled and a great number of wounded lay outside where I was obliged to operate in the falling snow. Only a man who has seen death staring him in the face can appreciate the nature of my task.

'My comrades gave in one after another; I alone had the strength to remain at my post until all the wounded in danger of losing their lives had received my help. During all this time I never once felt the call of nature, nor did I suffer from hunger, thirst, or the need to sleep.

'I did not feel the cold, which had frozen the feet and fingers of many about me; my hand never lost its precision. My operations were all done happily and without accident.'

The cold was, indeed, so intense that the instruments frequently fell from the hands of his assistants during the operations. Nevertheless, Larrey was still able to carry out several delicate and difficult procedures including amputations at the shoulder joint and sutures of facial wounds. Thanks to the cold, he needed to tie only the major arterial trunks to arrest haemorrhage, and not one of the wounded was lost from bleeding on the long route of evacuation.

Once the soldiers had been operated on 'their cries gave way to a surprising calm and a kind of internal satisfaction'.[15] But in dressing stations elsewhere, humanity was ill served. 'Arms to the left. Legs to the right.' The orderlies stood and shouted while nineteen-year-old conscript 'surgeons' hacked and butchered.[16] Bodies and limbs were cast aside to be trampled on by cavalrymen seeking straw for their horses, and when they found it they would even bed their mounts among the wounded—truly men ceased to be men when they could no longer fight.

During the afternoon the Russian right wing had unexpectedly attacked the French left in front of Larrey's casualty station. The first sign of trouble was a group of soldiers fleeing by the barns. Those of the wounded who were still able, took to their heels; those who were not, tried in vain to follow. M. Pelchet, the administrative officer in charge of the ambulance and a reliable man, stilled the panic with the aid of his orderlies. Larrey, as imperturbable as ever when operating, completed the removal of the leg he was amputating, rose to his feet, looked around him, and calmly announced his intention of dying with his casualties if he could not save their lives. Most of his assistant surgeons stayed with him and a very pale Auguste Frizac said: 'Monsieur Larrey, you shall not die alone. We shall not desert you.'[17]

Then, through the swirling snow came the cavalry of the Guard at full gallop, the gallant Lepic at their head. The Russian column was cut to pieces. Lepic had paid his debt.

When the commotion inside the barns had died down and the operating had begun again, Larrey was called outside to an officer. He went to the stretcher and lifted the snow-covered horse blanket. It was Hautpoul. He had been hit in the right thigh by a large iron bullet (biscayen) and carried to Percy's dressing station. In character, Percy said the limb could be saved and refused to amputate; however, since he judged the wound to be serious he informed Napoleon who sent the General to Larrey with one of his aides-de-camp. Larrey examined the patient. The wound was large, the femur fractured, and the soft tissues disorganized, but the femoral artery was undamaged and Hautpoul was in fair condition. Larrey urged immediate amputation; yet Percy had said the leg could be saved and Hautpoul clung to this straw. He refused amputation and Larrey could do no more than apply a simple dressing. Hautpoul was evacuated the next day. He reached Vornen, the first village on the road to Warsaw, and could go no further. He died on the third day.[18] A one-legged cavalry officer could not have fought for his Emperor; it was better to die.

Another casualty was an unnamed colonel who received a ball in his foot. When his turn came for operation, he could not stop his leg shaking and surgery was well nigh impossible. Larrey struck him a hearty slap on the face. The Colonel, who had never

Larrey at the Battle of Eylau, February 8, 1807. On the left, at the entrance to the ruined barn, is a flying ambulance

Louis Charles Antoine Desaix

Jean Lannes

Géraud Christophe Michel Duroc

Félix Hippolyte Larrey

been so insulted in his life, almost choked with anger: 'Sir, you take advantage of my state in a most cowardly manner. I demand satisfaction.'

'Colonel,' Larrey answered, 'accept my apologies. I understand you and I knew full well that such an insult would make you think of your honour and forget your wound. The operation is done and here is the ball I have removed. Give me your hand.'[19]

All the Guard and a great many of the line who had been severely wounded were operated on and dressed within 12 hours. 'We spent what was left of the night on the frozen snow around our bivouac fire. At daybreak the next day we resumed our work among the wounded of the Guard, and attended also to many of the line and to the Russian prisoners. I had the most severely injured of my own casualties transferred to a large house in Eylau.'[20]

While Larrey was at the house that morning a staff officer arrived with an order from Napoleon. He was to report immediately to embalm the body of General Nicolas Dahlmann. 'Return, Sir,' said Larrey looking up a good six inches to stare the other in the eye, 'and tell His Majesty that I shall not abandon 700 or 800 wounded of whom I might perhaps be able to save a half, to occupy myself with a dead man, however glorious his memory.'[21] Despite his devotion to Napoleon, Larrey made no bones about where his duty lay.

When on February 15 his work at Eylau was finished, Larrey wrote to Charlotte:[22] 'I have worked unceasingly night and day, nearly always sleeping in bivouac in the midst of the wounded and suffering the greatest privations. But, at last, I have finished. Today I evacuated the last convoy of wounded to Inowroclaw. I am thoroughly worn out physically, but my mind is happy and at peace. I have done my job efficiently and my ambulance distinguished itself—in fact, it was the only one that gave real service. I have saved the lives of a great number of men whose fighting qualities are above praise and I am well content. Furthermore, the Emperor and all the army witnessed and approved my conduct.

'I shall have the happiness, I hope, of telling you about these events and of proving that I am worthy of your love and affection.

This is, I think, the end of our campaigns; in a fortnight we shall know what is in store for us, but as things stand at present I believe we shall fight no more and that by Easter or Trinity Sunday I shall be home.

'Have patience then, beloved. My health has not been affected and there is nothing the matter with me that several days' rest in a large town will not mend.'

The evacuation of the wounded of the Guard succeeded only because of the organization Larrey had fought for. The removal of the other casualties verged on the barbaric and drove Percy to despair. The numbers of wagons and sledges was utterly inadequate. The wounded—often with their clothes cut or shot away, or stripped of their greatcoats and boots by human vultures —were lifted on ladders and dumped into carts. Those who could not be moved were abandoned and those who fell off were left to become snow-covered mounds at the roadside.

Meantime, 'the main body of the army pursued the enemy through the immense forests that extend northwards to Plegel [just south of Königsberg] behind which the Russians rallied and took up a defensive position. By now a thaw had made the roads impassable and this, together with the exhaustion of our troops, no doubt persuaded the Emperor to fall back to winter quarters on the banks of the Vistula. Accordingly, we set out from Eylau on February 17.'[23]

As they were leaving the town, Napoleon noticed quite by chance that Larrey was not wearing a sword. 'You haven't your sword, Larrey?' 'Sire, it was lost when the Russians overran the baggage wagon.'

'Here is mine. Accept it as a reminder of the services you rendered me at the battle of Eylau.'[24]

Larrey could find no words to express his emotions. The sword was now a symbol of martial glory and its award an honour reserved for the fighting man. Napoleon may have given way to impulse, but more likely the gesture was itself symbolic of his despair at the fate of the wounded—even an emperor's hands are sometimes tied by a corrupt and incompetent administration. But as his soul dipped deeper and deeper in wasted blood, the remnants of his conscience drowned. Already he was losing his sense of proportion: while in Warsaw in December, he had told Pierre Daru, the Quartermaster-General, statesman, and poet, to bring the army's ambulances—men, vehicles, equipment— up to a new, and perhaps adequate, strength. Yet where in the depths of a desolate Polish winter could any man find the material requirements, let alone the trained surgical personnel? Larrey's spirits as well as his vitality were at a low ebb, since, besides his sword, he had lost all his personal possessions during the battle. Only two shirts, several handkerchiefs, and the clothes he stood up in—all torn and dirty—remained.[25] His own special case of surgical instruments and his apparatus for making coffee were gone; but what he particularly regretted were Charlotte's letters, which he constantly re-read, a book of Demoustier's poems, and, most of all, Isaure's first letter which said, quite simply:

'Papa, I love you.'

In his own letters home he had been urging Charlotte to take care of herself during her pregnancy, and to write frequently to let him know how she was progressing. But, towards the end of February, he learnt the sad truth which further contributed to his depression.

'It now appears certain that you were not pregnant,' he wrote on February 26,[26] 'for your sister [Émilie] has written to me on February 3 that you were no more sure of your pregnancy than in the first month. Don't worry, as I had thought it was without doubt a pseudopregnancy.'

It seems that she was really suffering from lax abdominal musculature as, later, Larrey wrote advising her to take more exercise and to wear a body bandage to keep her stomach under control.[27]

And, to add to it all, he was peeved with his relatives and annoyed with Percy. With the sort of enthusiasm that can so easily become misinterpreted as officiousness he always tried to get his relatives into good positions. He had recently found a new post for his brother, Claude, and had been working for a long time to have him named a member of the Legion of Honour. Claude did not take kindly to it. 'In spite of all I have done,' Larrey wrote to Charlotte on March 12,[28] 'my brother clearly indicated to my nephew [i.e. Claude's son Auguste], that he felt the greatest resentment towards me—he appeared to be jealous of the favours that I had shown my uncle and his children and even of those that I had shown his own poor child.' And on the thirtieth:[29] 'I don't know why Alexis [his cousin] does not write. . . . You would be sad to learn that with the exception of three or four letters from your sisters and from Valet, you are the only one from whom I have received consolation in this unhappy country.'

He then gave vent to his feelings about Percy: 'M. P, who did not arrive until the end of the battle, and who did not appear at the previous ones, is now praising himself and his colleagues. Yet it was I who directed the service and performed nearly all the operations; it was my assistants and the surgeons of the Guard who dressed the greater part of the wounded of the army. But I do not wish to speak of this any more.'

In the middle of March the Emperor shifted his headquarters westwards from Osterode nearer the Vistula to a place called Finkenstein. Here Percy made another attempt to have the medical services of the army formed into an independent corps. He had already planted the idea in Napoleon's mind after Eylau when he had also suggested that Larrey's ambulance divisions might be extended to cover the entire army, but the imperial thoughts were otherwise engaged. And now Percy had no better luck. The Administration would certainly never accept the revolutionary plan without a fight and Napoleon had no intention of declaring war in that quarter. Nevertheless, the Emperor felt it advisable to give the surgical services some form of recognition and on April 7 Larrey wrote:[30] 'I believe that it is his intention to give me the title of general and of Commander of the Legion of Honour.' (Previously he had ranked as colonel.) The intentions took some time to materialize and he had to wait until May 15 before he could confirm the news.[31] 'Monsieur Percy has been promoted to the same grade, but what pleases me most is the citation I received: for *the creation and organization of the light ambulances which have saved the lives of so many gallant soldiers.* Because of this new title I am now ranked among the general officers.' But Ribes and Jouan were raised to a higher grade—so far as public honours were concerned, it paid to be in the personal service of His Majesty.

And Larrey was fated to have to wait until the eleventh hour to enter the personal service of the master he idolized. In Paris, Professor Pierre Lassus, one of the surgeons of the imperial household and professor of surgical pathology at the School of Medicine, had died. Sabatier and others of Larrey's friends had put his name forward for appointment to the chair. Charlotte even joined in by canvassing on his behalf. When Larrey learned of these events, he wrote to her (on April 7):[30]

'Why go to so much trouble to get me a post which no one wishes me to have because they do not consider me worthy? You would suffer yourself, my beloved, and you would not wish to see your poor love humiliated and discouraged for ever.

'However, I have not the same views on the appointment of surgeon consultant that the worthy old man also left vacant, as this suits me and is my due. I had not a moment's hesitation in making my request for it directly to His Majesty the Emperor, who received me with the best possible grace and gave me to hope that it will be mine. If he grants it me, I shall be very content and will consider myself honourably recompensed.'

This particular problem was resolved when the Administration interfered and told Larrey he must choose between the appointments as he could not have them both. He unhesitatingly opted for surgeon to the Emperor.[32] So, over the next few weeks he was constantly urging Charlotte to do all she could to help him in Paris since he suspected that Boyer, despite an outward show of friendship, was trying to get the appointment for someone else.[33] This proved all too true and, towards the end of May, Larrey began to feel the real strength of the opposition. On the twenty-second he wrote to Charlotte:[34] 'Quartermaster-General Daru has fallen in with the schemes of M. B [Boyer] who is jealous of my success and of the intimacy that enabled me to have the first chance. He has delayed his report, dealing with my place as consultant, because he tells me it has to be made in conjunction with that of physician consultant which is also vacant. For this purpose he wishes to take the advice of Dr Corvisart and has accordingly written to Paris. Although His Majesty promised me this place, I am beginning to fear it will escape me.' And escape him it did, since the Emperor, influenced again by

I

Corvisart, went back on his word and appointed Antoine Dubois.

Meantime yet another position had become vacant in Paris, this time in the Academy of Sciences. Charlotte and Sabatier went to work once more and, by gaining the support of two of the most influential members, had virtually won the election for Larrey. But he would have none of it. 'I am upset,' he wrote to Charlotte on May 15,[35] 'that M. Sabatier has put me in the same company as men so well known as Percy and Chaussier. My God, beloved, why the enthusiasm? I am only forty and practically unknown in the academic world. I shall learn with more pleasure than pain that the vacant seat has been awarded to someone worthier than myself. In return, dear Laville, I shall always be content if I hold the first place in your heart.'

Thus Larrey withdrew his name and Percy was elected. 'I am pleased above all that M. Percy obtained the votes and that he triumphed over the schemes of Dr C [Corvisart],' he wrote on May 29.[36] 'This adds to the honour of military surgery.'

As he was writing, the Russians unexpectedly attacked the French advance guard despite the opening of peace negotiations. Napoleon marched out and, after fighting the indecisive battle of Heilsberg, routed the enemy at Friedland. The Imperial Guard took no part in this latter battle (though seven or eight men were hit by stray bullets) which was fortunate for Larrey as he arrived late. His favourite horse, Coco, had been killed and the replacement he had bought had been wounded almost immediately.[37]

The Russians surrendered at Tilsit on the Niemen. Here, such was Larrey's fame in the allied camp that he was asked by the Czar and the King of Prussia to put on a display. The two monarchs were vastly impressed and Alexander presented the creator of the flying ambulance with a valuable ring. But the campaign had taken its toll of Larrey's physical resources and on June 24 he wrote to Charlotte from Tilsit:[38] 'It is as much the after-effects of the snows of Poland as of the sun that we have had on this campaign that has darkened my complexion. This same cause has considerably weakened my sight—to the point that I am quite myopic. You will find me much changed, beloved.'

So, when the imperial headquarters and the Guard moved to Königsberg, he was thankful to find lodgings with a wealthy banker, by name Jacobi, whose kindness and consideration quickly restored his vitality. But before leaving for home he was instructed by Napoleon to investigate a problem that had arisen among conscripts arriving from France to fill the gaps left in the ranks after Eylau. Many of these lads, who were scarcely eighteen, found marching difficult and painful and had to be admitted to hospital. The trouble was their youthfulness since the epiphyses at the ends of their femurs were still in the normal process of uniting to the main body of the thigh bone and in a number of instances could not stand the strain of long marches, day after day, with a heavy pack.

Larrey reported his findings in detail. 'Napoleon understood perfectly my anatomico-physiological observations,' he noted, 'and hastened to make the matter the subject of a senate decree. A law was passed making the age of recruitment at least twenty, and this law has been rigidly observed ever since'[39]—or it was until 1813 when Napoleon became desperately short of cannon fodder.

At the end of July Larrey left for home and late in October reached Paris where he resumed his duties at the Hospital of the Guard.

Larrey entered Spain for the second time in his life at the beginning of March 1808. The first experience, almost 14 years previously, had been deeply disturbing, but in this second one the vicious, senseless cruelty of mankind left a permanent scar across his memory. And, as he rode out of the foothills of the western Pyrenees into a world so different from the rest of Europe he was aware of a sense of foreboding—a presentiment that Napoleon's design to 'liberate' Spain by the mere presence of his army, ostensibly marching to reinforce Junot in Portugal, was doomed to failure.

He had been called from Val-de-Grâce by Marshal Bessières and ordered to set out after a column of the Imperial Guard marching to join the main force under Murat at Bayonne. Before leaving Paris, on February 11, he managed to persuade the Minister of War to grant him an advance of 750 francs on arrears of pay owing since October 1807—the paymaster of the army in Germany was running true to form, and without the money Charlotte would have been left in even greater financial turmoil than was her usual lot.

The journey to Bayonne was made with all Larrey's ancient speed and direction. His companion on this occasion, Auguste Frizac, at twenty-three a surgeon of considerable promise, readily agreed that the best route lay through Toulouse—his father, one of Larrey's old teachers, was professor of surgery at the university. Larrey himself wanted to visit his Uncle Alexis and then travel on to see his mother.

'My poor mama almost died with delight,' he wrote to Charlotte.[1] 'It was more than half an hour before she could say anything because of her tears, and then the first words she spoke were to ask about my wife and my Isaure. "I am so happy to see you," she said. "But I should die contented if I could see this lovely

Laville and her pretty child. I have put by for them a fine set of napkins which I crocheted with thread I had spun myself. There are a dozen of them." To my pleasant surprise I found her hale and hearty with scarcely a grey hair despite her sixty-nine years.'

This letter was written on March 6, the day after his arrival in Bayonne where, as the only inspector-general present, he was ordered by Murat to take charge of the army's medical services and to inspect the hospitals of the line on the route to Burgos and Madrid. He hurriedly bought himself two extra horses, and with Frizac and cousin Alexis (who had joined him at Toulouse) for company, set off for Spain—but not before unburdening himself of his money worries to Charlotte:[1]

'The heavy expenses incurred on the long journey and the money I gave my poor mother left me with only 25 louis [a louis was worth 20 gold francs], but happily my name is well known in this town and several merchants have offered me loans which I shall accept to pay for my horses.

'I have written to the Minister asking him to pay you my salary as inspector; if this is not done, I shall be extremely annoyed.'

The Guard was travelling rapidly and Larrey had only a short time in each city for his inspections—a tragedy as conditions in the Spanish hospitals were hygienically atrocious and the wards were full of young, untrained recruits suffering mostly from dysentery and typhus who had been left behind by the advancing French army. Larrey did what he could to remedy the situation and where possible installed Frenchmen to replace the local doctors and orderlies whose ideas were positively medieval.

They reached Burgos on March 27. Here Larrey learnt from Ribes, who had come direct from Paris, that Charlotte was pregnant again—genuinely so this time—and that the baby was due in September. During the coming months the child was rarely out of his thoughts—Larrey was convinced the baby would be a boy; his name, Hippolyte,[2] was already chosen, but during one of the spells of misery that Spain inflicted on him, he wrote to Isaure saying 'I have added Félix in the hope that he will be happier than his father'.[3] News also arrived of the revolution at Aranjuez where the people had prevented the flight of King Charles and his family to South America, forcing him to abdicate and placing his son, Ferdinand, on the throne.

After five days' rest in Burgos the Guard moved on to Madrid where it arrived on April 7. Here Larrey received confirmation from the Minister of War of his appointment as inspector-general in charge of the invading army's medical services—though not of the commensurate salary. The job was no sinecure. As more and more French troops converged on the capital the number of sick increased to such an extent that emergency hospitals had to be opened (there were more than 2,000 patients in the main hospital alone) and the quartermaster-general asked Larrey to extend the area of his inspection to the towns around the city.

It was at this stage that Napoleon's scheming began to go awry. He had successfully tricked Ferdinand into meeting him at Bayonne where he had made him prisoner and forced him to sign away the Spanish throne, but once again he had underestimated the quality of a people. The Spaniards had centred their hopes on Ferdinand in a fierce wave of patriotism, and now they vowed not to rest until the last foreigner had been driven from their country.

'There had already been several unpleasant episodes in the towns through which I had passed and these made me decide to cut short my tour of inspection. I arrived at the gates of Madrid on May 2, the day of the revolt, at eleven in the morning. The situation was extremely hazardous; musket- and cannon-fire could be heard everywhere. But I did not hesitate to enter the city since I was anxious to take charge of the hospitals.

'Having seen that my nephew (Auguste Larrey) was safe in the trustworthy hands of my host, the Marquis of Belgida, I remounted and rode straight for the hospital which was menaced by a mob. We were just in time to shut the hospital gates and to arm the surgeons and convalescents. We also arrested a number of Spanish orderlies who had already assaulted some of our sick and had wounded two or three medical officers.

'Several shots fired from the windows and over the gates persuaded the rioters that we meant business, and they withdrew from under the hospital walls. Our troops eventually swept them all from the streets and restored order. We received the wounded of both nations; their numbers swelled rapidly, and by nightfall we had admitted 300—of whom 70 came from the Imperial Guard.'[4]

The savagery with which Murat put down the revolt was vividly captured in Francisco de Goya's painting '3 May 1808' which portrays the cold-blooded shooting of hostages. The patriotic fervour of the inhabitants was inflamed and, though nothing serious happened for another three months, Larrey always wore his sword during the daytime and never ventured out after nightfall.

Yet, casualties from the uprising notwithstanding, Larrey's greatest problem at this time was still disease. Added to the inevitable dysentery, typhoid, and typhus was an illness known as Madrid colic which was, in fact, chronic lead poisoning due to a combination of the soft water dissolving lead from the pipes, lead in the local wines, and the use of poorly glazed pottery. Among the sufferers from the colic, many of whom died, was Murat who created a terrible fuss when he believed the attack heralded his last hours. With Larrey's help he pulled through and was convalescing nicely when news arrived of his appointment as King of Naples. This pleased him not at all since he had fully expected to be given the crown of Spain. An alarming fever consequently interrupted his progress, but on June 29, languishing in a litter and attended by a physician, he set out for France where the spa waters of Barèges completed his recovery.

René Savary now took command of the army for the short time until the arrival of Joseph Bonaparte, erstwhile King of Naples. Joseph was proclaimed King of Spain on July 22 and at the celebratory bullfight 15 bulls were sacrificed—though evidently not enough to placate the angry Spanish gods. Even as the French were relaxing, confident that the whole country would soon be theirs, the Spaniards showed their teeth. Against all the odds an army under Francisco Castaños had instilled panic into General Pierre Dupont de l'Etang and forced him to surrender at Baylen on the twenty-third. The ferocity of a simple people had combined with the fear of a stark and hostile land to demoralize the invader. Then, as if the news had passed along unseen wires, the people of several provinces rose in unison and marched towards Madrid.

'In haste we prepared our retreat and left the city on the night of July 31. Lacking transport for our casualties and being uncertain whether we would find supplies for them along the road to Burgos, we had to leave some of the sick of the line in the Madrid hospital.'[5] Despite all Larrey's efforts, the surgical services were below par. Surgeons, dressings, drugs, linen, and transport were in short supply as the Administration dug its toes in and refused to cooperate. Without the presence of Napoleon to reinforce his demands, Larrey was hamstrung. He did, however, manage to get all the wounded of the Guard (except for five who were unfit to travel) away from Madrid in his flying ambulances. For the rest, he commandeered mules and local Biscayen carriages which were particularly good in the mountains.

Accompanying the retreating army were some Spanish families who dared not stay in Madrid because of their commitment to the French. Their plight was tragic. 'My beloved,' Larrey wrote to his wife on August 11 after reaching Burgos,[6] 'we are unhappy, it is true. But if you could have seen these women from all strata of Madrid society—a great number are very rich and come from the highest ranks of the Spanish nobility and never go out except in their private carriages—if you could have seen them, having left in haste without even the most essential objects, marching with the soldiers in the sand and the dust under a broiling sun, what would you say? All these wealthy families are now without means of support or shelter. Some women, in advanced stages of pregnancy, dragged themselves painfully along, others led their little children by the hand; several babies were fed at the breast in the middle of the camp. What a caravan! It is difficult to credit such misery! And how to describe it? You should meet some of these unhappy women and they would tell you how they suffered.'

Larrey put their case to the senior officers, as a result of which they received regular rations and were found lodgings at night. He himself could not do enough for those who were ill—perhaps to purge the guilt of his countrymen who pillaged, raped, and burned as they retreated northwards. On one occasion he met a young mother carrying a child all but dead from starvation; he gave what aid he could and then put them both in his own carriage while he followed on foot to Aranda. When the vehicle, well known in the army, arrived in the town without him, rumour that he had been killed spread like wildfire, the more so since news of the slaughter of a number of medical officers arrived at the same time.

This rumour reached the Imperial Guard. And men, hard-bitten heroes of the bloodiest campaigns in history, broke down and openly wept, vowing the most terrible vengeance. The death of only one other man in the entire French army—Napoleon himself—could have provoked such a reaction. So when Larrey, his familiar little figure erect and dapper through all the trials and horrors of retreat in this alien land, marched into Aranda the town shook to the cheers of joy and it was Larrey's turn to give way to Gallic emotion.

Leaving Aranda, King Joseph passed Larrey at the wayside. He stopped to tell the surgeon of his pleasure that the rumour had proved false. The opportunity was too good for Larrey to miss.

'I rely on the Emperor, Your Majesty, and my country to assure the existence of my wife and children, for I am without fortune.'

'Calm yourself,' Joseph answered, 'my brother loves you too much to leave your family in need. You will be recompensed.'[7]

But neither Joseph's reassurances nor Napoleon's love could influence the Administration. The recompense was in the wrong direction and the reward a scarcely veiled insult. In June, the army paymaster in Spain had informed Larrey that he would combine the appointments of chief surgeon to the Guard and inspector-general but on a peace-time footing. So, as Larrey had, until then, been paid on a war-time basis, the overpayment of 1,500 francs would be deducted from his future pay! Moreover, the salary for the job of inspector-general would only be paid to Charlotte when the debt was settled.

Yet even this was too generous. On August 17, Larrey received another letter from the paymaster telling him that as he was merely acting as inspector-general until Percy's arrival, he had no right to double pay. However, said the paymaster, the Minister had agreed to grant him 400 francs in recognition of the extra service Larrey had given.

After marching around north-eastern Spain for the rest of August and most of September the Guard came to a halt at Vitoria where, among the mail awaiting Larrey, was a letter addressed in a childish hand: 'Oh joy, oh happiness, my dear Papa, Maman has given birth to a beautiful little boy. He is like an angel. I wanted to let you know as quickly as possible. Maman was delivered happily. I write to you from my aunt's where Maman sent me for fear of the birth. I am full of joy. I cannot write longer, for I am much unsettled. After tomorrow, I shall write you a longer letter. Adieu, my dear Papa, I am your little girl, I.L. Maman, my brother, and I do well.'[8]

Larrey could scarcely contain himself and even as he finished reading Isaure's letter he was on his knees thanking God. Then, happy beyond reckoning, he dashed into the streets to tell the news to all his friends. He eventually found himself at the king's residence and begged to be allowed to inform Joseph; but it was siesta time and the monarch was not to be disturbed.

Charlotte had not had such an easy confinement as Isaure implied, but Ribes had been there and had helped her through the difficult hours. An indication that all was not well came in Isaure's promised longer letter: 'My dear Papa, I have been slow in giving you news of Maman. At this moment, she has a moderate fever. I have not been allowed to see her for two days, but today the two days are over and I am able to see her. You may be more than certain of my wish to serve her and to provide her least desires. What has she not done in my young days to prove her love and affection for me. And what would I not do for so kind a mother. Also be sure that I shall do all that I can to bring her back to health.'[8]

But despite Larrey's elation, conditions in Spain weighed heavily on him. 'Since our arrival in this little town [Vitoria], where things are very bad on account of the great number of troops and other persons who are living here,' he wrote to Charlotte on October 15,[9] 'I have lost one of my horses which I have had to replace with a mule. The loss and the purchase cost me more

than 25 louis, which vexed me a great deal. My preparations for
the campaign and the refurbishing of my carriage are costing but
little less. Judge the contribution that I am making to the war with
my salary paid on a peace-time footing! Surely, if His Majesty
the Emperor does not compensate me according to my rank, I
shall not be able to continue much longer, for I cannot economize
even by a sou. My God, but these thoughts are painful to me. I
have been very patient, in spite of seeing every day many of my
grade—whom, I dare to say it, have rendered nowhere near such
important service as I to the state and to humanity—loaded with
favours and fortune. M. Renaud, among others, has received a
barony that brings in a fixed income of 10,000 francs, a gratuity
of 55,000 francs, the rank of general, and several decorations.
And your poor Larrey who kills himself to save the lives of others
has only pain and sorrow.'

Again, a fortnight later, he wrote: 'I have fallen once more
into sadness and melancholy; these are, my adored, the results
of my great sensitivity, nature's fatal gift.'[3]

But comfort for Larrey's troubled mind was at hand. He had
once said that he felt easy only when the Emperor was at the head
of the army, and now Napoleon was on his way to Spain with
130,000 picked veterans of the Grand Army. Austria and Prussia
had felt the weight of the Emperor's hand and could safely, he
believed, be left in the watchful care of his ally-of-convenience,
Alexander of Russia. He reached Vitoria on November 7, and in
his entourage was Percy. Larrey therefore resigned his temporary
appointment as inspector-general and was attached, by order of
Napoleon, to the advance guard of the army.

The Emperor quickly made his presence felt. Under his command the whole army took up its line of march for Burgos, where
there was a brief pause while the defending Spaniards were
soundly defeated, and then brilliantly but bloodily it crossed the
Somosierra Pass to Madrid. Here the inhabitants kept the gates
closed for two days before feebly surrendering.

With Napoleon in Madrid reorganizing the government of
Spain, Larrey believed the end of the campaign and his return
home to be imminent but it proved only a daydream when, on
December 15, he wrote to Charlotte suggesting that she might

soon come to Bagnères de Bigorre to meet him. 'There you will find my poste-chaise in which I can do 60 miles a day when it is drawn by three good mules. I shall accompany you as your aide-de-camp riding my little mare.'[3]

Larrey—and Napoleon—had reckoned without Sir John Moore's valiant attempt to save Spain. After the Spanish defeats he was thought to be retiring, along the way he had come, into Portugal. And, had the news that the Spaniards were preparing to defy Napoleon in Madrid not given him hope of helping them to save themselves, Moore would undoubtedly have done so. But by the time he knew of their weak-kneed collapse he had committed himself to an attempt to harass the French lines of communication.

Napoleon was just about to leave for Badajoz, on the road to Lisbon, when he heard of Moore's arrival in Valladolid. With characteristic speed he changed his plans. 'We left Madrid on December 22 and marched towards the Sierra de Guadarrama which we crossed on the twenty-third and twenty-fourth. At the foot of the mountains the temperature fell to 20 Fahrenheit degrees of frost.

'The wind blew straight out of the north and a great deal of snow had fallen in the previous few days. As we climbed into the mountains, the cold, already penetrating, increased perceptibly until men and animals, losing their balance, fell in the road or were swept away down the steep slopes in the flurries of fresh snow. Some just lay on the verges unable to rise. The flying artillery and cavalry were compelled to halt on a plateau about half way up and had to wait to tackle the remainder of the climb until the temperature rose, which it did the next day.

'Sleet and rain succeeded the terrible cold; with difficulty we marched to Medina del Campo and from there across country to Medina del Rioseco and Benevente. The continuing rains and the boggy ground, in which many carriages stuck fast, made the march yet more difficult, and when we halted we could find neither straw for the soldiers to lie on nor wood to make a fire.

'We reached Benevente a day too late, for the English army had just crossed the river and burned the bridge. However, our advance guard crossed at a ford and soon engaged the English rear-guard. A bloody contest ensued and, though the English were the superior force, our courageous chasseurs made themselves masters of the field of battle.'[10] A bloody contest indeed, but the English version differs in certain essential details. The hussars of the British and Hanoverian cavalry swept through the streets of Benevente, rejoicing at the chance to meet the enemy they had been eluding for so long, and drove the swaggering bear-skinned chasseurs of the Imperial Guard back into the river. Two hundred of the 600 French horsemen were lost to the Emperor that morning.

The English withdrew from Benevente on December 29, and the next day Larrey wrote home from the improvised hospital: 'It is pointless, my beloved, to tell you of our sufferings and privations, but the soldiers of the Guard take good care of me. They have an affection for me and never let me want for anything.'[3]

Benevente was the limit of Larrey's travail in the pursuit of Moore, and Napoleon went only a few miles further to Astorga. Here two things made him decide to turn back with the Imperial Guard. One, Moore had reached the mountains in time to avoid a battle on open ground, and two, a dispatch arrived telling of treachery in Paris and of Austria's opportunism in profiting from the Emperor's absence in Spain; war in central Europe was once again inevitable. Giving command of the pursuit—which ended at Corunna—to Soult, Napoleon returned to Valladolid from where, on January 16, 1809, he left for Paris.

'His Majesty departed the day before yesterday,' Larrey wrote to Charlotte on January 18.[3] 'We think he is making straight for Paris. However, the Imperial Guard is still here with the head-quarters staff. We have assembled our wounded and sick in a large hospital that I established on my arrival. I now await the staff from Madrid so as to organize the service properly; then I propose to ask Marshal Bessières for permission to return to Paris.' But he was out of luck and, far from obtaining leave, he found his duties increased.

'Marshal Bessières,' ran his letter of the twenty-fourth,[3] 'has not merely refused to grant me leave from the Guard, but on the contrary has just ordered me to resume the post of inspector-general of the hospitals of the line—these hospitals have fallen into a very bad state. I resisted as far as I could and said that, out of regard for M. Percy who would look unkindly on my supervision, it was impossible for me to take on the task. But as the instruction has been posted in daily orders by the Prince [Berthier], I cannot refuse.'

Nevertheless Larrey was becoming increasingly anxious to get away from the depressing atmosphere of Spain where everything—health, money, friends, and colleagues—seemed to conspire against him. He wrote to Charlotte asking her to persuade Napoleon to recall him to France, but he added: 'I believe that a spirit of intrigue and jealousy fermented by MM. D. . . and company is keeping me here to suffer all manner of unpleasantness.'[3] The M. D. . . was Antoine Dubois who had gained a position of influence in the Emperor's household and did not want to see that position challenged. In addition a rift was beginning to appear in the relationship between Larrey and Percy. For some while now Percy had been jealous of the efficiency of the Guard's casualty evacuation and in his latest attempt to induce Napoleon to form a proper medical corps he had 'borrowed' the concept of Larrey's flying ambulance. This upset Larrey and served to increase a growing resentment at the fact that he always seemed to be doing Percy's job—usually when it was in a sorry state.

And even when the Guard was preparing to leave, fate, in the shape of Marshal Bessières, was still against him. 'Alas! my adored,' he wrote on February 23,[3] 'it seems I am as far away from my family as ever; for the Marshal, instead of letting me go, wants to keep me here until the very last moment. And I fear that in departing last I shall have to follow the Imperial Guard and its ambulance with no chance of obtaining leave of absence, since we are assured that we must return to Germany.'

But it was home he returned to, and sooner than expected: 'Overcome by fatigue and much debilitated by a chill that began during the campaign at Benevente I contracted typhus from the English prisoners. Notwithstanding, on the third day [March 7] after the symptoms appeared, I set out for Burgos where I hoped to rejoin the Guard who had marched two days ahead of me. But I was seized with delirium along the route, and would certainly have died had it not been for the energetic help of my pupil and cousin, Alexis Larrey. I was carried insensible to Burgos where I lay dangerously ill for nine or ten days. However, at the first possible moment I arranged for transport to take me back to Paris and my family. I arrived on April 4 after a most trying journey.'[11]

16. *Wagram: A View over the Hill*

Napoleon had overreached himself. Like ordinary mortals, he could not be in two places at once, and impatience refused him time to consolidate his gains before moving on to fresh fields. Had he been able to rely on his marshals, the story could well have been different, but for the most part these men were born seconds-in-command who excelled only under the eyes of their Emperor. Left to themselves, they fell to petty squabbling. Thus Moore's army escaped from Spain when the greater urgency of affairs in Paris and Austria called Napoleon back across the Pyrenees. Yet still he persisted in piling up trouble for himself: not for the first time he disdained the advice of Talleyrand to regard the Continent as a United States of Europe with France as senior partner. Instead, he was determined to crush all peoples until they submitted to do his will. And, to make matters worse, the instrument of that will—his army—was rotting away.

At the top, the Revolutionary determination to put the world to rights had lost much of its momentum and when, after Friedland, Napoleon re-created the aristocracy the process was complete. At the bottom, the strength—so far as numbers were concerned—was kept up by conscription. Nevertheless, the recruits were poorly trained because time was short and, much more important, they were unwilling. In the middle, the backbone of the glorious Grand Army that had carried France and her Emperor to the conquest of Europe was being whittled away by battle and its companion diseases, and its effective strength reduced by the need to hunt out the most unwilling of the recruits within the frontiers of France itself.

It was as if Napoleon felt his years were numbered—and perhaps he may have had reason for believing this. He was thirty-nine; in twelve years' time he would be dead. There is nothing sinister about this in itself, even though he left behind him a trail of symptoms that have intrigued and confused historians ever since; depending on one's selection they can be attributed to a quite alarming list of diseases: tuberculosis, gonorrhoea with urethral stricture as a consequence, bladder stones, epilepsy, piles, peptic ulcer, stomach cancer, malaria, pituitary deficiency, hypogonadism, manic-depression, heart failure, and so on. Yet there is only one thing of which we can be really certain: a striking change in his appearance took place in his thirties. The young general in Gros's 'Napoleon Crossing the Bridge at Arcola', painted in 1796, is lean and craggy about the face, whereas 'The Emperor Napoleon Bonaparte' of Robert Lefèvre (1812) has full, smooth, practically unlined features, and a pencil drawing by Girodet, also in 1812, depicts a decidedly obese Napoleon. Other pictures, for instance by Gros and David, from about 1806 onwards trace the development of the alteration. Even so, portraits and contemporary descriptions tell us nothing more than that the Emperor was growing fat.

But if his body was going to seed, his brain showed no sign of working at other than full capacity. Indeed, the opening of the campaign in Austria in the spring of 1809 is sometimes cited as an outstanding example of his military genius. He left Paris on April 13 and arrived in Donauwörth on the seventeenth having outdistanced everything and everybody—including Josephine whom he left at Strasbourg. Messages had already been sent to Davout at Ratisbon (Regensburg) and André Masséna at Augsburg to bring themselves to order and unite their armies. This done, Napoleon launched a series of lightning attacks on the Archduke Charles of Austria who, in the belief that the French were still divided, had split his own forces. The Austrians were beaten at Abensberg on the thirteenth and at Ratisbon two days later; their centre folded and they retreated on Vienna.

Larrey was still convalescing in Paris when the campaign began, but without giving it a second thought he set out on April 22 to join the Imperial Guard. On the twenty-sixth from Strasbourg, where he paid his respects to Josephine, he wrote home:[1] 'My health is perfectly restored and I believe I am already putting on weight again.' He caught up with the Guard at Napoleon's headquarters at Schönbrunn (near Vienna) on May 12 and, ever

K

the optimist at the start of a campaign, wrote Charlotte,[2] 'Here is the end of our hardships and our misery. I hope that you will be my Baroness; until then be my constant and faithful love'— the first indication that Larrey knew Napoleon was contemplating making him a baron.

Although he was greeted by the Guard with enthusiasm and affection Larrey noticed a change: there were few battle-scarred veterans and even fewer of his devoted Egyptians. Most of the Old Guard were away fighting the demoralizing war in Spain and to take their place Napoleon had chosen the fittest, strongest, and most literate from among the recruits. This Young Guard was well equipped and in a short time had developed a fine esprit de corps.

The retreating Austrians evacuated Vienna, cutting the bridges across the Danube. The French at once improvised a crossing at the place where the river is broken into a maze of channels by numerous islands, one of which, Lobau, is of considerable size (about two miles by two miles at its widest points). By masking their true intentions, they induced the Austrians to leave Lobau poorly defended. 'On May 20 and 21 the Imperial Guard and several other units took possession of the island and at once threw bridges across the remaining channel to the left bank. The attack on the enemy's advance posts began with spirit, but the outcome at the end of the day was indecisive. Nevertheless, our troops remained on the left bank and the next morning (the twenty-second) covered the landing of the Guard and other units from Lobau. However, half the army were standing impotent on the right bank, unable to cross to the island because the bridges had been swept away. Despite this a general attack was ordered; the brunt of the terrible battle of Essling was borne by the infantry of the Guard who fought with courage and valour. This engagement, too, was indecisive and during the night we fell back to the island of Lobau—a difficult feat on account of the small number of bridges and their flimsy construction. My field dressing station was at the edge of a wood on the left bank and here we operated on all the severely wounded, both of the Guard and the line. The less serious casualties and those who could safely be moved were carried as quickly as possible to dressing stations on Lobau.'[3]

Towards the end of this second day of slaughter whilst walking back to the imperial headquarters Lannes remarked to his old sergeant of the Revolutionary armies, General Pouzet, how sick he was of continual killing and how he himself had had, that very morning, a premonition that this would be his last battle. Canister shot was raining down from above and as he turned to ask his companion's opinion of the phenomenon Pouzet was hit in the head and killed instantly. Lannes was grief-stricken. Oblivious to the entreaties of his aide-de-camp, Antoine Marbot, he wandered away in a daze until he came to a ditch, some hundred yards away, where he sat down lost in his misery. A quarter of an hour later he looked up as a party of soldiers carrying a body halted in front of him. The covering cloak fell away from the dead man's face: it was Pouzet.

'Is this terrible sight to follow me everywhere?' his voice shook. Then he rose, moved further away along the ditch, and sat down once more with his legs crossed and his head buried in his hands. Less than a minute passed before a ricocheting ball hit him in the legs. Marbot ran to him.

'It is nothing,' said Lannes. 'Here, give me your hand and help me to my feet.' But he collapsed in agony. Marbot summoned some soldiers to carry the Marshal off the field and they, seeing him uncovered, took the cloak from Pouzet's corpse and laid it over Lannes:

'This was my poor friend's,' said he. 'See, it is covered with his blood. I shall not use it. Rather, drag me along as best as you can.' And so he was carried the short distance to Larrey's dressing station.[4]

Larrey found him to be severely shocked with a shattered left knee and a nasty wound of the muscles of the right thigh. For a moment he was emotionally unsettled at the appearance of his great friend and, because he felt he could not trust his judgment in the circumstances, he called Yvan, Paulet, and one or two other senior surgeons into consultation. Yvan was the only one who advised against amputating the left leg—the Marshal's strength of character would see him through, and anyway to operate in such hot weather was asking for trouble.

'My other comrades were unanimously in favour of immediate amputation, but none was willing to do the operation since there seemed so small a chance of recovery. But I remembered several successful results in similar cases and, encouraged by a glimmering of hope, I decided to operate myself. The operation was completed in less than two minutes and he showed little sign of pain. I applied the usual dressings and then accompanied the Marshal to the island of Lobau where we were met by the Emperor.'[5]

Napoleon, determined to extract the last ounce of drama from the situation, leapt from his horse and through his tears said, 'Lannes, it is I, do you remember me?'

'Yes, Sire, but in two hours, without doubt, you will have lost your best friend.'

'No, Lannes, you will live. Larrey shall save you as he did Fugières in Egypt. Is that not so, Larrey?'

Then embracing the wounded man and, in the process, staining his white waistcoat with the Marshal's blood, he said, 'You will live, my friend, for I could not bear the sadness of being separated from you.'

'I trust I shall,' Lannes replied, 'if I can still be of use to France and Your Majesty.'[6]

When the Emperor had left, Lannes inquired about the military situation and requested Larrey to have a look at Marbot who had been slightly wounded. Larrey then entrusted the Marshal to the care of Surgeon-Major Paulet and returned to his dressing station which had by now been withdrawn to the island.

'It was not without regret that I left this courageous warrior, but I was the only inspector-general on the field of battle [Heurteloup, now Surgeon-in-Chief to the Grand Army, was among those stuck on the right bank] and a great number of wounded were awaiting attention. I separated, as far as possible, those of the Guard from those of the line, but we gave of our best to all without distinction. The medical officers of the ambulances and of the different corps of the Guard co-operated with each other and we did not rest until all the wounded had been operated on and dressed. Fortunately sufficient instruments and dressings had been brought to the island by the ambulances under the command of M. Pelchet.'[7] On the fourth day after the battle the bridges were restored and the wounded transported to hospitals prepared by Heurteloup at Ebersdorf and Vienna. For the wounded of the

Guard, Larrey appropriated a superb barracks at Reneveck.

Meantime Lannes had been evacuated from the island by boat and taken to Ebersdorf where he was lodged in a tiny room in a brewer's house—on one side was the brewery and on the other a damp, unwholesome courtyard. Larrey visited him at the first opportunity. 'I found him extremely weak, greatly depressed, and as pale as death. His thoughts were jumbled and his speech incoherent. He complained of heaviness in the head and a sense of oppression. He was restless and sighed frequently.'[8]

Larrey modified the treatment and this helped the Marshal to sleep more peacefully. On the next day when Larrey called to dress the wounds, Lannes seized hold of him and said, 'I feel I shall die. But if I am to live, you alone can save me. So don't leave me again, my dear Larrey.'[9]

But despite this touching plea he had to arrange for the seriously wounded to be cared for. He returned as quickly as he could. For the next twenty-four hours Lannes seemed much improved and Larrey began to hope for his recovery—even though his colleagues still feared the worst. Then, during the sixth night after operation Lannes developed a high fever. It was septicaemia, and three days later, on May 30, Jean Lannes, Duke of Montebello, was dead. Larrey had not left his side for those three days.

When Napoleon was informed he came to the brewer's house and embraced the dead Marshal; he stayed in the sordid little room for more than an hour.

That night Lannes' body was taken to the castle of Schönbrunn where at daybreak and at the Emperor's express command a desperately sad Larrey began to embalm his old friend. Decomposition was progressing rapidly, making difficult a task that was already dangerous on account of the septicaemia.

A week or so later Dominique Denon, the military artist and Director General of the Louvre, visited Vienna and Larrey suggested that Lannes' death might make a good picture.

'I hope he will like the idea of painting the touching scene where the Emperor embraced his gallant friend who was lying on a stretcher a few moments after operation,' Larrey wrote to Charlotte on June 14.[10] 'In that case I could figure honourably in the picture.'[11]

Denon was impressed with the dramatic possibilities and on his return to Paris asked Ribes for details. Ribes, in turn, wrote to Larrey. On July 18 Larrey replied, adding a note: 'At the request of M. Denon, the military artist, who wishes to portray the death of Lannes, Larrey sends these items of information to his friend, but expresses the formal wish that his name should not be mentioned. However, he takes the opportunity of asking to figure in the picture'[12]—a request that was granted.

On his return from the castle to the hospital at Reneveck, Larrey found infection rife, especially tetanus and hospital fever which were the main causes of the dreadfully high mortality rate. But this was of no concern to Napoleon who knew that he must fight again, and that the fate of his Empire hung on the outcome. He summoned reinforcements from Italy and the Rhine while Larrey speedily cleared the hospitals in the area, sending those men who were of no further use to the army back to France.

But despite knowing that his name was definitely on the list of those to be made a baron (and had been there since the beginning of the year),[9] Larrey's personal lot was no happier than usual when on a campaign.

'I am, moreover, very badly billeted and very badly fed,' he unburdened himself to Charlotte on June 23.[13] 'It grieves me to tell you that while I was writing my last letter to you at five in the morning, in my work room, someone took my watch and case of surgical instruments from my dressing table. Such an irreparable loss in this country has caused me the greatest worry. I have searched in vain. It is probably the German domestics as all these people are extremely light fingered.' His despair was not eased in any way by the fact that he was now paid in paper money and was losing heavily on the deal.

On July 1 these worries were temporarily forgotten when Napoleon made his move and by the evening of the fourth his entire force was assembled on the island of Lobau. 'A fleet of small boats carrying 3,000 sailors under the command of Captain Baste was then launched to cover the crossing of the last [and narrowest] stretch of river and to attack the enemy's advance posts entrenched on the left bank. A violent storm had been brewing and at the precise moment that the signal to attack was given it broke over our heads. The sound of the artillery on both sides was drowned by the almost continuous claps of thunder, and hail and rain fell in torrents. So intense was the darkness that we could only get our bearings during the flashes of lightning. Yet despite these formidable obstacles our troops gained the left bank, captured the enemy batteries and deployed rapidly over the flat and open countryside. By this time several bridges had been thrown across and the whole army reached the other side without difficulty.

'The enemy, staggered at our speed, smartly withdrew to a new position before Wagram. Here, that same evening, we fought a general though indecisive battle. Both armies remained facing each other during the night, and at daybreak on the sixth we renewed the attack. The enemy at first put up a stout resistance, although the efforts of their right wing, cramped by the Danube, were feeble. Soon, however, the left wing gave way, while their centre was steadily thinned by the fire of the light artillery of the Imperial Guard. At length, the Austrian lines were overwhelmed, their divisions scattered or destroyed by the terrible execution of our guns, and victory was complete.

'With my flying ambulance I followed the movements of the Guard until the final moment of the battle. We dressed the wounded, as we found them, on the field of battle; but when the numbers became too great I established an advanced dressing station in the nearest village to which the wounded of the Guard and a great many officers of the line were brought. Before nightfall some 500 casualties were gathered at this dressing station. The majority had been gravely injured by cannon fire and required major surgery.'[14]

These 500 were the lucky ones. Once again the arrangements for dealing with casualties from the line regiments were a disgrace. Many men were not recovered for four or five days and lay, lost among corn ready for harvesting, suffering the torments of hell, dehydrated by their wounds and the heat of the sun, and compelled to drink their own urine. Some lay burned in the blackened stubble where fire—despite the storm—had swept through the crop. And great numbers were attacked by fever since they could not drag themselves away from the decomposing bodies of those killed at their side or fallen across them.

'I saw,' Larrey noted,[15] 'these unhappy men covered in insects and virtually unrecognizable as a result of the swelling produced by the stings. The sort of flies that we see around butchers' shops were there in swarms, biting and devouring these men, driving them mad with pain and thus redoubling their suffering and their torture—which already were insupportable.'

Larrey's simple account of the victory ignores the fact that the issue was in doubt for a long time and only by a complete disregard for human life did the French win through. The battle of Wagram was largely an artillery duel—which explains the exceptionally large proportion of horrifying injuries; indeed, at one stage batteries of French cannon were less than 300 yards from the Austrians and firing at a rate of two rounds a minute. The Austrian centre weathered the bombardment remarkably well until Alexandre Macdonald firmly gripped the nettle and advanced at the head of eight battalions. He achieved his objective; the Austrians broke and fled, but of the 15,000 Frenchmen who began the attack only 2,000 or 3,000 remained on their feet to survey their triumph. Macdonald, the son of a Scottish Highlander who had fled to France after Culloden, was created a marshal on the field.

The full extent of the destruction and mutilation of humanity on those two days in early July 1809 will never be known. The casualty figures for both sides vary from authority to authority and sometimes the estimates for Aspern-Essling and Wagram are combined. Nevertheless it is probable that at Wagram the French lost about 23,000 killed and wounded (from an army of 180,000) and the Austrians about 19,000 (their army numbered some 130,000 men). After the battle about 7,000 men on each side were missing.

And once again the value of immediate amputation in saving life was abundantly confirmed, not least when it was the major undertaking of disarticulation at the shoulder. Larrey operated at this joint 3 times after Essling and 11 times after Wagram: 12 of the men recovered to enjoy perfect health, including Augustin d'Aboville, colonel of the light artillery. A cannon ball had made an appalling mess of his right shoulder. 'His pulse was scarcely perceptible and he seemed to be at death's door. Indeed, for a moment, I hesitated to operate as I doubted whether he could survive the amputation. But operate I did, more with the hope of easing his agony than of saving his life.

'To my great surprise the operation, which was rapidly done, was wholly successful. Had it been delayed a moment longer, though, d'Aboville would never have received the laurels he so richly deserved.'[16] But what Larrey wrote in his *Mémoires* for public consumption did not always agree with his private feelings. After the battle Napoleon called for a report from Larrey.

'Is d'Aboville dead?' he asked.

'No, Sire.'

'But how can that be? I saw him carried, dying, from the field.'

'Sire, I have operated on him. I performed a disarticulation at the shoulder joint, and from that moment on he became fully conscious and seems a little improved.'

'Will you save him, do you think?'

'Sire, I cannot say. It is possible that this is but a momentary success and that he will not see the morrow.'

'How can I help you save him? Ask anything!'

'I think probably a reward for his courage would have the greatest effect.'

'So be it. Larrey, go and tell Colonel d'Aboville yourself that I make him general, baron, and commander of the Legion of Honour.'[17]

Larrey took great care of his patient. He evacuated him to Vienna on a specially prepared stretcher to save him the bumping and jolting of a carriage. He visited him every day, put two surgeons at his disposal, and later had an ingenious steel shoulder cap made and fitted. When, in the autumn d'Aboville left Vienna for France he sent Larrey a little wooden box and a letter of thanks—written by a friend.[18] In the box was a diamond of such poor colour that Larrey took it to a jeweller who valued it at five louis. He promptly returned it.

'I hope you will forgive me sending it back,' he wrote to Charlotte on October 13,[19] 'but I am sick of being humiliated. I have never received such an affront.'

'What!' exclaimed d'Aboville when he opened the package. 'Is he practising some new kind of economy?'[17]—a cruel reference to Larrey's well-known impecunious state. But the story quickly spread throughout the army and gained for Larrey a great deal of sympathy.

Yet if these mighty amputations lacked nothing for drama, there was one extraordinarily moving moment during the horror of the evening of July 6. A grenadier sought out Larrey and finding him produced, like a rabbit out of a hat, an eighteen-month-old child with a slight wound of the shoulder which he asked the surgeon to dress. It took a lot to surprise Larrey, but he could scarcely believe his eyes. While doing the dressing he asked the soldier to explain.

Apparently, after the advancing French army had passed through Wurzburg a young widow was discovered wandering distractedly among the troops. She was utterly lost and almost demented with fear. The French directed her back to the town but in her bewilderment she ran off leaving her child behind. As the army was marching on, this grenadier took charge of the child. He made a leather pouch to serve as a portable cot which he slung from his back, and before an engagement he dug a hole in which he hid the pouched infant. All had gone well until Wagram. Fortunately the child's injury was not serious, but Larrey was so touched by the grenadier's humanity and obvious concern for the child that he gave him a napoleon (a gold coin worth 20 francs) and organized a whip-round among his colleagues. (After the peace treaty was signed, the Guard returned through Wurzburg where the grenadier found the widow and to her immense delight gave back her child.)[20]

After the battle of Wagram the French pursued the fleeing Austrians and cornered them on July 11 at Znojmo. However, before any serious damage was done a parley was held and an end to hostilities agreed upon.

This news struck right through the army like a thunderbolt. Spirits were high after Wagram and the men reckoned they had Austria at their mercy and could finish her off once and for all. Larrey noted in his own copy of his *Mémoires*:

'Hostilities ceased after a nocturnal visit by the Prince of Liechtenstein to Napoleon. Acting on behalf of the Emperor of Austria, the Prince offered him Marie Louise, the Emperor's daughter, as wife. Never did anything have such a disastrous effect on the morale of our soldiers. [Whether or not the offer was ever made is open to doubt, but that does not alter the general situation.]

'I saw, with astonishment, a great number of our horse grenadiers break their long swords in despair. There was no doubt at all that the Austrian army and their Emperor himself were about to fall into our hands.

'In truth, such a result would have achieved a general peace and would have been for the good of France. As it is, this marriage has been the cause of all our disasters.'[21]

When the talking started the French withdrew and headquarters were established at Schönbrunn and Vienna where they remained until the treaty was signed on October 14. During this time Larrey prepared a report for the Emperor. At Aspern-Essling and Wagram 1,200 of the Guard had been wounded; by August 600 had been returned to their units. Two hundred and fifty (including 38 amputees) had been sent back to France; only 45 soldiers had died.

This was a magnificent achievement that Napoleon could not ignore. At long last Larrey received official notification of his title of baron—although he was only one of four medical officers to receive the honour: the others were Percy, Desgenettes, and Heurteloup. Larrey's barony was in Swedish Pomerania where the estates yielded a revenue of 5,000 francs a year. Admittedly this was a niggardly sum compared with the amounts many others received, yet it helped to stave off his chronic financial worries. 'I wish our children to divide this income between them,' he told Charlotte in his letter of August 27[22]—as sometimes happened, he was officially informed about the income before the title.

With the peace treaty signed, the French army retired home. Larrey himself left Vienna on October 31 to shepherd the remaining wounded on their journey and arrived in Paris on November 18. During the campaign he had shown, once again, what an efficient medical service could do. Yet Napoleon, with incredible obtuseness, failed to profit from the evidence before him. It was not so much his marriage to Marie Louise, as Larrey believed, that led to disaster, as his continued failure to follow up his instructions to the Administration regarding the medical services.

For two years Larrey and his Charlotte lived together in their house in the cul-de-sac Conti undisturbed by the demands of war—even though the Peninsula remained a running sore in the flesh of France. They took part in the glittering splendour of life at the imperial court, which, that spring, gave itself over to a grand celebration. Josephine's sacrificial divorce had been concluded and on April 1, 1810, her liberated husband married Marie Louise, daughter of the Habsburg Francis of Austria and niece of Marie Antoinette.

The new Empress soon became pregnant—the raison d'être of the whole affair—and this meant a royal accoucheur had to be appointed. At the end of October, Antoine Dubois was named which left a vacancy among the surgeons of the imperial household. Larrey, quick to respond, wrote to Corvisart recalling his previous request in 1808 and reminding the physician of the Emperor's promises: 'The appointment was conferred on M. Dubois in my absence. I did not protest, but now that the post is again vacant I beg you to consider my application with justice and kindness.'

But again Corvisart had someone else in mind whom he did not hesitate to recommend to Napoleon. The Emperor, torn between hurting Larrey and offending his first physician, took the easy way out and simply said that Dubois should remain surgeon to his household. Corvisart then wrote to Larrey telling him of the decision, but went to great pains to confuse the true reason: 'The Emperor regards the appointment of consultant physicians and surgeons to his household as a reward and as an honourable retirement for elderly physicians and surgeons who have distinguished themselves in the difficult exercise of their art, whereas military physicians and surgeons have their own particular reward. [Corvisart shed no light on the nature of this.] You see,

Larrey and Napoleon

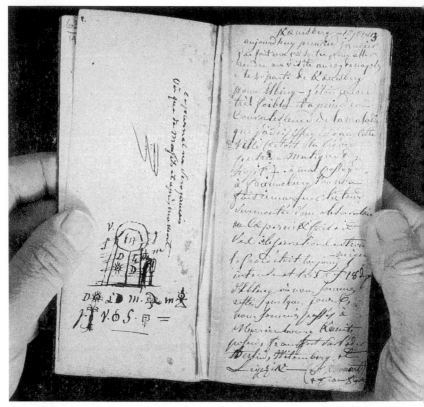

The opening page, January 1, at Königsberg, of Larrey's campaign journal for 1813

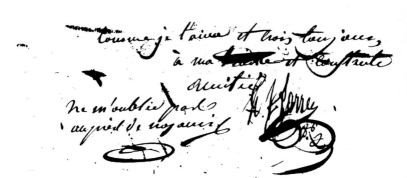

The last two lines and Larrey's signature from a letter to his wife, February 15, 180

Monsieur le Baron, that unless I had been informed of your request I would never, during your absence, have dreamed of presenting you to His Majesty in the capacity of consultant surgeon—and that is all I could have done, since the choice does not rest with me.'[1]

Larrey had returned, on New Year's day 1810, to the Hospital of the Guard where he worked as hard as he had ever done in the field to improve the lot of his patients. No aspect of their comfort, diet, treatment, or other needs was too trivial for him to bother about, and, because the Emperor was a frequent visitor to the hospital, he managed to persuade the Administration to meet his demands. One especial concern was the staff; not only did he acquire a sufficient number of disabled veterans as nursing orderlies but he was insistent that they were of the right calibre. When he ran up against the Administration over the appointment of surgeons, he got his own way by writing to the Minister of War (in November 1811) saying that he would find it most difficult to answer for the surgical services of the ambulances and units of the Guard if he was not consulted on the selection of, at least, the senior surgeons.[2]

And, as he had done on his return from Egypt, he spent many of his evenings writing in his study, surrounded by diaries and notes kept throughout his career. The result was the first three volumes of his memoirs which ended with his return to Paris after Wagram. Presenting the first volumes to Napoleon, he then sent copies to all the sovereigns in Europe—to the Czar of Russia, to the kings of Prussia, Bavaria, Naples, Spain—and to many other notables besides. The response was overwhelming. Letters of thanks were for the most part accompanied by gifts of considerable value. Alexander sent a ring of great price, Frederick William a bejewelled snuff-box with a portrait of himself on the lid, and others diamond-encrusted miniatures of themselves and more snuff-boxes and rings. Larrey's worth and the quality of his mercy were greatly appreciated, and held in high esteem outside France.

But no sooner was his task finished and the memoirs published than Larrey learnt of preparations being made by the government for another war, almost certainly in some distant sphere. 'My fears on this point were speedily confirmed when I received, quite unexpectedly, an order of departure accompanied by the decree (dated February 12, 1812) appointing me Surgeon-in-Chief of the Grand Army. I was no longer in doubt that a new campaign was about to open.'[3]

18. *Moments of Decision*

Before leaving to join the headquarters at Mainz, Larrey personally selected the surgeons for the Guard's ambulances and put Paulet, his deputy, in charge. Then he emerged from the comparative shelter of Gross-Caillou to face up to the harsh realities of the job that had once been Percy's.

In the years since Wagram decree after decree had—apparently for reasons of economy—cut back the army's medical services to a level scarcely adequate for peace, let alone war. The number of medical officers was now so low that ambulance divisions were allowed only 8 surgeons instead of the usual 15. Medical orderlies and stretcher bearers were in short supply (and not exactly dedicated), and medicines, dressings, bandages, and other equipment were totally inadequate. Yet this is what had been decreed and the Administration was well satisfied.

Larrey's foreboding of trouble ahead was strengthened when he saw the signature on his orders at Mainz: Joinville, temporary Quartermaster-General and the man whose feathers he had sorely ruffled at Austerlitz. But he was not the only Frenchman to take a gloomy view of the future. Most of Napoleon's advisers had warned him of the dangers of invading Russia; yet he would not listen and they watched with mounting anxiety as the largest army ever seen in Europe took shape. Forty tried battalions crossed the Pyrenees from Spain and were replaced by raw recruits. Prince Eugène marched into Germany with 50,000 Italians. Contingents came from all the subjugated states of Europe, and the two uncertain allies, Prussia and Austria, provided 30,000 men apiece—though Napoleon should have known better and demanded more, since he was leaving two still powerful forces in his rear who would certainly turn against him should things go wrong. The Grand Army of France was close on half a million strong, yet barely 200,000 were French. Cohesion and motivation were not its most remarkable attributes.

On the other side, Alexander was at war with Turkey. Even so, he knew where the real danger lay, and since 1810 had stationed the bulk of his forces on Russia's western frontier. When Napoleon sent an envoy to warn him of the consequences of inadequately supporting the continental blockade, Alexander gave his answer in the clearest possible terms. Showing the envoy a map, he said: 'I know that the Emperor Napoleon is a great general; but you see I have the advantage of space and time. There is no remote corner of this vast country to which I will not withdraw, no distant part that I will not defend, rather than agree to a shameful peace. I do not attack, but I will not lay down my arms as long as there remains a single foreign soldier in Russia.'[1] But Napoleon had made up his mind and was not to be warned off.

At Mainz Larrey found that most of the troops had already crossed the Rhine and were marching swiftly towards Prussia. He also discovered that 'the object of the expedition was unknown, although it was generally supposed that we would embark on the Baltic to invade England or to journey to some more distant country'.[2] Napoleon's secrecy was perfectly understandable since he intended to fall like a whirlwind on the two Russian armies, defeating them piecemeal, and then march triumphant to Moscow living off the land as he had always done before. For such a campaign he had all the supplies and transport he needed. But if events did not go as planned. . . . However, even had Larrey known their destination and guessed at the horrors that lay ahead, he would not have been able to prise one more stretcher, one more roll of linen, one more bandage out of the unbelievably stubborn Administration.

Headquarters left Mainz on March 8 and together Larrey and Desgenettes (Physician-in-Chief to the Grand Army) travelled north-eastwards across Germany to Berlin. Along the way they did what they could to improve the state of the hospitals and to prepare them for the reception of whatever casualties might be forthcoming. They reached Berlin on April 2 and at once Larrey gathered all the surgeons of the army together to assess their capabilities.

'The inexperience of the surgeons creates more casualties in the army than the enemy batteries,'[3] Napoleon had written in January that year, and he was uncomfortably close to the truth. Students were being squeezed through medical school by the strong grip of the Administration to emerge with some theoretical knowledge though completely lacking in experience. Larrey was therefore obliged to organize crash courses in military surgery and the practice of operating.

'Before leaving the capital, I formed six divisions of flying ambulances, personally assigning the eight surgeons to each. The surgeon-majors in command exercised their divisions each day in surgical operations and bandaging. The standard of discipline was high.

'We left Berlin on April 30 and on May 10 arrived at Posen [Poznan] still unaware of our destination. Throughout this time the army had been growing in strength and masses of artillery and supply wagons were pouring in from every direction.

'The Grand Army soon arrived at the Vistula where a count made during the crossing gave us about 400,000 men with roughly equal numbers of infantry and cavalry.'[4] But of that 400,000, 60,000 were admitted by their commanding officers to be sick; the true figure was probably double this.

On June 3, the day after he had rejoined his army, Napoleon received the reports of the various departments and then announced, at last, the purpose of the campaign. The invasion of Russia now began in earnest. But as soon as the Grand Army crossed the Niemen the weather declared its allegiance. The 60-or-so-mile march to Vilna was made along roads that scarcely merited the name and there was no shelter from the continuous rain. These conditions sent the sickness rate soaring even higher and contributed to the death of appreciable numbers of horses. But the weather was by no means the only menace to health. Vast quantities of the local schnaps were drunk and many of the Young Guard died.

Napoleon dallied a fortnight in Vilna instead of pursuing the enemy with all speed, as once he would have done and as his plan demanded. He marched out of the city on July 10 and on the twenty-seventh came to Vitebsk, the capture of which resulted in some 750 French wounded who were treated on the field of battle, though Larrey complained bitterly about the lack of first-aid dressings. After a very short while the stocks in the flying ambulances were exhausted and the surgeons had to use the soldiers' linen and even their own shirts. The fourgons containing the reserve supplies straggled far behind and the only explanation the quartermasters gave was that if Larrey chose to move so fast they washed their hands of all responsibility.

On the day after the fall of Vitebsk Napoleon visited the hospitals taking an exaggerated interest in the casualties, enquiring after their needs, and leaving a trail of decorations and rewards behind him. All the while he studiously avoided saying a word to his Surgeon-in-Chief—so completely alien to his usual behaviour—until, at the end of the visit, he faced Larrey and severely reprimanded him for his negligence in failing to order up the medical supply wagons. Larrey tried to justify himself but Napoleon simply turned on his imperial heel and walked away. This was the first time Larrey had been blamed for a medical deficiency and he took it badly. Quietly seething, he sat down and compiled a report for the Emperor, including copies of his letters to the quartermasters, which proved beyond argument that the Administration was responsible for the delay of the fourgons, and for the absence of linen, food, and drink. He also took the opportunity to unburden himself of his indignation at the Administration. For a long time, he wrote, its authority had been prejudicial to the well-being of the wounded and had seriously hampered the surgical services.

'Sire, if the surgeons were invested with the necessary authority to grant the soldiers all the comforts that humanity decrees is their right, Your Majesty could rest easy in your mind. But the military surgeon is obliged to struggle ceaselessly against the existing state of affairs. Indeed, the same spirit which pervades the Administration has destroyed the schools of military surgery in France; has promulgated regulations harmful to the medical officers; and without doubt has been the reason why we have lost so many good surgeons who, during past campaigns, gave proof of their skill and courage to His Majesty. Now, disheartened, they have left the military service.'[5]

In the margin of this lengthy report Napoleon scribbled: 'Refer to the Quartermaster-General to learn why linen was lacking on the field of battle.' But he did nothing constructive to help the situation, although when he realized he had maligned Larrey he had no hesitation in making amends. At a reception later in the week he noticed Larrey across the room and at once pushed his way through the gathering to clasp the surgeon's hands in genuine affection.

'Good,' he said, 'now I know what really happened. But you should never have doubted what you must surely know: that I regard you as one of the best servants of the State and as my friend.'[6]

In a turmoil of indecision Napoleon delayed the departure from Vitebsk until August 13, by which time one part of his plan had been thwarted. The two Russian armies, under Bagration and Michael Barclay de Tolly (a Livonian of Scottish descent), had linked up at Smolensk on August 3. The situation was becoming tense; Napoleon was unhappy about wintering in Lithuania—his mixed bag of an army would lose its impetus and disintegrate—yet he was beginning to sense the dangers of going on. But go on he did, hoping that the elusive victory would lie over the next hill or across the next river.

The Russian rearguard put up a brief but determined resistance at Krasnoe which cost the French 500 wounded. To look after them—and the large number of wounded Russian prisoners—Larrey had to leave 'several surgeons' in the town. Smolensk was reached on the seventeenth. Its capture was 'one of the bloodiest fights I have ever witnessed'.[7]

Once again the materials for dressings were soon exhausted but this time Larrey did not have to resort to the soldiers' own linen as he found that one of the buildings chosen for a hospital harboured the city's archives: the paper was a passable substitute for linen and bedding, while the parchment made excellent splints. Bark fibre from birch-trees, used instead of lint and absorbent tow, completed the improvisation until the supply fourgons arrived. Fortunately, a good quantity of brandy, wine, and miscellaneous medicines had survived the burning of the city and been rescued by the ambulance personnel before it could be looted.

Despite the terrible difficulties, all the necessary surgery was performed within twenty-four hours, Larrey's personal contribution including eleven amputations at the shoulder joint. Nine of these eleven patients recovered completely; the other two died of dysentery—as at Vitebsk the means of subsistence failed suddenly after a month.

With the capture of Smolensk, the moment of decision had come for Napoleon. In his heart he knew he should go into winter quarters—despite the risk of disintegration—and he had gone so far as to order administration units to be set up in Lithuania which were to pay particular attention to the problem of provisioning his army. But still he hankered after a decisive battle, and when intelligence arrived that the Russians were preparing to fight at Dorogobouje, 50 miles ahead, the temptation was more than he could resist. Having checked that his wings were secure, he marched out with the centre which consisted mainly of Frenchmen and included the Imperial Guard. Everyone expected him to return to Smolensk after the battle. Larrey certainly thought he would, and was convinced that the approaching autumnal rains would in any case prevent a major advance to the north.

When Napoleon ordered him to join headquarters, he therefore felt it reasonable to argue that he would be far better employed seeing to the desperate needs of the 10,000 French and Russian wounded in the Smolensk hospitals. 'No,' said the Commander-in-Chief, for he knew the value to morale of Larrey's presence.

'I obeyed,' Larrey noted in the margin of his copy of his *Mémoires*,[8] 'but not without regret and reluctance, foreseeing all the misery that would be ours and the hardships I would have to bear.' However, the foresight was the sort that comes in retrospect—this volume of the *Mémoires* was published in 1817—since he departed with only one ambulance division and two favourite pupils. The other five divisions and all the surgeons of the reserve he left in Smolensk.

While Larrey was arguing, the advance guard had had trouble with the Russian rear-guard at Volontina, 16 or so miles away on the road to Moscow. In consequence, surgical aid arrived as darkness fell after the engagement. 'The enemy had four times more dead than the French, and doubtless this success—or the hope of soon fighting a decisive battle—led Napoleon on in pursuit. As I intended to follow him, I quickly dressed the wounded, amounting to 600 or 700, but I had to leave the ambulance division behind to take the casualties back to Smolensk.'[9]

The full extent of Larrey's predicament now becomes clear. As surgeon of the Imperial Guard he had wounded the Administration's ego on more than one occasion and had gained almost complete control of the evacuation of the Guard's casualties. Where he was dependent on the quartermasters for supplies and personnel, Napoleon's influence smoothed the path. But once he was promoted to Surgeon-in-Chief of the Grand Army, the Administration had got him where it wanted him and was prepared to turn the screw and go on turning until he was crushed completely. It would show the Surgeon-in-Chief that he had no military rank or authority—despite his fine general's uniform—and was merely the Administration's whipping boy. And as if this were not enough, Larrey was now faced with the problems of ever-lengthening lines of communication and the impossible strain this placed on his surgical personnel.

As well as the surgeons of the ambulance divisions, there were the regimental surgeons. They helped on the field of battle, but stayed with their regiments—they were not involved in the business of evacuation. So there was Larrey at Volontina endeavouring to cope with one undermanned ambulance division, seeing the advance continue, and receiving no support from the rear. On the day after the fight, Napoleon sent a despatch to Smolensk: 'Write to the Quartermaster-General and say that the ambulance service is very bad. It is unbelievable that although the advance guard was engaged yesterday, the reserve surgeons, the ambulances, and the empty carriages from your headquarters and elsewhere, have not been sent to gather up the wounded. The Administration has no direction.'[10]

For the best of reasons, Larrey had decided to take with him just one ambulance division. That was gone and so it was that he caught up with the army at Dorogobouje with only his two assistants. Dorogobouje was in flames and deserted. Viazma was in flames and deserted. Barclay was doing his job well.[11]

Yet still Napoleon drove on, lured further and further into the entangling net of Russia. Gzhatsk, the next town, was burning fiercely; but as the French arrived, the heavens opened and some of the wooden buildings were saved to give the headquarters staff and the officers of the Guard a roof over their heads. Here, too, the troops had a brief respite from hunger when a store was found to contain bacon and biscuit and the surrounding fields to be full of large-headed cabbages.

The rains, which seemed to have come to stay, made the roads impassable for the artillery and forced the army to halt. Then, unexpectedly, the wind swung round to the north-north-east bringing with it dry weather. 'During the delay, we received information that the Russian army had at last taken up a strongly entrenched position on the heights of Mojaisk by the River Moskova. Orders were given to prepare for a major battle and the Commander-in-Chief told me to make my arrangements accordingly.

'I was greatly disturbed by this news.'[12] And well he might have been, since he was facing the prospect of evacuating the casualties from the bloodiest clash in history with only himself and two pupils.

19. *Borodino*

Prince Michael Golenischev-Kutuzov had chosen the ground for the forthcoming battle, and he had chosen well. The Russian army was entrenched along the crest of a hill that extended from the Moskova river and the main road to Moscow on its right to the old Smolensk road and the forests disappearing away into the distance on its left. A deep stream—a tributary of the Moskova—flowed north-east along the foot of the hill, adding greatly to the defensive strength of the position. On its west bank about half way along the Russian front was a little village. Its name was Borodino.

Before setting out from Gzhatsk, Larrey had managed to extricate himself from his immediate difficulties by robbing Peter to pay Paul. Leaving the infantry regiments with a surgeon-major, one assistant surgeon-major, and one under-assistant surgeon-major, and the cavalry regiments with a surgeon-major and one under-assistant surgeon-major, he ordered the remaining regimental surgeons to report for duty with headquarters. This manœuvre brought 45 surgeons under his immediate command. Then luck also took a hand. The halt at Gzhatsk was prolonged for 24 hours during which time several ambulance fourgons arrived.

The march to Borodino took 36 hours. Both men and horses arrived in a state of near-exhaustion from lack of food. The neighbouring villages were empty and the abbey of Koloskoi six or seven miles away had little to offer. There was even a shortage of water; the troops had to draw their supply from the stream in the face of the Russian guns.

'Nevertheless our advance guard deployed and, at two o'clock in the afternoon of September 5, attacked the enemy front line which was forced to fall back on the second. We captured several redoubts with their cannon intact. The Russian resistance was, in fact, crumbling when darkness fell and we were obliged to break off the fight. Both sides resumed their respective positions.

'During the night I had our wounded dressed and evacuated without delay to the forward hospital at the abbey of Koloskoi.

'The sixth was spent resting and reconnoitring the enemy lines. I organized the preparation of dressings, instructed my surgeons in their duties, and saw to the distribution of medical supplies and equipment. The placing of the general headquarters and the headquarters of the Guard was done by Napoleon himself; but before making my bivouac with them, I rode along the whole length of the line giving my instructions to the surgeons in charge of the corps and divisional dressing stations.'[1]

Larrey was up before dawn on the seventh moving his advanced dressing station into an area about 250 yards square behind the centre of the line and close to the headquarters' tents. He later reckoned that on that day 127,000 Frenchmen and 140,000 Russians came face to face. (Only the Grand Army's centre was engaged at Borodino. Its wings—intentionally 300 miles away—were already beginning to fold. In the north, the left, which included the Prussian contingent, were under pressure from Louis Wittgenstein; it gave way late in October when its component parts lost all cohesion. In the south, the right with the Austrians under Karl Schwartzenberg were quietly wintering and doing no harm to anyone. This gave General Tormasoff a comparatively free passage from his recent war in Turkey through Minsk and on eventually to capture the strategically vital bridge across the Beresina at Borizov.)

When the sun rose at six o'clock, the battle opened with a general attack. Prince Eugène (Beauharnais) commanded the left wing (of the centre), Prince Josef Poniatowski the right, and Ney, Davout, and Junot the centre. The Emperor and his Guard were stationed behind the centre.

'The artillery of both sides—more than 2,000 pieces—opened up simultaneously. Our troops advanced stubbornly through the enemy's cross-fire to capture their foremost redoubts. The left wing routed the defenders of one of the strongest positions on the road to Moscow, and pressed on to Mojaisk [behind the Russian right]. The centre, under the immediate command of

Marshal Ney, withstood the murderous fire of numerous batteries and redoubts before capturing an almost inaccessible position that held the key to the enemy defence.

'General Caulaincourt [brother of Louis], in command of one assault, was killed at the first redoubt. Generals Charles Morand and Lausnaberg, who succeeded him in turn, were both wounded at the same redoubt. Their loss seriously slowed the progress of this column which had great difficulty in even holding its gains. Nevertheless, Prince Poniatowski's attack on the right was successful and the entire enemy line was weakening. Without a doubt it would have been completely beaten had our reserve been called upon to help the central column; as it was, the front was too broad and our men physically exhausted. Indeed, for some moments the outcome was in the balance. But our troops drew on hidden reserves of energy, closed their ranks, and swept the Russian army before them to become masters of the field. The bloody battle had lasted from six in the morning to nine o'clock at night.'[2]

Yet the French victory was not decisive; the Russians put up a stout resistance and withdrew in good order. The only trophies the French had to show for the day's work were 700 or 800 prisoners and 20 or so shattered cannon. Had Napoleon committed the Guard in the afternoon—as his officers repeatedly begged him to do—Russian defeat would have become Russian disaster. But he was acutely conscious of his distance from France and was determined to keep the elite of his army intact and use it only as a last resource in a truly desperate situation. He was also acutely conscious of his bladder. His customary difficulty in passing water had become embarrassingly painful—probably an attack of cystitis, maybe a consequence of urethral stricture or bladder stones—and life that day on horseback must have been agony. As well as this he had developed an irritating dry cough which interfered with his breathing. However, it would be rash to attribute Napoleon's failure to annihilate the Russians at Borodino simply to physical illness. This may have played a part, but the real reason for his caution and indecision was faulty judgment—a disability he had demonstrated already on this campaign. For want of a better way of expressing it, his luck was running out and he probably knew it. At Austerlitz seven years earlier he had said, 'One has only a certain time for war. I shall be good for another six years; after that I must stop myself.'[3]

That evening, when a dispirited Napoleon was inspecting the battlefield, a horse trod on a wounded man. One of those in the Emperor's entourage remarked that it was only a Russian, which brought the rebuke: 'There are no longer enemies after a victory, only men.'[3]

Larrey estimated that on that bloody day between 12,000 and 13,000 Frenchmen, including 40 generals, and more than 20,000 Russians were killed or wounded. Approaching two-thirds of the 9,000 French wounded passed through Larrey's own advanced dressing station and it was only his habit of treating first those in greatest need, regardless of rank or nationality, that prevented utter confusion. Because of the small number of adequately qualified surgeons, he had to perform all the difficult operations himself as well as supervise the work of all the other dressing stations. And from time to time he was called upon to operate under fire in the front line.

'I continued, without rest, to operate on the difficult cases until late into the night of the eighth. Our work was made more difficult by the very cold and cloudy weather. The prevailing northerly winds were strong, by reason of the approaching equinox, and I had the greatest difficulty in keeping a wax taper burning throughout the night. However, I only had real need of it when applying ligatures to arteries. Without exception, my surgeons proved their courage and devotion, while those of the corps and regimental aid posts performed their duties in exemplary fashion.

'The wounds received in this battle were generally serious since they were nearly all the result of artillery fire or of muskets discharged at point-blank range. Moreover, the Russian cannon-balls were larger than ours. A great number of men injured by the artillery fire required amputation of one or two limbs, and during the first 24 hours I performed about 200 operations of this nature.

'Two only of the eleven soldiers whose arms I removed at the shoulder died during evacuation. The others reached Prussia and Germany safe and healed. The most remarkable of these was a major from one of the infantry regiments of the line. Immediately after the operation he set out for France; soon afterwards he lost his horse but he did not allow this to interfere with his progress and in three and a half months had reached Paris with the wound fully healed.'[4] (The officer sponged the discharges away from the surface of the dressing every day; otherwise nothing else was done until the original bandages were removed in Paris.)

Among the amputations was Larrey's sixth and last removal of a leg through the hip joint; it was also the most successful. The patient was an under-officer of dragoons who had been hit in the left groin by a bullet which had destroyed the muscles on its passage through the tissues to shatter the head and upper part of the femur. After operation the man was taken to the abbey of Koloskoi and then evacuated in stages to Vitebsk, from where the surgeon-major in charge wrote that the patient was in good health and the wound almost fully healed. The under-officer journeyed on into Poland and Larrey never heard of him again, although he always hoped for news and thus for proof of complete recovery from the operation.

Two hundred amputations by one man in 24 hours is a physical tour de force as well as a surgical record that will never be beaten. But let this not be taken as evidence that Larrey was too ready to chop off limbs. His master's military judgment may have failed, yet Larrey's own surgical judgment remained sound and balanced through all the dangers, fatigue, hunger, and bodily discomfort of that ghastly battle. Nowhere was this shown more brilliantly than in his treatment of General Claude Pajol.

Pajol was shot in the left forearm. Both bones were broken and the fractured ends fragmented. It was the sort of injury where even the most conservative of surgeons would probably have advised amputation—especially in the frantic conditions at the dressing station. But Larrey believed that tidying up and immobilization would save the arm; so, despite the difficulties, he débrided the wound, removing all foreign bodies and all fragments of bone not attached to periosteum. Then he bandaged and splinted the forearm and supported it with a sling. Larrey later looked after the dressings himself, even during the retreat from Moscow, and was well rewarded by seeing the injury heal well and the shape and movements of the arm return to normal[5]— further indication of his concern for his patients, since bony union and healing of the wound were all most surgeons bothered about (but did not always achieve); appearance and function were left very much in the lap of the gods. Thanks to Larrey, Pajol was able to lead his cavalry into glorious action in the campaigns in Saxony and France.

And as if 9,000 wounded Frenchmen were not enough, Larrey had plenty of the enemy to deal with as well. Most upper class Russians spoke French fluently and whenever their wounded officers fell into French hands they demanded to be taken to Larrey's dressing station.

The large numbers of wounded presented a tremendous problem as everything was either in short supply or totally lacking: food, dressings, straw, blankets, tents, and carriages. Flying ambulances took the wounded from Larrey's dressing station to the villages and the abbey of Koloskoi, but they too were insufficient for the task. And when the men arrived at the limited number of places suitable for temporary hospitals they found the cavalry had been there first; all the forage had been eaten and no straw was left for beds. Even the abbey, a fair sized complex of buildings where most of the wounded were taken, had tragically little to offer beyond shelter.

'However, many essential items, such as bread, flour, beer, medicines, and material for dressings, might have been obtained from several places where we had found supplies. I did indeed ask for this to be done and the necessary orders were given, but as usual the execution of such measures depended on so many people that nothing was achieved. The surgeons, sole attenders on the wounded, were thus compelled personally to wash (or have washed in their presence) the linen that was already in use so that the dressings might be renewed daily. The majority of the wounded owe their recovery to the tireless zeal and industry of my colleagues.'[6] The Administration simply sought ways of avoiding their responsibilities and of profiting from the situation.

During the few days that Larrey was at Borodino and then at Mojaisk he created such a fuss about the conditions and supplies, complaining to Daru, the Quartermaster-General, and to Napoleon himself, that he managed to persuade the quartermasters to set up stores in the abbey of Koloskoi and at Mojaisk. For a while rations were distributed more or less regularly. But once Larrey was safely on his way to Moscow, the Administration showed its true colours. Only those wounded who could pay—be they French or Russian, officers or men—were fed. The rest, if they were incapable of helping themselves, just starved.

And this was not all. The medical orderlies, such as they were, were purloined by the Administration to attend to its own comforts. As a result dressings were not done, wounds became infected, and hospital gangrene killed like no human conqueror. The dead remained unburied. Many of those who survived these barbarous torments died when the barns and warehouses where they lay were set on fire by incendiaries. Small wonder that those who could, dragged themselves away. Soldiers who had had legs amputated made themselves pegs out of any pieces of wood they could find, just to escape the horror of the so-called hospitals. The risks of hobbling painfully back home were greatly to be preferred.

Nothing on God's earth—or in His heaven—can ever excuse the despicable conduct of the French Administration. So steeped was it in selfish inhumanity that it intercepted the surgeons' reports to Larrey from as far back as Kovno lest he learn of the true situation and complain to the Emperor.[7] Only on the retreat as he arrived at one town after another did he discover what had been happening.

So, at Borodino were revealed in stark reality the two extremes of human character. In between was the great mass whose lot in life throughout the ages is simply to know suffering and to bear it with a greater or lesser degree of equanimity.

'Alexander will sue for peace only after a major battle,' Napoleon had said at Vitebsk. 'If needs be I shall go in search of this battle, even as far as the holy city, and I shall win it. Peace awaits me at the gates of Moscow.'[1] And here he was at those gates, far from home, troubled in mind and body, and desperately in need of that peace. The battle had been fought, yet away in St Petersburg Alexander had no intention of coming to terms; he could afford to play a cat-and-mouse game with the invader.

The progress of the advance guard under Murat had been disputed, and so on the morning of September 14 Napoleon mounted his white horse fully expecting the last few miles into the city to be furiously contested. But the countryside was deserted; the effect on a tired and hungry army was unnerving.

Then, with only two hours of daylight left, they came to the top of a rise and saw the holy city at their feet. All past dangers and hardships, all present fears and hungers were forgotten as battalion after battalion halted, stupefied by the almost spiritual beauty of the scene. The slanting rays of the sun were caught by the metalled roofs of hundreds of churches and palaces and thrown back in a dazzling display of many-coloured fires. The men broke ranks and all they could say was 'Moscow! Moscow!' Napoleon had his emotions under a tighter rein: 'So here at last is this famous city,' then, after a pause, 'and not before time.'[1]

But as the day slipped away the glamour faded and the capital seemed dark, silent, and menacing. Napoleon's anxiety returned to infect the army and the troops became difficult to control, the more so as many young conscripts were still drinking themselves literally to death with local schnaps. When Napoleon reached the suburbs his worst fears were confirmed by reports that the retreating Russian rearguard had taken practically the entire population with it. To all intents and purposes, Moscow had been abandoned. And that night the fires began. They were quickly extinguished and were at first thought to be a result of indiscipline and drunkenness among the French, but when they broke out with renewed fury the next night the truth was clear. 'The cause was justly attributed to the deliberate actions of the criminal classes who had been released from prison by the departing Russian army.'[2]

(The burning of Moscow according to Philippe de Ségur, Napoleon's aide-de-camp, had been planned by its commandant, Feodor Rostopchin, who feared one of two things; that a dishonourable peace would be extracted from his Emperor or that French propaganda would incite a revolution. Nevertheless, in a hand-written comment in his *Mémoires*,[3] Larrey disputed that it was Rostopchin who had had the idea of burning the capital and said that it had been ordered in London and set in motion from St Petersburg.)

'The Commander-in-Chief with headquarters and the Guard left the Kremlin [not without difficulty in getting the horses through the burning streets] for the castle of Peter the Great about four miles outside the city on the road to St Petersburg. I remained, with a few of my colleagues, in a stone-built house in an isolated area near the Kremlin.

'Our own soldiers, suffering greatly from hunger and thirst, incurred all manner of risks to acquire food, wine, spirits, and other articles of greater or lesser usefulness from burnt cellars and shops. They ran through the streets mingling with the inhabitants and loaded with everything they could snatch from the wreckage. Thus, in eight or ten days this magnificent city was reduced to ashes, leaving only the palaces of the Kremlin, some of the larger houses, and the churches, all of which were built of stone.

'The army was in a state of great consternation as it was generally supposed that we could no longer obtain sustenance, cloth, or other necessities of which there was the most urgent need.'[4]

Napoleon had reached Peter the Great's castle late on the night of the 16th. In the morning he announced his intention of marching on St Petersburg, but at that moment the report came in of Kutuzov's march south and west to cut the road to Kalouga.

Here was an opportunity to catch the defeated Russian army and crush it completely; at the same time as protecting his right flank he would take Kalouga and Toula, the granary and arsenal, respectively, of Russia, and open a safe route to Smolensk. Then someone proposed returning to Vitebsk. The net result was that the once decisive Napoleon did nothing and on the twentieth, after the fires had died down, he returned to Moscow.

The journey back gave him increased reason for worry—the lack of order and discipline was obvious. In fields thick with mud, men warmed themselves at fires built of valuable furniture, ornate window frames, and richly gilded doors. Soldiers and their officers, blackened with smoke, sat around in luxurious arm chairs or slept on elegant sofas up to the springs in mud. And at their sides were piles of cashmere shawls, rare furs from Siberia, and cloth of gold from Persia. On the road itself he met bands of soldiers dragging their booty behind them or driving before them, like beasts of burden, a crowd of Russian peasants bent double beneath the weight of plunder.

'On our return, headquarters were again established in the Kremlin and the Guard occupied some nearby houses which had escaped the flames. Everyone resumed their duties.

'Searches were ordered and stores of flour, meat, salted fish, oil, brandy, wine, and spirits were discovered. Some was issued to the troops, but the rest was left to deteriorate or be burnt or pillaged—the expressed desire to save it for the future was merely an excuse for taking no action. These stores would have been most valuable and would have met the needs of the army for more than six months, had it remained in Moscow. More attention should also have been paid to the collection of cloths and furs so as to manufacture winter clothing. The soldiers themselves gave no thought to future needs but instead were concerned only with gathering wine, spirits, gold, and silver—everything else was disregarded."[5]

This behaviour was due not so much to greed as to the belief that they had already paid for all they took in terms of the dangers and hardships they had suffered. Regrettably, all the resources still existing after the fire were lost through this irregular pillaging.

On September 25, Larrey advised Napoleon that if he was

intending to leave Moscow he had better do so at once or not at all—to delay a retreat could only have disastrous consequences. But if he intended to remain, there were enough provisions to see the army through the winter.[6] Daru was at this meeting and agreed with Larrey—an event so unusual in itself that it must give added weight to the truth of their assertions. In addition Larrey recommended slaughtering all the horses that could not be fed and salting them for food. But when Napoleon called a council of war his marshals and generals were more anxious to enjoy the delights of Paris than spend an uncomfortable winter in Moscow. They advised leaving.

So yet again Napoleon seethed with indecision for two or three days before giving the order to lay in provisions, and to help the morale of the senior officers he had one of his aides draw up a list of actors at the Comédie Française who could come to Moscow without upsetting the Paris programmes.

Meantime Kutuzov was busy sustaining Napoleon's belief that Alexander was ready to negotiate a peace and relying on an inexhaustible fund of excuses why the preliminaries could not be signed. Towards the end of the first week of October, with the situation verging on the ridiculous, Napoleon sent General Jacques Lauriston as an emissary to Kutuzov bearing a personal letter for Alexander. Lauriston, the son of an exiled Scot, had been on a mission to Russia before the invasion and was held in some esteem by the Czar, yet even he was duped before Kutuzov agreed to a truce until a reply could come from St Petersburg—which the Russian emphasized could not be in less than a fortnight. Although the main body of the Russian army observed, in a sense, this truce, large bands of Cossack irregulars hovered around the French encampments and gave the foraging parties little peace. Murat's cavalry was slowly being whittled away in these skirmishes.

'General Kutuzov took advantage of the truce to regroup his forces and to strengthen them with fresh recruits. His advance guard gradually—and with seemingly peaceful intent—closed with our own. When the truce expired [October 17] Murat found himself surrounded and was put to flight with the loss of some of his men and several pieces of cannon. But he quickly

M

rallied and broke through the encircling Russian column to gain a favourable position. From here he launched a violent counter-attack on the enemy cavalry and rescued the cannon and soldiers taken in the first engagement.'[7]

Napoleon was reviewing his troops in the Kremlin when an aide-de-camp brought him the news. At once he seemed to recover all his lost energy and decision. Orders poured from him, ranging from over-all strategy to the smallest details; all were co-ordinated, all necessary. But unfortunately he was poorly served by Berthier who during this whole critical period, ignored details and initiated nothing on his own account. Since Vilna, most of the troops had bartered their winter clothing for food; the march had destroyed their footwear; and their uniforms bore the evidence of battle. Yet only on October 17, after the first snow had fallen, did Berthier begin to think about issuing leather jerkins.[1]

The general uncertainty of the situation was reflected in Larrey's action during the previous two or three days of evacuating to Mojaisk under a strong infantry escort all the sick and wounded who could be moved. Only 1,200 patients were left behind—a great achievement considering that 20,000 of the 110,000 combatants with which Napoleon entered the capital had been sick or wounded. Thanks to the care and skill of Larrey and the other surgeons the Emperor was able to leave at the head of more than 100,000 fighting men. But before he went he decided to teach the Russians a lesson and take from the Kremlin churches anything and everything that would serve as a trophy. He justified his action on two counts: his right as conqueror, and on the fact that the Russians had consigned their treasures to the flames when they set fire to the city. The greatest trophy was the gigantic cross which the French removed with difficulty from the tower of Ivan the Terrible. This was regarded by the Russians as a kind of talisman for the safety of their Empire. Napoleon intended that henceforth it should protect his own from the dome of the Invalides in Paris.

And so, before dawn on October 19, Napoleon, momentarily revitalized maybe, but lacking the judgment of old, rode out of Moscow. 'We march on Kalouga, and Heaven help anyone who finds himself in my way.'[1]

'Fear of rations failing and memories of their recent hardships made my colleagues look to the future. They loaded provisions on horses and into carriages, and our orderlies filled their knapsacks with rations. The army itself, however, had never been so encumbered with baggage as it was on its departure from Moscow.'[1] In addition to their rich and varied plunder—reflecting Moscow's importance as a trade centre between East and West—the French took with them 550 cannon and 2,000 artillery carriages; and, further slowing the procession, were some 30,000 non-combatants—among them French residents of Moscow, men, women, and children, and several Russian girls who had thrown in their lot with the enemy.

Napoleon had marched out along the old Kalouga road—the one being covered by Kutuzov—but after the first mid-day halt he changed his mind and turned west across country for the new road. As if this was not a difficult enough manœuvre in itself, it began to rain and threw the entire column into disorder with everyone desperately trying to save his own share of the treasure from the clinging mud.

'On the evening of the twenty-third the enemy abandoned his position and marched to intercept us. Prince Eugène, in command of the advance guard, was ordered to make for Malojaroslavitz, a small town in a mountainous gorge through which Kutuzov's army would have to pass. Due to the treachery of his guides and the bad state of the roads, he reached this town two hours after the enemy. The Prince, nevertheless, crossed the rivers and launched a bold attack up the mountain-side. After a bloody fight he gained possession of the gorge, but it was too late—the greater part of the Russian army had already passed through. The Russians lost upwards of 6,000 men; we had nearly 2,000 wounded who were dressed on the field and later transported in the rear of the army in private carriages brought from Moscow.

'Headquarters and the Guard reached Malojaroslavitz as the battle ended and while the enemy troops were being pursued beyond the gorge some miles along the road to Kalouga. The captured cannon were spiked and the artillery wagons burned. The wounded Russians were carried, on my instructions, to the town; but as I could not wait to see that the necessary attention was given them, I departed in the hope that they would receive it from their fellow countrymen.

'We did not at first know which direction we should be taking, but we headed for Borowsk. After passing this city we marched through a pleasant, fertile, and well-populated area. It would have been advisable to continue in this direction and on through the Ukraine, but Napoleon, wishing no doubt to save the large numbers of wounded and sick left at Mojaisk, Koloskoi, Gzhatsk, Viazma, and elsewhere along the route of the advance, and being aware that Tormasoff had cut his communications with Borizov, decided to return the way we had come.'[2]

Although Kutuzov's threat to the southern route was more apparent than real—he was retreating south himself, licking the wounds of Malojaroslavitz—the danger to Napoleon's lines of communication was growing fast. The left wing of the Grand Army had been beaten by Wittgenstein at Polotsk on October 19 and was retiring on Smolensk. The right wing under Schwartzenberg had done nothing to hinder Tormasoff's advance north and by staying at Slonim had left the army's escape route fully exposed. Nevertheless to show he had not forgotten the Emperor Schwartzenberg sent a dispatch proudly announcing that he was covering Warsaw.

To his later expressed regret, Napoleon allowed himself to be swayed by those of his generals who feared the dangers of both an unknown route and the presence of Kutuzov on their flank. Davout's forecast of what they would meet along the other road made no impression: 'A desert of sand and cinders,' he had said, 'where convoys of wounded will add to our embarrassment; where we will find only desolation, blood, skeletons, and starvation.'[3] But his words were remembered a few days later when they reached Mojaisk. As the army realized what lay ahead, an already tottering morale began its fall into the abyss. Any semblance of co-ordination ceased to exist; each unit marched on its own with its commander acting independently. Napoleon, through the inadequacies of Berthier, lost touch.

'On our arrival at Mojaisk,' Larrey wrote in his campaign journal,[4] 'I hastened to visit the hospitals we had set up on our way to Moscow; they held about 2,300 patients who were mostly up and about. All the wounded from the battle of Borodino were in good enough surgical shape and had received regular medical attention. But I have no praise for the conduct of the Administration. I found the greater part of the wounded in extreme destitution; they had no equipment, no books, no bread, no meat, no light food, and no beer or wine. These unhappy men had not even had a regular distribution of gruel, bad beef or horse-meat soup, or of the cabbage stalks which the walking wounded had gathered from the fields. The paillasses and straw that served for beds were rotting and infested. Those who were unable to fend for themselves lived in appalling filth. When we moved on we had to abandon a few who were seriously ill but I left several medical officers with them.'

With the departure from Mojaisk the north-east wind began to blow and the temperature fell rapidly. Borodino was passed in silence. No one stopped at this vast sepulchre where 30,000 half-decomposed corpses now lay as their own memorials frozen amid the litter of battle. But as Larrey passed the flames of a nearby village, three Russian officers, on whom he had operated during the battle, came to thank him for what he had done. Their wounds (two had lost a leg apiece) were healed and they were about to be evacuated with the French but they begged to be allowed to stay. Larrey agreed and gave them money to buy, from travelling Jews, a few much needed necessities until their own countrymen arrived. Then, clasping their hands and advising them to make themselves scarce until the French were gone, he entrusted to their care the wounded soldiers who were being left behind.[5] As Louis Thiers remarked in his *Histoire du Consulat et de l'Empire*, 'God alone knows whether they paid this debt contracted with the best of men.'

'My inspection of the abbey at Koloskoi, where we had 700 wounded, was extremely distressing. It would be difficult to describe the terrible state of the patients, particularly of those in the stables and barns; they were rotting on a dung-heap, surrounded by corpses.'[4] Like those everywhere else, they had had little or nothing to eat and their wounds had been dressed infrequently because of the lack of linen. A number of men in sore need of surgery were operated on either by Larrey himself or under his personal supervision; eventually he evacuated all but 40 to Viazma. Later, to his sorrow, he learnt that a short while after his departure, the abbey buildings had been reduced to ashes.

'The delay at Koloskoi meant that I had to march every night to catch up with headquarters. The lack of resources was already great; it snowed hard and the cold increased daily. The march was extremely difficult; the soldiers suffered much in bivouac; and it was now that the disorganization of the army began.

'The Emperor at this time put at my disposal his carriages and wagons for the wounded. His household doctors, my friend Ribes, and Yvan were ordered to follow and give assistance.'[4] Larrey later noted, 'In this way I transported more than 2,000 wounded. I obtained an order from the Emperor which obliged every officer, every cantinier, every refugee from Moscow who had a carriage to take one or more of the wounded with him.'[6] Regrettably the cantiniers and vivandiers did not welcome the additional weight on their already overloaded (with plunder) vehicles and some of them threw their passengers into the ditches. Those few who were caught in the act were shot.

'The army had already eaten the food brought from Moscow, and the stores at Mojaisk were scarcely sufficient to meet the needs of the advance guard.'[4] And at Viazma the now familiar pattern of desperately neglected casualties and lack of supplies was repeated, though the troops did receive an issue of flour and a very small quantity of bread. All the transportable wounded in the town were got away safely, but as the rearguard, under Prince Eugène, was about to enter it found itself cut off and compelled to fight through a large corps of Cossacks and Russian infantry—the Russian advance guard under the command of Michael

Miloradovitch. Kutuzov was unwilling to risk another major engagement, preferring to rely on the weather to achieve his victory for him; so it was left to Miloradovitch, 'the Russian Murat', to harass and demoralize the retreating French.

This engagement outside Viazma, fought in a thick mist, cost the French 4,000 men and the Russians 6,000. However, 'the convoy of wounded and the rear-guard's equipment suffered much in the combat; I lost a great number of casualties who had been well on the way to recovery, together with several of my medical officers. Furthermore, the majority of the French families from Moscow who were travelling with the rear-guard and those unfortunate enough to be wounded in this fight had to be abandoned at the wayside, where they were slaughtered by Cossacks and Russian peasants.'[4]

Leaving Viazma on November 2 Ney's corps replaced, as rear-guard, that of Davout and Prince Eugène which had become seriously weakened. The weather improved and this, combined with the hope, encouraged by the officers, that once they reached Smolensk and its storehouses the worst of their troubles would be over, raised the men's spirits. But on the sixth as they marched out of Dorogobouje the heavens firmly allied themselves with Kutuzov. A freezing mist enshrouded the army and soon snow began to fall in huge flakes. Thin, damp clothing froze on the soldiers' backs. Breathing became harsh and the exhaled air froze in their beards. Snow clogged under their footgear and men fell over the least irregularity; if they could not get up, they died where they lay. The horses, too, had difficulty keeping their footing as they had not been shod for winter. With each mile that passed the breakdown of discipline became increasingly evident. At Mikalewska the useless spoils and treasures of Moscow, everything that might impede the march, were thrown into the the lake of Semlewo. The mighty cross of Ivan crashed through the ice and no one shed a tear as it sank. Yet many threw away their arms to save their plunder.

During the ten days between Viazma and Smolensk, Ney was continually in action to give Napoleon time to rally. He stood and fought outside Smolensk when he could have found safety inside, solely to gain for his Emperor another precious 24 hours. His most testing moment had come at Dorogobouje where, thunderstruck, he found himself falling back on abandoned cannon and bands of men (from generals downwards) wandering in weaponless disarray. When, for a time, it seemed that his own corps might be infected he seized a musket and fought like a most uncommon common soldier at their side.

'Throughout the march to Smolensk, we found only the huts which had been built for the relays of dispatch riders. Such houses as there were hardly sufficed for the Emperor and two or three senior officers; as a result we had to sleep in bivouac. It was at this period that we felt hunger most intensely. The country, entirely destroyed, offered no resources [the swathe of desolation was 20 to 25 miles across] and the army had already lost most of its equipment. Happy the man who was able to find fresh horse meat. I saw soldiers fall upon horses dead for several days and dissect them down to the bone. Unhappy the beasts that wandered during the night or were inattentively guarded by their masters; they were killed, disemboweled, and dismembered. The liver and heart were the most sought-after delicacies, and were often the cause of bloody scuffles between soldiers who had together carried off and killed an animal. Officers had not the slightest influence over the men: personal interest was the sole motivating force throughout the army; brother no longer recognized brother; husbands no more heeded the wives who till then had shared their privations and hardships; children, even, were abandoned.

'I was astonished, on the approach to Smolensk, at the sight of a young woman pushed to extremes by her hunger. She threw herself into the midst of a group of soldiers who were disemboweling a native horse and, even though she was wearing a magnificent fur cloak lined with white satin, plunged her hands into the animal's belly to tear out the liver. But without a knife she was forced to use her teeth. At last she emerged with a piece of the delicacy and ran off to roast it at the first bivouac fire she could find. Alas! how many of these unfortunate women succumbed to the tragic effects of their overpowering need. *Nearly all our wounded died from hunger.*

'At last we arrived at the promised city. The cold was extreme—

the temperature had fallen to zero Fahrenheit. But what a terrible shock awaited us. There was scarcely food enough for the small garrison and for the sick in the hospitals.'⁴ And even that was plundered.

The first to reach Smolensk had been a disorderly rabble who found the gates shut in its face. When these men were told they would have to wait for the arrival of the Guard, they broke down the gates and looted the stores. No one would hold *them* back just so the Guard could have the pick of the food.

'A small number profited for a short while from this pillage, but the rest of the army was condemned to suffer. The sick were deprived of their accustomed rations, and for the two days that we spent in the town, I had the sad experience of seeing many of our wounded and of my medical officers go without any food at all. I shared, among 30 of them, a sack of flour that I had managed to buy at an exorbitant price.'⁴

Larrey did what he could to help the casualties, operating when necessary, but lacking transport he could not evacuate them all and was obliged to leave 50 surgeons behind as well as a number of medical officers with frost-bitten feet.

'We departed from Smolensk on November 14. The 100,000 fighting men who had marched out of Moscow were now reduced to about 37,000. The remainder were dead or followed in utter confusion: 50,000 or 60,000 men of all ranks, of all corps, and of all arms straggled along in smaller or larger groups. The wind was set in the north-east and the temperature fell to 44 Fahrenheit degrees of frost. The march to Krasnoe, about 72 miles, was extremely painful as we had no shelter or provisions. The villages along the way were all totally burned. Moreover, the enemy who had attacked our rear-guard at Smolensk, and given me a large number of casualties to operate on and dress, tormented us on all sides. We had only three or four hours' rest a night, always in bivouac, and marched without pause for the remaining eight to ten. Cold *and above all hunger* were the sole causes of death along this part of the retreat. Those of my colleagues who had adopted the habit of walking and who had saved a little coffee and sugar suffered the least; the continual exercise prevented the limbs becoming numb and maintained warmth and function in the organs, whereas those who travelled on horseback or in carriages were soon paralysed with cold. If they then approached a bivouac fire they were struck by gangrene. I saved myself from this fate by marching always on foot and by depriving myself of the luxury of warmth.

'The baggage wagons and the artillery parks were attacked several times and scattered by the Cossacks with considerable ease owing to the icy roads. Once I found myself surrounded by one of their bands; I owe my safety to the help of several grenadiers of the Guard who saw my plight and threw themselves upon my attackers. By great good fortune a ball struck a Cossack who would probably have killed me.

'On our arrival, on November 17, at Krasnoe we were surrounded and had to engage the enemy at practically all points. The Imperial Guard—the only unit of the Grand Army still intact—sustained the brunt of the attack and fought with such success that in less than two hours the battlefield was covered with Russian dead and dying. We were in very great danger and several of my colleagues were killed or wounded at my side. But the courage of my surgeons and of those who came to our aid was truly admirable. The French women who had left Moscow with us and had shared our privations and dangers, carried devotion to the point of heroism dressing the wounded under cannon fire. Outstanding among them was Madame Aurore Bursay,[7] directress of the Moscow theatres, who left the field only with the last of the wounded.'[4]

This battle at Krasnoe was motivated by Napoleon's fear that, with Ney and Davout cut off, Kutuzov would launch a general attack. So, rousing himself from his lethargy, he had taken the initiative with all his former flair and energy. Marching on foot at the head of the Old Guard, he inspired 15,000 cold, hungry, dispirited Frenchmen to beat 60,000 Russians and so save the rear-guard—but at the relatively terrible price of 4,000 dead.

'The army resumed its march but on its arrival at Orcha was greatly dismayed to find itself separated from Ney's rear-guard; in fact we believed his corps to be completely lost. We had already left the town thoroughly depressed when, at the next halt, I was one of the first to hear that the Marshal was safe. To protect the army, Ney had fought continuously with a corps badly reduced by the losses it had sustained; its cavalry was totally destroyed and very little artillery remained. Nevertheless it had battled with superhuman courage. The enemy cavalry encircled this little body and, supported by infantry which pressed hard on Ney's rear and flanks, called upon the Marshal to surrender.'[4] Five thousand Frenchmen with six cannon faced 80,000 Russians and 200 cannon.

Even as their envoy spoke, the Russians opened fire. This served merely to harden Ney's resolve: 'A marshal of France never surrenders,' he said to the envoy, 'and since one does not negotiate under fire, you are my prisoner.'[3] Then he calmly assessed the situation before giving the order to his remaining troops to fight their way out. With truly incredible valour displayed over two days and nights this steadily dwindling force eventually battled its way back to the main body.

The delight of the army at Ney's return was inexpressible and temporarily raised morale. Napoleon, too, gave him a warm welcome: 'My eagles are safe! I would have given three millions of my treasure for the ransom of such a man.'[3]

Across the Dnieper for the last time, conditions deteriorated yet again as a rise in temperature turned the roads to mud, though at Tolecsehyn the French found a warehouse containing a considerable quantity of flour, bread, and brandy which was distributed and raised their spirits for a while.

'Marshal Victor who had come to meet us [with a little push from Wittgenstein] now rejoined the army and replaced Marshal Ney as the rearguard. We reached Borizov without difficulty, but Tormasoff's army, newly arrived from Turkey, was waiting for us at the crossing of the Beresina. They had cut the bridge.'[4]

22. *The Last Days of the Grand Army*

Charles Oudinot also linked up with the main force at Borizov. Neither his nor Victor's men could believe their eyes when they saw the so-called army straggling back to the Beresina—tattered bits of carpet and women's cloaks were as common as greatcoats, and all were filthy, scorched, and holed from the bivouac fires. At first they shared their rations and spare clothes, but the utter demoralization was catching and soon began to weave its evil spell.

Despite the reinforcements, the situation was bleak; strong Russian forces faced the French across the river and were closing rapidly on their rear. Any thought of crossing at Borizov was out of the question as there was no hope of repairing the 600-yard-long bridge. The best possibility seemed to lie with a ford downstream; but then one of Oudinot's patrols reported seeing a peasant on horseback cross at Studzianka a few miles upstream where the river was just over 100 yards wide and about six feet deep. So, on the night of November 23, part of Oudinot's corps, artillery, and engineers occupied the left bank at Studzianka. The next day 300 soldiers and a great crowd of stragglers were sent to the ford downstream to gather materials and create the impression that they were about to build a bridge. At the same time a staff officer gathered several local Jews and by discreet questioning left them with the inescapable impression that the French were indeed intending to cross at the downstream ford.

Building the bridge at Studzianka was beset with difficulties and it was not ready until the 26th. The previous night had, however, been full of incident, mostly favourable to the French— the only unfortunate happening had been the disappearance of the Studzianka ford when the river level rose unexpectedly. Oudinot had left Borizov to take up his position at Studzianka. Napoleon himself had followed shortly after to spend the night

'The Battle of La Moskova (Borodino)', September 7, 1812, by Louis François Lejeune, 1775–1848, general and artist. Larrey is seen in the centre
foreground treating General Morand who has been severely wounded in
the lower jaw

'Bivouac at Molodetschno during the night of December 3–4, 1812', by Johannes Hari, 1772–1849. 'On the morning of December 3 Napoleon arrive at Molodetschno. . . . A quantity of food was found there; fodder was abundan the day fine, the sun bright, the cold supportable.' (Ségur, p. 406)

at the Radziwill castle half-way between the two towns. Here
Murat, who thought the end was near, pleaded with Napoleon
to escape while there was yet time, but the Emperor indignantly
refused to abandon his army in its hour of greatest need. Meanwhile, on the other bank Napoleon's star flared brightly: the
Russians had been deceived. Admiral Paul Tchitchakoff was
moving in force downstream out of Borizov; and, except for one
infantry regiment and 12 cannon, had abandoned his position
at Studzianka.

Two corps of the French army crossed by the bridge on the
26th and established themselves on the right bank. By 4 in the
afternoon a second bridge was completed 200 yards further upstream to take the artillery and baggage wagons, but twice during
the night it broke away, holding up the evacuation for seven
hours. It broke for the last time during the afternoon of the 27th.

Napoleon crossed shortly before this disaster and with him
the Imperial Guard and the 600 men who were all that remained
of Ney's corps. The disordered mob around the bridgeheads
took fright when it realized that the Guard was crossing and a
passage had to be forced for the Emperor. Larrey had already
crossed with headquarters but when the vehicular bridge was
finally swept away he knew his ambulances would have to be
abandoned on the left bank. 'Twice I recrossed this fatal bridge
[the footbridge] to try to find my equipment and to send across
some cases of surgical instruments of which we had the greatest
need. The third journey all but cost me my life and if my name
and person had not been known, I should never have returned.
I found myself caught up in the moment of greatest panic with
no prospect of escape. Death was very close when happily I
was recognized. My name was shouted. All at once everyone
turned to help me. Passed from soldier to soldier, I was carried
right up to the end of the bridge and thus I rejoined headquarters.'[1]

A few months later Larrey wrote to Charlotte telling her how
much he had owed to the ordinary soldier throughout the retreat:
'Ribes can tell you that in the midst of the army—and above all
of the Imperial Guard—I could not perish. In truth I owe my
survival to the soldiers. Some ran to my assistance when, surrounded by Cossacks, I was about to be killed or taken prisoner.

Others helped me to my feet and supported me when, from physical exhaustion, I fell in the snow. Still others, seeing me tormented by hunger, shared with me such rations as they had. If I approached their bivouac fire, they would make room for me, and I was even wrapped in straw or their coats. How many generals and senior officers were rebuffed and sent away without pity by their own soldiers! But at the name of Larrey all rose to their feet and welcomed me with a respectful friendship. Anyone but I would have perished at the Beresina when I crossed for the third time at the most dangerous moment. But hardly had I been recognized than I was seized by strong hands and passed from one to the other, like a bundle of rags, to the end of the bridge. Generals following behind me, though saying they were accompanying me, were stopped and disappeared for ever before my eyes. Beloved Laville, these signs of the love of the army for me are the greatest rewards I could wish for.'[2]

On the evening of November 27, as Victor assumed the increasingly perilous defence of the remaining bridgehead, Wittgenstein debouched from the hills and cut the road between Borizov and Studzianka. But with the strange perversity of panic, the French simply abandoned the bridge and bivouacked in Studzianka. No one crossed that night.

The next morning the Russians took the offensive simultaneously on both sides of the river. On the right bank at Borizov, Tchitchakoff, with 27,000 men, attacked Oudinot, Ney, and Poniatowski, with scarcely 8,000 between them. Yet the Russians were put to flight. Among the French wounded was the sixty-year-old Pole, General Josef Zayonscheck, a veteran of Bonaparte's Italian campaign and a great character in the army. His courage and daring in action were matched only by his affectation, since he would prepare for battle as if for his wedding. He perfumed himself from head to foot, dressed in his finest uniform, adorned his hands with rings and his person with jewellery, and wore his most precious sword. At Borizov his luck ran out with his perfumes and he was hit by a ball in the right knee. The joint was shattered and the vessels and nerves torn; it was a grave injury demanding immediate amputation through the thigh. Help came to him where he lay within range of the Russian cannon. Larrey knelt beside the general and, as it was snowing hard, instructed four soldiers to hold a large cavalry cloak high over the leg. In less than three minutes the operation was completed.[3] Zayonscheck was evacuated to Vilna by sledge in the care of Larrey's sole remaining pupil who was authorized to put at the general's disposal a fine new carriage, left by Larrey in the town, for the remainder of the journey to Warsaw. There the stump healed rapidly and soon afterwards Zayonscheck was named by Czar Alexander as prince and viceroy of Poland, a responsibility he discharged with dignity until his death in 1826. Yet in changing his allegiance he did not forget the man who had saved his life. In the summer of 1814 he wrote thanking Larrey for his help and asking whether he should return the carriage to Paris or sell it in Warsaw. Larrey answered, but heard nothing further until in 1819 he received a letter in which Zayonscheck apologized for the delay. He had sold the carriage for 1,800 francs and had banked the money in Larrey's name. His letter ended: 'I embrace you and thank you from the bottom of my heart.'[4]

Throughout the 28th, on the left bank of the Beresina, Victor's 6,000 held the 40,000 of Wittgenstein and remained in command of the heights of Studzianka, though there must have been times when they wondered whether it was worth the effort. At first light the frantic mob bore down on the bridge and there, once again, chaos reigned. If such were possible, the insensate confusion intensified when stray shot began falling in their midst and they heard the noise of fighting on both banks. Men hacked paths for themselves to the bridge; others drove their carriages, still loaded with plunder, pell-mell through the mass; but humanity was not quite dead for among all the selfish, brutal, panic-stricken horror, a few stood by their officers or sacrificed their own chances by attempting to save a wounded comrade.

Victor began his retreat at 9 in the evening and his men had to cut a way through the people they had so recently been defending. But whether paralysed by fear and cold or reluctant to run the risk of losing their plunder the mob refused to follow. The last chance of crossing passed unappreciated. At 8 the next morning Jean Baptiste Éblé, the builder of the bridges, set fire to his handiwork. Men and women, many clutching desperately to their children, flung themselves across the ice and into the freezing waters to be swept away by the current, or turned to face the slender mercies of their Russian captors.

On the 29th 'the army continued its march by little-frequented tracks that led through immense forests as far as Smorgoni where we rejoined the main road. Since our crossing of the Beresina the weather had grown steadily colder and at Smorgoni the temperature was minus 8 degrees Fahrenheit. It was here that the Emperor left the army to return to France, having handed over command to Prince Joachim.'[1]

Napoleon would have preferred Eugène to be in command but Berthier, old, sick, and tired, was proving more than usually obstinate. At first he handed in his resignation because Napoleon was leaving without him, and then he refused to serve under anyone less than a king.[5] So the King of Naples it had to be.

'I hope you will obey him as you would myself,' were the Emperor's parting words to his generals, 'and that harmony will reign among you all'[5]—hopes that were doomed even before they were uttered.

Travelling under the name of M. Reyneval, he left Smorgoni on December 5, taking with him Caulaincourt, Duroc, and Georges Mouton, Count of Lobau. He believed that his presence in Paris was as indispensable for France as it was for his tragic army. Only there could he wield the stick over Austria and Prussia, and only there could he raise the new army of his dreams. But although he left detailed orders, his departure opened a void that the flamboyant Murat could not fill. The days of the Grand Army were numbered.

'The march from Smorgoni to Vilna was terrible, and in this short distance [about 75 miles] we lost more than 10,000 men from hunger and cold. During the night of the eighth/ninth the temperature fell to minus 35 degrees Fahrenheit. This was disastrous for our wounded, the young men, and for nearly all the horses. Nothing was more distressing than the sight of our bivouacs the next morning; they were surrounded by bodies that at first glance one took to be sleeping, but were in fact frozen to death. Those who escaped this fate, remained in a profound torpor, scarcely able to help themselves or to speak, and seeming thoroughly dazed. They ignored each other and if we had not had to make forced marches, I believe they would all have perished.

'Nevertheless, in the midst of these creatures, starving and frozen stiff, without arms, clothed in the most bizarre fashions, and shuffling mindlessly along, several companies of the elite of the Guard aroused amazement and admiration by their bearing. They had retained their weapons, their cloaks or greatcoats, their horses and their gloves, and they entered Vilna as if on parade.

'As for myself, although I am one of the most robust men in the army, it was only with the greatest difficulty that I reached Vilna on December 9. I was at the end of my tether and near falling, like so many others. But the warm welcome I received from the grey sisters of the Charité hospital and their kindness and comfort restored me to life. I shall never forget them. Yet, alas! how many men, exhausted by hunger, fatigue, or struck down by congestion of the blood, will remain in this town. Among their number is my colleague, Baron Desgenettes, who until then had borne the rigours of the campaign extremely well. On the night of departure we separated at the lodging of Count Daru, believing that we would meet up again on the road the next day. It seems likely though that when the time came to leave he could not find the strength, and so took the wise course of staying with the university professors.

'Vilna contained some very large stores of food, clothing, and other supplies, but a sudden attack by the Cossacks threw the army into confusion. The doors of the warehouses were forced and everything was freely plundered by both soldiers and inhabitants. The immoderate use of the great quantities of spirits that were found, hastened the demise of many among them.'[1]

Until the arrival of the disordered army at the gates, no one in Vilna had known of the disaster. Napoleon had deliberately kept it from the people lest they would side with the Russians and turn on the French garrison. But once they had recovered from the shock of realizing that Napoleon's genius was not infallible, the inhabitants, many of whom were Jews, took the sick and wounded into their homes, clothed and fed them and tended to their needs. Unhappily, when the French moved out the townsfolk robbed and stripped those of their guests who remained and flung them into the streets—perhaps giving vent to their true feelings, perhaps fearing the wrath of the Russian army since anyone caught harbouring the enemy was dispatched forthwith to Siberia. Of the 25,000 sick and wounded left in Vilna only 3,000 lived into January; hunger, cold, disease, and horrifying brutality killed all but the most resilient.

On the 10th, after several hours' sleep, Larrey inspected the hospitals. 'I gathered all the sick surgeons and the senior wounded officers at the Charité hospital to be looked after by the good sisters. In all the hospitals I left, besides the sick medical officers, a sufficient number of surgeons of all grades to ensure satisfactory treatment. I gave them letters of recommendation to the chief medical officers of the Russian army. Then, during the night I set out again just after the Imperial Guard, on foot and leading my horse by the bridle.'[1]

During the French retreat, and particularly in its later stages, the Russians suffered too. Kutuzov's 120,000 were reduced to 35,000 at Vilna, and Wittgenstein's 50,000 to 15,000. And, like so many of the French, these men also knew the mental as well as the physical effects of the cold. Benumbed and stupefied, they were often incapable of distinguishing the French who marched with their disorganized columns. Woe betide any Russians who became separated from the main body for they ran the risk of being attacked by their prisoners and robbed of rations, uniforms, and weapons; the French would then return unrecognized to the ranks.

After leaving Vilna Larrey lost sight of his friend Ribes with whom he had been making the awful journey. 'I was getting worried, when at the approach to Kovno [Kaunas] I recognized him quite by chance in the middle of a seething throng. He showed every sign of being in the last stages of physical and mental exhaustion. A little bread, some sugar, and several sips of rum that I still had with me, helped him reach the town. I brought him to the hospital where a small room had been kept for me; it was difficult to heat, but it did have a bed which was just what my friend needed. Some broth and warm sweetened wine that I managed to procure brought life back sufficiently for him to continue the journey on my horse, though he still had to be led. I was happy to do this; indeed I believe it was what saved me.'[1]

Ney covered the retreat into Kovno with the rear-guard—the fourth that he had seen whittled away around him. But with the frontier so near, the last 60 men felt they had had enough and Ney found himself deserted. Alone he entered Kovno and here gathered his fifth rear-guard from among the foreign recruits of the garrison. But at the sound of Russian guns, they took to their heels. Ney, on the bridge over the Niemen, stood firm. Shamed into action, 30 soldiers rallied and two or three pieces of artillery were brought up. Fighting all the way, Ney was the last to leave Russian soil.

From then on the army marched without a rear-guard, but thankfully the Russians, uncertain whether Prussia was friend or foe, slackened their pursuit.

'After crossing the Niemen the troops of the different nations in our army dispersed to their own lands. Only the French took the road to Gumbinnen. Here we found supplies, above all of food in great variety for which we had to pay exorbitant prices; but what is money when one is in need?

'Three thousand of the elite of the Guard, as many infantry as cavalry, and all from the southern provinces of France, were the only ones who had withstood the cruel hardships of the retreat. They still had their arms, their horses, and their military bearing. Marshals the Dukes of Danzig and of Istria [Francis Lefebvre and Bessières] were at the head and Princes Joachim and Eugène at the centre of this troop—all that remained of an army of 400,000 men. The honour and glory of French arms were enshrined in this small elite corps.'[1]

23. *The Phoenix Rises*

Herr Jacobi, the Königsberg banker, was not best pleased to hear an insistent knocking at his door. It was late on December 21 and there were 50 degrees of frost outside. At length, deciding the caller would not go away, he opened up to find himself face to face with a small man holding the reins of a horse. It was hard to say who was leading which, but without his horse's support the man would certainly have fallen. Jacobi asked him several questions but could get no answer. At last the man opened his cloak to reveal the uniform of a senior French officer, neat and correct for all its well worn look. From a pocket he withdrew a letter and handed it to the banker. Like all the citizens of Königsberg Jacobi hated Napoleon and would lose no sleep if he never saw another French uniform, yet when he read the name on the letter, he opened his arms and half carried Larrey into his home. Since 1807 when Larrey had been Jacobi's guest after Tilsit, the two men had remained friends and had corresponded regularly.

In the morning Larrey was up before daylight, for there was work to be done despite his exhaustion. He was stiff, his feet were swollen, and he was scarcely able to hobble, but he spent that day and the next visiting the hospitals in the city, which had become a general clearing station for all the casualties sent back from Russia—there were nearly 10,000 of them. To add to the problems typhus was epidemic. Larrey worked like a man possessed; he organized the surgical staffs, advising on the treatment of conditions such as gangrene and frostbite which abounded in the wards; he initiated the further evacuation of those patients who could travel to their respective corps along the Vistula; and he prepared preliminary reports for Murat and Daru.

'I had scarcely finished these arrangements when I was suddenly struck down by typhus. The fever made rapid progress and in a few days I was dangerously ill. I owe my recovery to the efficient and tireless care of my host and respected friend, M. Jacobi. This wise old man knew from experience the best remedies and how to administer them. I rapidly became convalescent and was able to leave my bed for the first time on New Year's Eve.

'That same day we received news of Macdonald's retreat. Initially he had marched on Riga in a combined operation with Yorck, the Prussian Commander-in-Chief, but the separation of these two army corps [Hans Yorck, in fact, had come to an arrangement with the Russians] compelled Macdonald to withdraw on Königsberg. On December 31, the hospitals, arsenals, and magazines were speedily evacuated, and preparations made for the departure of headquarters. On January 1, the troops began to leave. Macdonald's rear-guard, under his personal command, entered Königsberg on the evening of the second with the enemy hard on his heels. I summoned all my strength and set out with Dr Bourgeois, one of my valued assistants, who gave me a great deal of help.'[1]

In Prussia, unlike the behaviour further east, the doctors did all they could for the French sick and wounded. As Larrey noted: 'Nearly all our sick have been left in the care of local doctors who are truly worthy of our trust.'[2]

Larrey rejoined headquarters at Elbing and at Posen Murat decided to desert the army leaving the command to Eugène who, as Larrey remarked, enjoyed the confidence and friendship of the troops. When Napoleon heard of this change of command he wrote to Murat: 'I suppose you are one of those who think the lion is dead. If this is your belief, you will soon find it false. You have done me all the harm you could since I left Vilna: the title of king has turned your head.'[3] And less than a month later Napoleon lost his Austrian troops as well when Schwartzenberg defected.

Despite his considerable debility on the journey westwards Larrey was already giving thought to the rebuilding of the army's surgical services. He wrote to all the known surviving medical officers, to the corps commanders, and to the Surgeon-in-Chief of the Russian army to discover the fate of his surgeons. He had, however, heard nothing of Desgenettes and although he imagined that the physician's reputation would ensure his safety, he was nevertheless most uneasy. Since the Physician-in-Chief of the Grand Army was a very important person, Larrey set in motion a number of diplomatic wheels to secure his release if he was still alive. He put the case to Prince Eugène; he asked Berthier to make enquiries of Kutuzov; and he wrote personally to the Czar. Alexander responded and ordered Desgenettes to be set free. The Physician-in-Chief arrived at the Magdebourg head-quarters at the end of March, but he showed no gratitude to Larrey. Although he knew of the trouble that had been taken on his behalf, he believed it to be his fame alone that had achieved the result. Had not Alexander said to him: 'Know that you have the right not only, as you say, to the goodwill but also to the gratitude of all nations.'[4]

Larrey was well aware of the man's tremendous conceit and usually made allowances, but this time Desgenettes had gone too far. From Leipzig on April 11, 1813, Larrey wrote to Charlotte:

'Without me, he would be no more than a memory in people's minds. When I asked His Highness the Prince of Neuchatel [Berthier] to approach Prince Kutuzov for his freedom, he replied, "Desgenettes! but he is dead; why do you want us to take these steps? His death at the hands of the Cossacks was seen at Vilna." I had to protest against this belief and to insist strongly that the favour be granted me. I owed it to my colleague. Too bad if he is not grateful to me.'[5]

But worse was to come. Desgenettes went straight back to Paris promising to claim for them both for loss of equipment. 'I am well pleased to learn that Desgenettes has received 2,000 francs indemnity,' he wrote to Charlotte on August 22. 'He had promised, when putting his claim to the Emperor, to speak equally for me and to request 2,000 francs for each of us. It appears he did not do so. That's that then.'[6] And so it was, as far as the friendship between the two men was concerned.

When Larrey arrived at Frankfurt-am-Oder on February 10, he at once began a detailed report for the Minister of War on the surgical services during the retreat from Moscow. Out of an original 826 surgeons of all grades, 275 were still serving on February 15, the date of the report; 30 were known to be dead; 137 were prisoners; 383 were missing; and one had taken his discharge. Larrey reckoned that most of the prisoners and of the missing could be accounted dead. Those few who did manage to survive and escape brought back tales of the most terrifying barbarity. One of them, Surgeon-Major Capron who escaped from Vilna, said that not even Christ's Passion could give an idea of what he had endured.[7]

The Russians were still advancing westwards. When they crossed the frozen Oder the French retired to Berlin and then to Leipzig which they entered on March 9. Here the French believed the campaign of the past year was at last ended, and they were indeed promised several weeks' rest. But before a fortnight had passed the skirmishing season opened in earnest and Eugène was compelled to manœuvre across Saxony to avoid a superior Prussian force which was moving to link up with the Russians near Leipzig.

Headquarters were established at Merseburg and on 'April 30 our advanced posts were engaged by the enemy. This was part of the attempt by the allies to cut off our small army and march on the frontiers of France. But their design was frustrated by the arrival of Napoleon at the head of fresh troops. On May 1 he and Eugène joined forces and from then on the two headquarters were united.'[8]

24. Saxony

In three months Napoleon had conjured up an army of 200,000 men of whom some 85,000 could be put in the field to oppose the 110,000 to 112,000 available to the coalition. For the most part the French recruits were adolescents lacking the training necessary for their commander-in-chief to carry out complex manœuvres, but to some extent making up for this by outstanding courage and enthusiasm—until the dream of glory wore thin. At Lutzen, their first battle, they would appear broken one moment, only to rally the next with the cry of 'Vive l'Empereur!' The same cry was on their lips as they submitted to the surgeon's knife and as they died. When their Emperor saw them in action he exclaimed, 'For 20 years I have commanded the French armies, but never before have I seen such bravery and devotion.'[1] Yet these qualities were not enough to save Napoleon's star. The French cavalry was greatly below strength and prevented him from pressing home his advantages to turn defeat into destruction.

Larrey was ordered to join the grand headquarters at Lutzen. He left Merseburg with his flying ambulances during the night of May 1/2 and reached the battlefield at midday. (On his arrival he was told of the death of Marshal Bessières while on a reconnaissance with Napoleon the previous evening. He was completely unmoved. Later he noted that the Marshal was 'the son of an army surgeon and jealous of the favour that Napoleon often accorded his surgeons and above all me. He was the most presumptuous man I have ever known.' Bessières had in fact used his position to undermine Larrey's status as Surgeon-in-Chief of the Grand Army and to sabotage Larrey's projects for reforming the surgical services.)[2]

'Catching a glimpse of His Majesty the Emperor, I walked to meet him though we were hidden from each other by the passing of a body of soldiers. The meeting thus happened suddenly.

I stopped at the sight of the sovereign who strode towards me and said, "Good morning, Larrey; there you are. How are you? You are welcome as you have arrived just at the right moment; the battle is starting. Go into the town and make ready for the wounded, then rejoin me here."[3]

'The enemy attacked with all his troops in line and so the battle began. The first clash was extremely spirited on both sides. Several of our battalions wavered and the outcome was uncertain. However, every Frenchman showed his courage. The young men stood firm.

'The battle continued throughout the day until at last, in the evening, we were victorious. The enemy lines were broken and his army routed. Dead and dying covered the battlefield. We gathered up the enemy wounded as well as our own. After the battle, the inhabitants of Lutzen gave welcome aid to our casualties. They brought linen, lint, and food on to the field and provided means of transport. They then received these men into their town and spared no effort in caring for them.'[3]

In the first two days and nights Larrey performed 18 disarticulations at the shoulder; 15 of the patients survived—a superb achievement. But he was badly hampered by shortage of staff since the campaign in Russia had taken a well-nigh irreplaceable toll of surgeons. In all, he had to perform or personally supervise 365 operations. And to make matters worse the Administration was up to its old bloody-minded tricks. One surgeon in command of an ambulance division complained bitterly afterwards that he had been ordered to Merseburg and compelled to stay there with his ambulances during the entire battle.[4] The supply fourgons were sent in the wrong direction by a quartermaster so that the compassion and practical help of the local Saxon population were godsends, as indeed they were throughout the whole campaign.

In their pursuit of the fleeing allies the French were held up on the left bank of the Elbe at Dresden by the destruction of the bridges. In the hospitals here Larrey found evidence in plenty of the unsatisfactory nature of Saxon amputating technique. (The Saxon surgeons cut through skin and muscle with a single circular sweep and sawed through the bone at nearly the same level. They then brought the skin edges together with sutures and adhesive strapping. The results of this tension in the stump were disastrous. Infection with gangrene could almost be guaranteed and the patients were in terrible pain.) He advised the Saxons to cut the sutures and release the tension but they assured him that the disturbance was only temporary and would not interfere with the eventual outcome. So far as Russian and Prussian soldiers were concerned, Larrey did not insist; but when he came to a French artillery officer he himself removed the dressings and sutures from the thigh stump. At once the officer felt greatly eased but infection had already set in and he died a few days later.

Only practical experience would convince the Saxon surgeons, so Larrey and his colleagues demonstrated their three cut technique on the many French wounded still requiring amputation. The success rate was impressive and effectively persuaded the Saxons to adopt the method.

'When the bridges were ready [two pontoon bridges had been built as well as the stone bridge repaired] the army crossed the river to continue the pursuit of the enemy. Headquarters and the Imperial Guard left Dresden on May 19 and reached the heights of Bautzen on the 21st. The enemy had taken up a position to the north and east of the town on a circular range of hills that merged in the east with the mountains of Bohemia. On the day of our arrival there was a brisk engagement that was ended by rain and the coming of darkness. The enemy line withdrew and took up a new position behind a series of prepared redoubts at the most exposed points. That day gave us 2,500 wounded whom we treated at the dressing stations I had organized in the neighbouring villages. These wounded were evacuated immediately to Dresden.

'Preparations were made for a fresh attack. During the night we approached the enemy positions and at daybreak the cannonade began and the battle became general. Violent attacks were launched by first one side and then the other. Several times their redoubts were entered only to be retaken. At length, after eight or nine hours' fighting victory was ours. The enemy position was captured and with it 40 or so pieces of cannon. That day we had 6,500 wounded.

'I had gone forward to follow the movements of the army and

so was able to dress the wounded where they lay. With the help of my flying ambulances they all received prompt attention and were evacuated to Bautzen where I went myself after the battle. We continued operating all that night and during the ensuing days.

'The conduct of the inhabitants of Bautzen towards our wounded was most praiseworthy. They provided linen for dressings and other supplies. Moreover, as transport to Dresden was non-existent, these good people managed to get the casualties to the city, 15 miles away, by using the wheelbarrows they all possess. These barrows are very long and capacious and were filled with straw. It was a strange sight to see this convoy proceeding in file and at a good speed along the side of the road which slopes downward all the way with only the occasional undulation. Several women followed with food for their husbands. [The idea for using these barrows came from Larrey who was always alert to the possibilities of local resources.]

'On the third day I set out from Bautzen to rejoin the army which was already a good way ahead. The advance guard and the Emperor's entourage had endured several attacks before arriving at Hainau. It was in one of these that the Marshal the Duke of Friuli [Duroc] was mortally wounded while in the Emperor's company.'[3]

Duroc had been carried by Yvan and Ribes to a nearby cottage where Napoleon stayed for some while at his side reflecting on the life hereafter. When he took his leave, the Emperor said, 'Fare-well, my friend, we shall perhaps meet again soon.'[5] He then returned to camp where he sat all night in front of his tent and, for the first time in his career, refused to attend to the army. When General Antoine Drouot asked for orders, he was told abruptly, 'Tomorrow—everything.'

Duroc's wound was distressing. A ricocheting cannon ball had carried away most of the skin of his abdominal wall. Several loops of small intestine were exposed and perforated. He asked repeatedly for Larrey.[6]

'I still had not rejoined headquarters. However, as soon as I arrived I hastened to see him. He was dozing. His eyelids were closed. I quietly approached the death bed and gently took his wrist to feel his pulse and to assess his condition.

'"Whose hand is this that touches me and makes me feel better?" he said in a weak, trembling voice. He opened his eyes and recognized me.

'"Ha! I was sure it was you, my dear Larrey. I have been asking for you for a long time and awaiting your attentions with impatience. See the state I am in; you cannot cure me this time. But give me something to end the terrible torture I endure. Do me the service of a true friend. Don't let me suffer any more, my dear Larrey. I rely on you."

'My friend was unable to continue, and I could not say a single word; my grief prevented it and I felt I would faint.

'As his weakness increased, my illustrious and unhappy friend closed his eyes again. But in the same instant he squeezed my hand for the second time and was without doubt bidding me eternal farewell. My friend Ribes, who I found at my side, took me and led me from the distressing scene. The Marshal died a few hours afterwards.'[3]

The loss of Duroc was felt deeply by both Napoleon and Larrey. Napoleon bought the cottage where his marshal died and put up a commemorative plaque: 'Here General Duroc, Grand Marshal of the Palace of the Emperor Napoleon, wounded by a cannon-ball, died in the arms of the Emperor, his friend.'[5] In his *Campagnes et Voyages*, Larrey wrote that 'the Emperor who had visited the Marshal some hours before me, lost in him the most loyal friend, the most trustworthy councillor, and one of the wisest and most intrepid of warriors'.[6] For Larrey himself a part of his life had come to an end. 'His name and those of Generals Desaix and Lannes are deeply engraved on my heart,' he wrote in his *Mémoires*, 'in gratitude for the friendship that these renowned and courageous soldiers always bore me.'[7] If a man is judged by the quality of his friends, then Larrey ranks high indeed.

After Duroc's death 'we continued our pursuit of the enemy who was retreating on Breslau. However, after an armistice and the preliminaries of a peace had been announced, the Imperial Guard and headquarters halted for some days at Neumarkt, a little town 18 miles from Breslau.'[3] Larrey liked the idea of this armistice little better than he had the one after Wagram. The troops were in great fettle and, in his view, could easily have driven the enemy back beyond the Oder and relieved the garrisons in the towns along the river. But Napoleon had other plans, and headquarters returned to Dresden.

Here, Larrey at once began a personal search for wounded Russians and Prussians who, he knew from bitter experience, would be hidden away somewhere. And, sure enough, in an attic of the Academy of Art he found 50 of them in a terrible state, without food, water, or fresh air and with their dressings neglected. Scarcely able to control his fury, Larrey stormed downstairs and into the magnificent salons where the Saxon orderlies were carousing with the French guard, gambling, smoking, drinking, and bedaubing the paintings. Calling down the wrath of God on their heads, he flung bottles, cards, paints, and canvasses out of the windows and had them sweeping the room and carrying in beds and bedclothes before they knew what had happened. He then operated on and dressed the casualties, leaving them sure of careful attention in the future.[8]

'I fully expect to be called before authority for having trod on its fingers and toes,' he wrote to his wife on August 3, 'but you know full well that having already fought against their influence, the quartermasters worry me little.'[9]

In fact nothing that obstructed the paths of righteousness was able to overawe Larrey. In the recent battles nearly 3,000 soldiers, mostly young recruits, had been wounded in the hands or fingers. A number of senior officers, inspired apparently by Soult, insinuated that these wounds were self-inflicted with the object of avoiding further military service.[10] Napoleon was inclined to agree in view of the numbers involved. Yet he should have known better than to trust his marshals' word in a case like this. Even during the current peace negotiations Metternich had said that surely the French army was weary of war. Napoleon had replied, 'My army, no; my generals, yes.'[11] If they could undermine Napoleon's confidence in his army they might yet achieve the result they wished.

Desgenettes and Yvan subscribed to the self-mutilation theory, and the principal surgeon of the twelfth corps pointed to the burnt sleeves of those wounded in the forearm and to the scorched and blackened skin of those wounded in the hand as indisputable evidence. But Larrey did dispute it—despite appearances, he said, only an examination of the circumstances could establish the truth. He had seen similar wounds inflicted by the enemy among young soldiers in Spain and on the first Polish campaign.

'An order of the day condemned two soldiers from each corps to be shot. This concerned me in so far as I had to choose those who, from their appearance or the character of their wounds, appeared the most guilty. These soldiers came from 12 corps inclusive of the Imperial Guard which meant that 24 individuals were condemned. However, the Provost Marshal, who was charged with executing the order, wanted four taken from each corps thus making 48.

'Whatever danger I might run, whatever disgrace I might incur, I resolutely declared that I was unable to find the least reason to suspect these brave soldiers who all appeared to me to have been wounded honourably.'[3]

When Larrey made his opinion known to the Emperor he was told to set up and preside over a court of enquiry. 'Go, Sir,' said Napoleon, controlling his annoyance, 'go, do your duty. Make your observations to me officially.'[12] Larrey and four other surgeons spent from the sixteenth to the nineteenth of June examining each one of the suspected soldiers. They concluded that every man was innocent and for three main reasons. First, the weapon drill of the recruits was hopelessly inadequate; when formed up in three ranks, those in the third rank had wounded those in the front two either by resting their muskets on the arms of their colleagues or by overestimating the kick of their weapon. Secondly, when attacking uphill—as they had had to do in the recent battles—the soldiers carried their muskets above their heads and thus their hands were the first parts of their bodies to be exposed to enemy fire. And thirdly, nearly all of them had other wounds besides those of their hands or forearms.[13]

When the findings were complete, Larrey presented the report to Napoleon. 'Well, Sir,' said the Emperor, 'do you still persist in your opinion?' 'I do, even more, Sire,' Larrey answered, 'and I shall prove it to your Majesty. These brave young men have been unworthily slandered; I have spent a great deal of time in a most penetrating examination and I can find none of them guilty. Every one has made his own report—there are numerous documents which Your Majesty can order to be examined.'[14]

Napoleon seemed agitated and began pacing up and down with quick little steps. Then he suddenly stopped and grasped Larrey's hand. 'So be it, M. Larrey,' he said with emotion, 'happy indeed is a sovereign in having a man like you at his side.' That night Larrey received a portrait of the Emperor in a diamond studded frame and was told that he was to receive a State pension of 3,000 francs.

'This day was one of the happiest of my life since I was able to save the lives of 48 persons and to preserve the honour and pride of French soldiers.'[3]

While he was in Dresden, Napoleon wanted to reward the surgeons for their conduct during the recent campaign by organizing them at long last into a proper corps. 'Consequently, he ordered a council composed of the quartermaster general, the adjutant general, and the inspector general of the surgical services to assemble under His Excellency the Minister Count Daru. It was to draft several resolutions relating to the medical services on the field of battle. An organizational scheme was proposed, based on the guidance given by the Emperor himself:

'First, a corps of military surgeons to be formed. An inspector general, with the rank of brigadier general, to form a senior council with the Minister in Paris and to supervise the entire ambulance service throughout the army.

'Second, the surgeons in chief of the army to have the rank of colonel.

'Third, the surgeons of the first class to have the rank of major.'[3] And so on down to second lieutenant. Five schools of military surgery were to be established and, from the beginning, a fully equipped and staffed battalion of ambulances was to be attached to the Grand Army.

However, as an indication of its true intentions, the Administration refused to pay the surgeons at Dresden or to give them lodgings. The reason, it said, was that the surgical services were without resources and so had nothing to offer the army. Next, possibly because Larrey was endeavouring to obtain compensation for his personal losses in Russia, the Administration suddenly decided to make a counterclaim on Larrey personally for all the ambulance equipment lost on that campaign. Larrey told the officials in no uncertain terms what they could do about it—the more feelingly as his barony was now part of Bernadotte's Sweden and the erstwhile French marshal had confiscated all pensions paid from there.

To reinforce the claim for a medical corps, Larrey, on August 6, 'presented a report to His Majesty—at his levee—dealing with the work of my service during the campaign. To this report I added a request that eight surgeon-majors and one surgeon should be decorated. After several questions the Emperor willingly agreed. On the same day I was officially informed that His Majesty had accorded me all I had asked, plus a State pension of 3,000 livres [confirmation of the pension he was granted after the court of enquiry] and a gratuity of 6,000. The decorations were distributed on the Emperor's birthday.'[3]

25. *Surgeon to His Majesty*

'The end of the armistice was fixed for August 15, the Emperor's birthday; nevertheless from the 11th of the month the enemy had been attacking our advance posts at various points and the renewal of hostilities was imminent. The celebrations were therefore curtailed and preparations for a new campaign speeded up. Unfortunately the quartermasters had been extremely sluggish about gathering material for the ambulances and had no wish to issue me with the light carriages or the pack horses needed to carry the first-aid dressings. We lacked practically everything.'[1]

And not only were the medical services in the field shabbily treated; the hospitals from Dresden to the Rhine and beyond into France were truly called the sepulchres of the Grand Army.[2] In August 1813 they held 35,000 sick but, as the days passed, they were inundated by crowds of boy-soldiers, sick and wounded, to whom youth denied strength and Daru bread. In such circumstances it is small wonder that typhus swept through the lines of evacuation like an avenging angel.

The start of the fighting was also the signal for the Swiss general, Henri Jomini, to desert. This had disastrous consequences when the allies acted on his advice and struck at Napoleon by picking off his lieutenants one by one. Yet, as if to compensate, one man returned to the Emperor's fold. Murat had been greatly impressed by his brother-in-law's recent victories and, with his own interests at heart, hurried from Naples to make amends. Napoleon forgave him his double dealing and put him in command of the cavalry where, at the forthcoming battle of Dresden, as always in the field, he distinguished himself and contributed greatly to the victory. But it was to be his swan song; after Leipzig he too deserted, seduced by allied promises.

'The army began its march towards Görlitz since the enemy had arrived there in strength. But acting on intelligence reports that a

o

considerable army was encircling Dresden, we promptly turned about and reached the city just in time. The enemy were already masters of the Pirna suburb and we were obliged to attack their positions there. They put up a stiff resistance. However, during the night our troops had an opportunity to deploy and the next morning we attacked again. The battle became general. It had been pouring with rain since the morning of the 25th [the previous day] but in spite of this hindrance our soldiers launched themselves fearlessly on the enemy, breaking them, destroying them, and putting them to flight. Before evening, victory was complete. We took 25,000 prisoners, 20 standards, and 30 or 40 pieces of cannon. About 6,000 of our men were wounded.'[1]

Larrey had set up his dressing station at the Pirna gate, and at the start of the battle had had no dressings. When he asked the quartermasters where they were, he was told that the fourgons had not yet arrived. At this he flew into a rage. 'So! You have none. I shall go to the Emperor and he will give them to me.' And off he galloped. On the way Mathieu Dumas, the quartermaster-general, stopped him and asked what all the hurry was about.

'I'm going to find the Emperor,' Larrey answered, 'to tell him that your agents undoubtedly think a battle such as this will produce no casualties. They have nothing prepared. I shall ask the Emperor for what they have forgotten—linen for my wounded.'

Dumas calmed him down and persuaded him to return to his dressing station. Within an hour Larrey had all the dressings he needed.[3]

'If the 27th had been a success for the army commanded by the Emperor himself, it had been a disaster for the first corps commanded by General Vandamme and one division of the fifth corps at Lowenberg. The first corps was surprised in the gorge at Toeplitz and destroyed almost completely. The fifth was likewise surprised and the division forming the advance guard perished entirely. These reverses nullified our successes and were the start of all our later misery. Marshals Ney and Oudinot had no more luck in their attacks on the Swedish army before Berlin.'[1] And neither had Macdonald who was defeated by Blücher.

During September numerous skirmishes and minor engagements took place in the countryside around Dresden. In one of these, on the 10th, Blücher's son was wounded and taken prisoner. Larrey dressed the wound and though his courtesy and efficiency were the same as he would have shown to any wounded man, this act was responsible for saving his life before two more years passed.

'Information that large numbers of enemy troops were grouping behind Leipzig to cut off our retreat and force us to capitulate, made us leave Dresden in a hurry on October 7. When we reached Leipzig, the two armies found themselves face to face and on October 16 a battle took place which I foresaw would be very bloody. It produced 5,500 wounded. All branches of the surgical service functioned well.

'Although the enemy was beaten in this action he received reinforcements (Bernadotte's army was brought in against us) and we were attacked anew on the morning of the eighteenth. The battle became bloody and general. The Guard were in the process of making victory complete and putting an end to our troubles when the Bavarians, the Saxons, and others deserted to the enemy. Our retreat began and before the day was out the Guard had abandoned the field and were withdrawing on Leipzig in the wake of the remainder of the army. I hurried on with the dressings and made most of the wounded find their own way back to Leipzig without delay. The more seriously hurt stayed with the ambulances on the battlefield.

'I set out with my light ambulances at 5 a.m. on the 19th and soon passed through the town [Leipzig]. Some hours later, the bridges were jammed by a great crush of people, a situation that deteriorated with the approach of the enemy. They were shelling our troops and several houses were destroyed. The Emperor, who had stayed to say farewell to the King of Saxony, was in serious danger and only extricated himself by the greatest good fortune. We learnt the full extent of the catastrophe in a bulletin which announced that 20,000 French had fallen into the hands of the enemy, together with most of the artillery; all our equipment and our ambulances were captured. This was one of the worst disasters of the war. The rest of the army was shaken and in disorder until we reached Erfurt.'[1]

The disaster was caused by the premature destruction of a vital bridge over one of the rivers. Napoleon had refused to burn the town and so a rearguard action had to be fought through the streets. The bridge was mined in readiness but the colonel in charge of the operation entrusted the job to a corporal and four sappers. As soon as he caught sight of the enemy the corporal set light to the powder leaving Poniatowski, Victor, Lauriston, Macdonald, Reynier, and their men at the mercy of the coalition. Poniatowski and Macdonald leapt into the river, but only Macdonald reached safety—Poniatowski could not swim. The others were taken prisoner.

Also among those captured was Desgenettes. Once bitten, twice shy, Larrey wrote to Charlotte from Mainz on November 7, 'As to Desgenettes, I confess that I have no desire to take the steps I did the first time when I was repaid for my help and concern by slander and abuse. I have abandoned him to the grace of God. He was within pleading distance of the Emperor Alexander, of whom he professes himself very fond.'[4] In due time Desgenettes was released.

From Erfurt, where Murat made his second and final departure, the army fell back on Hanau. Here 'we found our passage disputed by a Bavarian army more than 60,000 strong. We were thus faced with the choice between perishing or surrendering under un- favourable conditions. The Emperor preferred the former. Accordingly he regrouped his army and attacked the enemy with great fury. De Wrede and his army were beaten—the general himself was seriously wounded. Many of their soldiers were killed and the rest took flight. A thousand to 1,100 lay on the ground without aid as all our ambulances had been lost at Leipzig. I had, however, retained my instruments and we found a sufficient amount of linen in the victims' possession. I therefore rallied the surgeons of the Guard and those of the ambulance divisions who still remained and together we attended the wounded. These casualties stayed with us in bivouac during the night of October 29/30 before being evacuated to Hanau and Mainz.'[1]

The main body of the army arrived in Mainz on the night of November 1/2. After a short stay, Larrey set out to inspect the hospitals along the line of evacuation to Metz. His instructions for this came from the quartermaster-general, Baron Jean Marchand, a humane and reasonable man, to whom he submitted his report on December 10. Typhus was rampant and, if such a thing were possible, the hospitals were in a worse state than Larrey had ever known. He had done what he could to bring order to the situation; he had had the dead buried and had written to Marchand listing what was needed when it could not be obtained locally.

While at Mainz, Larrey had asked Napoleon for leave, but had been refused. He had then applied through official channels and again been refused. So, when he arrived in Metz he delivered an ultimatum and said if his request was refused again he would simply walk out. The Administration realized it had gone far enough and on December 27 Larrey was granted a month's leave —with pay. But on the twenty-sixth he had already started another tour of the hospitals, and although a messenger caught up with him on January 2, he went on to complete the inspection two days later.

On January 6 Marchand wrote to Daru about Larrey's latest report and suggested that as the vacancy in the Imperial household left by Heurteloup's death in 1812 had not been filled, Larrey's name should be put forward.[5] Daru agreed and at long last Larrey achieved his dearest ambition—surgeon to His Majesty the Emperor Napoleon.

Yet the appointment did nothing to ease his inner conflicts. 'I confess I have never had any desire other than that of helping the wounded, no intention other than that of doing right, and in all actions—most of which I did unobtrusively—I have had no other end than the well-being of these unfortunate men,' he had written, desperately searching his soul for spiritual ease, towards the close of his 1813 campaign journal. 'I have given no thought to personal gain and have remained poor until today. By neglecting my own interests I could easily have fallen into the hands of the enemy or perished in battle.

'What privations and miseries have I suffered to ensure that my wounded are efficiently treated; I often think that those who cling to conservatism must recognize the need for operation, even though it may call for ingenuity, yet fail to perform it through fear or some other equally futile reason. They are guilty men. To perform a task as difficult as that which is imposed on a military surgeon, I am convinced that one must often sacrifice oneself, perhaps entirely, to others; must scorn fortune and maintain an absolute integrity; and must innure oneself to flattery.

'I always have been, and doubtless always will be, the victim of my sincerity and openness. Often the Emperor has reproached me for being able to see merit in others yet not in myself. I do not even begrudge the ingratitude of some individuals to whom I have given greater or lesser service—even life itself. I am not vindictive. Indulgence is one of my milder affectations. I hate foolishness and politics. The truth, even when others cannot see it, marches always before me; I follow it blindly and am in danger of falling into the abyss if that is where it leads me.

'The misfortunes of others affect me strongly. Major disasters afflict my soul and plunge me into the deepest grief. I often think I can do something to help, and even attempt to remedy the situation. But such is my nature that I am thrown off balance and reason is no longer in control. In vain do I call for help upon the names of those whom I hold most dear. Yet they are always my true concern. I face up to the trials and tribulations of my life and bear them bravely only for the sake of my Laville whom I adore and of my children whom I cherish.'[1]

Larrey returned home on January 8, 1814, to find a tearful Charlotte awaiting him. She had been the victim of a confidence trick—to the tune of 30,000 francs, with no hope of redress—and the family had next to nothing to live on. The plight of the national coffers was little better and Larrey had yet again to battle for his pay. At length, on January 24, an order from the Emperor instructed the controller of the Imperial Treasury to pay him all that was owing. But by the time the money arrived, Larrey and his Emperor were once more in the field.

Europe was united against France. The armies of Prussia and Austria-Russia were gathering on her eastern frontier, preparing to conquer by weight of numbers if by no other means. On the morning of the twenty-fifth Napoleon left Paris and arrived at his headquarters at Châlons-sur-Marne in the evening. The next day Blücher and Schwartzenberg marched into France between the rivers Marne and Seine. They advanced separately, intending to link forces on the road to Paris. Napoleon, caught by the suddenness of the invasion, longed for the men away in the east, locked in garrisons along the Oder and the Elbe. One hundred and seventy thousand experienced troops were denied him. Yet one by one these garrisons tamely surrendered; only Hamburg (under Davout) and Magdebourg held out until the last days of the war. In the end it was the army of half-trained, half-armed conscripts, stiffened by the Old Guard (stationed at Troyes), that served their master more faithfully.

Larrey left Paris a few hours after Napoleon and followed him to Châlons; on the thirtieth he rejoined headquarters at Brienne where the French had just resoundingly trounced Blücher. He described the opening moves of this amazing campaign in a letter he wrote to his daughter from Troyes on February 25:[1]

'What momentous events have taken place, my dear Isaure, since we parted! At the first sight of the Emperor, the soldiers rose above themselves and, although heavily outnumbered, attacked the enemy's advance guard with great success. Already it is plain that France is by no means in the weakened state that everyone believes. The initial successes were achieved at Brienne where the Emperor had studied the basic elements of the art of war. Unfortunately, bad weather and the shortage of necessary supplies made us stop 24 hours too long here. The enemy, informed of our position by some traitorous citizens, made a surprise attack in considerable force. However, we were not defeated and retired in good order to the town of Troyes where we found the Guard waiting for us.

'The enemy swelled with pride at his achievement and, recovering his courage, advanced swiftly on all roads to the capital. With deceptive simplicity the Emperor let them advance, but his plans were skilfully laid. He led us along near-impassable roads to attack the flanks of the enemy columns commanded by the Prussian general. They were staggered by the first attack; their battalions were driven back by our cavalry; their squadrons were caught in the muddy swamps and perished; the artillery and baggage fell into the hands of the local inhabitants who were seeking reparation [they had been badly treated by the invaders]. In the end we put the entire army to flight, and then with all haste turned our attention to the second army which was advancing along a parallel route. We again made the cross-country journey by terrible roads. This second army, which had not had time to learn the news of its partner, did not reckon on seeing us. It was attacked with the same vigour and suffered the same fate. You have, no doubt, seen the prisoners from these two brilliant battles.

'Although we fought these two armies, a third—the most formidable—commanded by the three sovereigns, advanced by long stages and its advance guards were already at Fontainebleau and Guigne. We had to march night and day to catch up with them and stop their impudent progress. We arrived at Guigne during the night; we deployed, manoeuvred, and then charged suddenly on troops already drunk with the prospect of possessing our Parisian beauties. Never had the French attacked in a more spirited or resolute manner; the enemy squares were driven back in confusion and the superb Germans fell like a house of cards. The enemy army was routed; we pursued it as far as here [Troyes] and captured the baggage wagons, a part of the artillery, and the rear-guard.

'Now without doubt nothing can stop their flight, but we must not give them a moment's respite; thus we continue our march, and I trust that we will halt only at the very frontiers of France. It is necessary that these people retain the memory of our strength and courage. I hope also that when we reach these frontiers, peace will be made and that I shall be able—with the assurance of no further active service—to return and remain with you.'

The fight at Guigne on the 18th was the battle of Montereau, a mere 40 miles from Paris. In a note in his own copy of his *Mémoires* Larrey wrote: 'This memorable battle is one of those where one can judge the superiority of French troops over those of the German nations. An army of about 40,000 Austrians, entrenched between the river and the town of Montereau, was defeated in less than two hours by 10,000 to 12,000 Frenchmen.'[2]

Napoleon's genius shone as the sun at mid-day, yet this alone could not save Imperial France. His marshals had had enough and not even the sight of their Emperor personally directing the cannon could inspire them to one last effort. That effort had long since been made. The fruits of Montereau lay ungathered and Victor's follow-through in particular was so lethargic that Napoleon removed him from his command. But throughout this swift-moving campaign of lightning strikes, Larrey's evacuation of the casualties by road and river had been immaculate. And this with an ambulance service far below strength.

On February 27 Napoleon left Troyes to have yet another crack at Blücher who had pulled his army together and was again on the road to Paris. After several marches and manœuvres that, in Larrey's words, 'could scarcely be seen for their speed',[3] the French cornered Blücher on the plateau at Craonne, north of the River Aisne.

The Prussians were forced to accept a pitched battle which took place on March 7 and lasted all day. It was a bloody encounter. Among the wounded were Marshal Victor and General Sparre.

Victor may have lost his enthusiasm for command, but he

most certainly had not lost his courage. He fought like a hero that day until hit in the left thigh by a bullet which passed between the bone and the femoral artery. Larrey débrided the wounds of entry and exit and laid them open wide, since he was anxious lest suppuration or exertion would rupture the denuded artery. Healing was complicated and the Marshal was left with a traumatic neuralgia for the rest of his life.[4]

Sparre was hit in the right leg by a howitzer shell which carried away skin and soft tissues and fractured the middle part of the tibia. It was a wound that seemed to call for amputation and indeed Larrey's colleagues thought it essential. But Larrey believed he could save the leg, though instead of operating at once he turned to attend to the more seriously injured. (An irate Sparre later complained about this to Napoleon who, not unexpectedly, gave him short shrift.) When the General's turn came Larrey removed the larger splinters of bone and carefully débrided the wound. He then applied one of his special splints over the dressings and evacuated his patient by river to Paris. The splint was not touched for three weeks and healing proceeded uneventfully.[5]

The next few days were spent in several fruitless battles, leading up to the more serious attack on Reims which Napoleon took on the thirteenth. From there the allied army retreated south to Arcis-sur-Aube where 20,000 Frenchmen in vain tried to draw out five times their number in pitched battle.

The French retired across the river under fire but 'instead of proceeding to Paris, the army marched on St Dizier, so leaving the route to the capital exposed. The allied army took advantage of this to seize the roads, and merely pursued us with a corps of cavalry.'[6]

Napoleon's plans had gone awry. His intentions in going to St Dizier were to get much needed reinforcements from the troops still guarding the frontier and at the same time to induce the allies to follow him so that he, reinforced, could then sweep round and cut their communications. He very nearly succeeded. After hesitating, the allies did set off in pursuit; but a French courier was intercepted and that, combined with the news of the welcome awaiting them from the royalists, decided Alexander to march instead on Paris.

'We immediately gave chase, but as the bridges across the Seine were down we had to make a detour to Sens and to Pont-sur-Yonne. This held us back by 24 hours and the capital had just been surrendered when our advance guard reached Fontainebleau.'[7] A few hours more and Napoleon would have put the fear of God in the allies, but his marshals abandoned him and forced his abdication.

27. *Et tu, Larrey?*

'On April 11,' Larrey noted, 'Napoleon attempted to poison himself with a dose of opium given him by Yvan. He gave several convulsive movements, then vomited and expelled the poison.'[1] Yvan lost his head and the next day fled to join Ribes, Jouan, and the host of others who either abandoned or turned against their former Emperor. Larrey, however, remained with the imperial headquarters at Fontainebleau until the 20th when Napoleon set out for Elba. His loyalty while Napoleon was still on French soil is unquestioned.

In *Campagnes et Voyages*, published in 1841, Larrey tells how, at the moment of farewell, he begged to be allowed to join his master in exile. 'No, M. Larrey. You belong to the army, your place is there. Yet it is with deep regret that I leave you.'[2] Echoes of Larrey's words on Bonaparte's flight from Egypt—the old score settled; the slate rubbed clean. Perhaps, but only in the mind of an old man for whom dreams of what might have been had become what had been. The reality is shown in a letter he wrote on June 5, 1814, to Drouot, Napoleon's senior aide-de-camp on Elba.

'I cannot express the regret I have felt, and still feel, about your exile and that of the Emperor. If I had but thought, when I left Fontainebleau, that the Emperor's personal surgeon, M. Y [Yvan], was not travelling with him always to be at his side— as he should be—I would voluntarily have offered to follow him, assuming that he agreed. I even told my wife of this wish and she without saying anything to me first, wrote to His Majesty [King Louis]. In spite of the hope that the appointments of first surgeon to the troops of the Royal Household and of Inspector General are being held for me, I am still entirely willing to rejoin you if His Majesty will assure the continued support of my family. For, I confess to you, General, that as I have always dedicated half of

René Nicolas Dufriche Desgenettes

Pierre François Percy

Dominique Jean Larrey in later middle age

Dominique Jean Larrey, *c.* 1804

were those that had been infected by comparatively harmless bacteria that the body could fight, with the consequent production of pus. The presence of suppuration in general ruled out the presence of gangrene, so pus came to be regarded as a good thing and to be encouraged—the doctrine of 'laudable pus'.

5 Triaire, footnote p. 5 (campaign journal).
6 This name is more usually spelled Abbatucci. Larrey's spelling, particularly of proper names, was not of the best.
7 *Mémoires*, I, 74.
8 Soubiran, pp. 76–7 (Larrey's dossier, Historical Archives of the Army).
9 In all ages, most people are simply the children of their time; they accept things as they find them—pain, suffering, cruelty, sickness, for example—because these are as they have always known them. So, unless we can bring ourselves to understand that attitudes were utterly different—and based on long tradition—in Napoleonic times, we will never appreciate the quality of Larrey's difficulties or the significance of his achievements.

4. TOULON RETURN *pp. 27–31*

1 Bégin (1860), p. 106. Rochard, chapter 2.
2 Soubiran, p. 84. Until he took command of the Army of Italy (1795) the General spelled his name Buonaparte.
3 Soubiran, note p. 492 (Larrey's dossier, Historical Archives of the Army).
4 Val-de-Grâce, a monastery founded by Anne of Austria, wife of Louis XIII, in 1645, was converted into a military hospital in 1793.
5 Soubiran, pp. 90–2 (Larrey's dossier, Historical Archives of the Army).

5. THE FLYING AMBULANCE *pp. 32–41*

1 Wellcome.
2 Wellcome. Letter of August 15 from Larrey to his wife.
3 Soubiran, p. 95.
4 *Mémoires*, I, 151–2. (See *Appendix* p. 259.)
5 *Mémoires*, I, 152–8.
6 Soubiran, pp. 96–7.
7 *Mémoires*, I, 174.
8 Triaire, p. 18 (campaign journal).
9 The medical services were not alone in their dissatisfaction with the Administration, though they were certainly the worst served. The case for the Administration can be summed up by saying that it was constantly required to economize, was chronically short of staff, and suffered from a distinct lack of men of the right calibre.
10 *Mémoires*, I, 181.

6. ARMY OF THE ORIENT *pp. 42–52*

1 Triaire, p. 21 (campaign journal).
2 Triaire, footnote pp. 23–4 (Larrey's correspondence in the Bibliothèque Nationale).
3 Triaire, footnote p. 32 (a Larrey note).
4 *Campagnes*, p. 350.
5 *Mémoires*, I, 192–3.
6 *Mémoires*, I, 196.
7 *Campagnes*, p. 299.

8 Triaire, p. 45 (a Larrey note).
9 Triaire, p. 48 (a Larrey note).
10 Triaire, p. 52 (a Larrey note).
11 Triaire, footnote p. 53 (a Larrey note).
12 *Campagnes*, pp. 366–7.

7. SHACKLED BY UNBREAKABLE CHAINS *pp. 53–58*

1 Triaire, p. 57. (After Miot, J. F. *Mémoires pour Servir à l'Histoire des Expéditions en Égypte et en Syrie*, p. 79.)
2 Triaire, footnote p. 58.
3 Triaire, p. 62.
4 The ophthalmia was not a single infection but a variable mixture of trachoma, spring catarrh, gonorrhoeal infection, and secondary bacterial infection complicating any of the other three. Unfortunately the climate itself favours the transmission of trachoma and even today the prevention of the disease is still one of the major health problems facing Egypt and the Middle East and many other countries besides. Larrey's treatment was successful insofar as it helped to prevent secondary infection. He used soothing eye washes and compresses to treat the inflammation and ulcers of the cornea, and for some of the complications he resorted quite successfully to surgery. Regrettably his recommendations for treating gonorrhoeal ophthalmia were very much in line with contemporary thought. Because the sudden cessation of gonorrhoeal urethral discharge seemed often to be followed by ophthalmia, the best cure for the ophthalmia was considered to be the re-establishment of the urethral discharge by inoculating gonorrhoeal matter. 'Much confidence ought to be placed in the inoculation,' he wrote in his *Mémoires* (**1**, 210 and 215), 'as we possess a specific which will cure the gonorrhoea in a very short time.' Heaven knows what catastrophes this led to, particularly as the distinction then between gonorrhoea and syphilis was vague in the extreme.
5 *Campagnes*, p. 338.
6 *Mémoires*, **1**, 231.
7 Triaire, footnote p. 71 (campaign journal).
8 Triaire, footnote pp. 72–3 (Larrey's correspondence in the Bibliothèque Nationale).
9 Triaire, footnote p. 85 (Larrey's correspondence in the Bibliothèque Nationale).
10 *Mémoires*, **1**, 276–7.
11 *Mémoires*, **1**, 278.
12 Triaire, pp. 86–7. Larrey gave the grateful English captain a sum of money and asked him to have it forwarded to Charlotte. She received it safely a few days after the captain had arrived in London.
13 *Mémoires*, **1**, 279.

8. EXODUS *pp. 59–69*

1 This explanation for the Syrian expedition is by no means generally accepted, though it fits in with my reading of Bonaparte's character at that time. The more popular explanation is that the expedition was simply a local affair to subdue the Pashas and thus to secure Bonaparte's Syrian front— which was indeed what he stated in a letter to the Directory.
2 *Mémoires*, **1**, 281–2.
3 Busquet *et al*.

4 *Mémoires*, **1**, 288.

5 Triaire, pp. 93–4.

6 Triaire, footnote p. 93 (a Larrey note). This defence of Bonaparte's action by a man of Larrey's humanity illustrates most forcibly how moral standards can differ at different times.

7 Desgenettes, p. 51.

8 Desgenettes, p. 49.

9 *Mémoires*, **1**, 294.

10 Triaire, p. 98 (a Larrey note).

11 *Mémoires*, **1**, 296.

12 *Mémoires*, **1**, 298–9.

13 *Mémoires*, **1**, 300.

14 Triaire, footnote p. 110 (a Larrey note in his own copy of his *Mémoires*).

15 *Mémoires*, **1**, 303.

16 Triaire, p. 102 (a Larrey note in his own copy of his *Mémoires*).

17 *Mémoires*, **1**, 305–6.

18 The British surgeon, Percivall Pott (1714–1788), said 'that amputation in the joint of the hip is not an impracticable operation (although it be a dreadful one) I very well know: I cannot say that I have ever done it, but I have seen it done, and am now very sure I shall never do it, unless it be on a dead body.' Quoted by Guthrie, G. J. *On Gun-Shot Wounds of the Extremities Requiring the Different Operations of Amputation, with their After-Treatment*, p. 116. London; Longman, Hurst, Rees, Orme, and Browne. 1815—Guthrie successfully performed this operation at Waterloo.

19 *Mémoires*, **2**, 182–4.

20 *Mémoires*, **1**, 308.

21 *Campagnes*, p. 298–9.

22 *Mémoires*, **1**, 309–10; *Campagnes*, p. 292.

23 As recognition of their services, both Larrey and Desgenettes were awarded gratuities of 2,000 francs each.

24 *Mémoires*, **1**, 312–13.

25 Triaire, p. 113.

9. ALARMS AND EXCURSIONS *pp. 70–76*

1 One blind soldier from Verdier's division lost touch with his friends and was wandering aimlessly about calling for help. Suddenly a hand took hold of his and a woman's voice said, 'Hold on to the tail of my horse and don't let go; he is a gentle animal and will do you no harm. Come I shall look after you.' The man could not believe his ears. 'Is this an angel who leads me?' 'No, only an Italian. I am Madame Verdier, your general's wife.' Throughout the whole of the terrible withdrawal this courageous woman helped the surgeons with their dressings, giving her linen to make bandages and ekeing out the pitiful rations of the sick and wounded with her own provisions and water. She never rode while there was a wounded man walking. (Desgenettes, p. 104.)

2 *Mémoires*, **1**, 355.

3 Desgenettes, p. 99.

4 Triaire, p. 117.

5 O'Meara, vol. 1, pp. 331–3.

6 *Mémoires*, **1**, 366–7.

7 Triaire, p. 125.

8 'I explored all the tortuous passages of the Great Pyramid and carved my

name, as many others had done, on the stone that forms its apex' (*Mémoires*, **2,** 3).

9 *Mémoires*, **2,** 4–7.
10 *Campagnes*, p. 297.
11 *Campagnes*, p. 371. Simple and obvious though it may now seem, the method of artificial feeding through a stomach tube had then only recently been introduced—by John Hunter in 1790. Larrey may well have been the second person to adopt it. In Murat's case the tube almost certainly prevented an abscess forming in the internal throat wounds.
12 *Campagnes*, p. 372.
13 *Campagnes*, p. 341–2.
14 Triaire, p. 146 (a Larrey note in his own copy of his *Mémoires*).

10. HOMEWARD BOUND pp. 77–84

1 Triaire, footnote p. 151. Kléber's letter was written on September 26, 1799.
2 *Mémoires*, **2,** 9–10.
3 *Mémoires*, **2,** 10–11.
4 In the pursuit of the Turks after the battle of Heliopolis (March 20, 1800), Larrey saved the life of one of Mourad Bey's Mamelukes (the Bey had become an uneasy ally of the French). He refused to accept any reward, so a bewildered Mourad sent him twelve beautiful slaves convinced that he had found something no man would reject. But Larrey distributed them all among his delighted colleagues—he himself was 'free from the passions of men of my age and of the soldiers of my time' (Soubiran, p. 150).
5 Kléber was assassinated by 'Soleyman el-Haleby, an educated but fanatical young philistine' (*Mémoires*, **2,** 98–100).
6 The settled conditions brought about by Kléber had had one inevitable result—an increasing number of soldiers were admitted to hospital with syphilis. 'To prevent the spread of the disease I proposed to General Menou that he should establish a civil hospital to receive prostitutes suffering from venereal disease, and also those who were pregnant that we might stop them inducing abortions. General Belliard, the commandant of Cairo, prepared a large house where we collected all the women suspected of having had intercourse with French soldiers. Those who were free from infection were sent away, the remainder were admitted and treated. We also made regular searches throughout the barracks and every infected soldier was sent to the hospital where he stayed until cured. These measures had the desired effect and the patients of both sexes were restored to health' (*Mémoires*, **2,** 107–8). The quality of health to which the patients were restored is problematical: the treatment of syphilis in those days relied on heavy doses of mercury, both internally and rubbed on the surface of the body. It was carried to the verge of poisoning and in the hot climate of Egypt the danger point was often passed with consequent irreparable damage to the kidneys (chronic nephritis) and nervous system (mercurial palsy or the shakes).
7 *Mémoires*, **2,** 104–5.
8 Wellcome.
9 Wellcome.
10 Soubiran, pp. 152–3 (Larrey's correspondence in the Bibliothèque Nationale).
11 Larrey's pleasures included an investigation of ancient Egyptian embalming—he, incidentally, preferred the contemporary technique. His only

recreation was his horses. (Letter to his wife written on November 24, 1801, while in quarantine at Toulon. Wellcome.)

12 *Mémoires*, 2, 255.
13 Triaire, footnote p. 172 (a Larrey note in his own copy of his *Mémoires*).
14 *Mémoires*, 2, 294.
15 Wellcome.

11. ORDERS AND DEGREES . . .' *pp. 85–91*

1 The commission was delivered to Larrey on March 22, 1802.
2 Letter of November 24, 1801, to his wife (Wellcome).
3 Soubiran, p. 167 (Larrey's correspondence in the Bibliothèque Nationale).
4 Except for changes in the style of his references to Napoleon, this history was repeated verbatim in volumes 1 and 2 of Larrey's *Mémoires*.
5 Larrey's thesis was dedicated to Villemanzy.
6 During the seventh assault on Acre, Eugène had been hit in the head while standing at Bonaparte's side. The ball had damaged his right orbit and grooved the temple. With Larrey's treatment, the wound had healed rapidly. As Larrey rather ingenuously noted, Beauharnais was the one among the senior officers who took the greatest liking to him (*Campagnes*, p. 295).
7 Triaire, p. 190 (journal).
8 *Paradise Lost*, Book 5, lines 789–90.
9 Corvisart was one of the outstanding figures of French medicine, and earned himself a place in medical history quite apart from his relationship with Napoleon. He fell from favour when he opposed Napoleon's marriage to Marie Louise; later he advised the Empress not to accompany her husband to Elba.
10 Triaire, footnote p. 183 (a Larrey note).
11 *Mémoires*, 2, 313–14.
12 Triaire, footnote p. 192.
13 *Mémoires*, 2, 314–15.

12. AUSTERLITZ *pp. 92–102*

1 Triaire, p. 198 (Larrey's correspondence in the Bibliothèque Nationale).
2 Triaire, p. 197.
3 Hassenforder (1957). An undated letter written from Augsburg (Val-de-Grâce collection).
4 Triaire, pp. 199–201.
5 *Mémoires*, 2, 326–7.
6 Triaire, footnote p. 204.
7 Hassenforder (1959).
8 Triaire, pp. 206–9.
9 *Mémoires*, 2, 330.
10 Triaire, pp. 212 *et seq.*
11 *Campagnes*, p. 398.
12 Triaire, footnote p. 214 (Larrey's correspondence in the Bibliothèque Nationale).
13 Hassenforder (1957). (Val-de-Grâce collection.)
14 The colonel, François Louis Morland, had been shot in the head and chest while leading the first charge against the Russian Imperial Guard. Afterwards Napoleon believed him to have been the hero of the day and wished to bury his body in the crypt of a monument planned for the terrace of the

R

Invalides. The monument was never built and Morland, magnificent in his uniform, found his way to a room in the hospital of the Imperial Guard where he stood side by side with Colonel Barbenègre of the seventh hussars who was killed at Jena and also embalmed by Larrey. So perfect was Morland that a female relative thought he lived and embraced him. She promptly fainted when she realized the truth. Doubtless the two corpses would be in the hospital yet, had not their families, in a belated show of grief in 1818, claimed them back. Larrey tried to keep them but was overruled by the then Minister of War.

15 *Mémoires, 2,* 346.
16 *Mémoires, 2,* 339.
17 Hassenforder (1957). The letter was written on Christmas eve (Val-de-Grâce collection).
18 Jean Rapp, one-time aide-de-camp to Desaix, and a true friend to Larrey, had been wounded at Austerlitz but had fought on to the end before allowing Larrey to attend to him.
19 Hassenforder (1957). (Val-de-Grâce collection.)
20 There were two Paulet brothers, but their Christian names are lost. When referring to 'Paulet', nowhere does Larrey distinguish between them.

13. JENA *pp. 103–8*

1 *Mémoires,* I, 228. *Clinique Chirurgicale,* I, 406–7.
2 Soubiran, pp. 162–3.
3 The Prussians at Jena were only a strong covering force. At the simultaneous battle of Auerstadt, Davout's corps of 26,000 alone routed the main Prussian army of 63,000 which was under the command of the Duke of Brunswick.
4 *Mémoires, 3,* 3.
5 *Mémoires, 3,* 3.
6 Wellcome. Written from Halle.
7 Triaire, p. 230 (a Larrey note).
8 Triaire, pp. 231–2 (Larrey's correspondence in the Bibliothèque Nationale).
9 Wellcome.
10 *Mémoires, 3,* 8–9.
11 Wellcome. Written from Berlin. Many of Larrey's letters, both to his wife and his daughter, at this period were written on the Queen of Prussia's writing paper.
12 Throughout his correspondence Larrey called his wife Laville, usually with an added endearment. This letter of November 1 is the only occasion that I have been able to find (certainly in the whole of the Wellcome collection) where he uses her Christian name, Charlotte. Both Triaire and Soubiran refer to her by her other name, Elisabeth, but provide no documentary evidence to support their choice.
13 Wellcome. Written from Berlin.
14 Wellcome. Written from Berlin.

14. THE FROZEN WASTE OF EYLAU *pp. 109–21*

1 *Mémoires, 3,* 25.
2 Wellcome.
3 On January 18 he wrote home saying that he had lost his hat in the mud of Poland and asking Charlotte to send him the trimmings and ornaments of a colonel of the grenadiers of the Guard for his new one. In this letter he

also said that he was sending her a parcel of furs including seven sable skins which had been very expensive but would last a long time (Wellcome).

4 Wellcome. Larrey was most aggrieved because all his letters and packets had been opened and scrutinized before he received them.

5 *Mémoires*, **3**, 35.

6 Hassenforder (1959).

7 *Mémoires*, **3**, 36.

8 Triaire, p. 241.

9 *Mémoires*, **3**, 36–7. (There were, however, no Russian redoubts at Eylau.)

10 Triaire, p. 242 (a Larrey note).

11 Triaire, footnote p. 204 (a Larrey note).

12 *Campagnes*, pp. 359–60.

13 *Mémoires*, **3**, 37–8.

14 Triaire, footnote pp. 251–2.

15 *Mémoires*, **3**, 39.

16 Soubiran, p. 202.

17 Letter of February 15, 1807, written to his wife from Preuss-Eylau (Wellcome).

18 Triaire, footnote pp. 245–6 (a Larrey note).

19 Debénédetti.

20 *Mémoires*, **3**, 42.

21 Soubiran, p. 204.

22 Wellcome.

23 *Mémoires*, **3**, 58–9.

24 Triaire, p. 255.

25 Letter of February 26, 1807, written to his wife from Osterode. He admitted that he had been unwell after Eylau and said that he was indebted to Frizac who had stayed with him (all other surgeons had accompanied the wounded) and to Percy who had lavished care and attention on him in a truly friendly manner (Wellcome).

26 Wellcome (the same letter as mentioned in Note 25).

27 Letter of May 6, 1807, written to his wife from Riesembourg (Wellcome).

28 Wellcome. Written from Osterode.

29 Wellcome. Written from Osterode.

30 Letter written to his wife from Riesembourg (Wellcome).

31 Letter written to his wife from Riesembourg (Wellcome).

32 Letter dated May 6 written to his wife from Riesembourg (Wellcome).

33 Letters dated April 16, May 15, and May 22 written to his wife from Riesembourg (Wellcome).

34 Wellcome. Written from Riesembourg.

35 Wellcome. Written from Riesembourg.

36 Wellcome. Written from Riesembourg.

37 Letter dated June 19 written to his wife from Tilsit (Wellcome).

38 Wellcome.

39 Triaire, footnote p. 272 (a Larrey note).

15. THE 'LIBERATION' OF SPAIN *pp. 122–33*

1 Soubiran, pp. 225–6 (Val-de-Grâce collection).

2 On September 6, 1808, Larrey wrote to his daughter from Miranda: 'If it is a little boy you will call him Felix Hyppolite' (Wellcome). Until 1829 at least Larrey persisted in spelling the name Hyppolite (or even Hypolite). By 1835 he seems to have resigned himself to Hippolyte (Wellcome collection).

R*

3 Hassenforder (1957). (Val-de-Grâce collection.)
4 *Mémoires*, 3, 137–9.
5 *Mémoires*, 3, 241–2.
6 Hassenforder (1957). (Val-de-Grâce collection.) Triaire, pp. 286–7.
7 Triaire, footnote p. 287. (From a letter to his wife written from Miranda on September 6, 1808.)
8 Soubiran, p. 236. (From Bérenger-Féraud, L. *Le Baron Hippolyte Larrey*. Paris; Fayard, 1899.)
9 Soubiran, p. 231 (Val-de-Grâce collection).
10 *Mémoires*, 3, 251–3.
11 *Mémoires*, 3, 271–2.

16. WAGRAM: A VIEW OVER THE HILL *pp. 134–45*

1 Wellcome.
2 Wellcome.
3 *Mémoires*, 3, 276–7.
4 Triaire, p. 305 (a Larrey note.)
5 *Mémoires*, 3, 279–80.
6 Triaire, p. 309 (a Larrey note).
7 *Mémoires*, 3, 280–1.
8 *Mémoires*, 3, 282.
9 Letter dated June 14, 1809, to his wife written from Vienna (Wellcome).
10 Wellcome. Written from Vienna.
11 A month earlier (in his letter of May 12) he had asked to figure in Girodet's picture of the revolt in Cairo.
12 Triaire, footnote p. 310 (Larrey's correspondence in the Bibliothèque Nationale).
13 Wellcome.
14 *Mémoires*, 3, 346–9.
15 Soubiran, p. 254 (manuscript in the Bibliothèque Nationale).
16 *Mémoires*, 3, 355.
17 Triaire, p. 324 (a Larrey note in his own copy of his *Mémoires*).
18 General Desvaux. A copy of Larrey's reply to this general is attached to his letter of October 13 to his wife in the Wellcome collection.
19 Wellcome. Written from Vienna.
20 Triaire, p. 326.
21 Triaire, p. 327.
22 Letter to his wife written from from Vienna (Wellcome).

17. INTERLUDE *pp. 146–8*

1 Soubiran, p. 363.
2 Soubiran, p. 266 (Larrey's dossier, Historical Archives of the Army).
3 *Mémoires*, 4, 2.

18. MOMENTS OF DECISION *pp. 149–56*

1 Leroy-Dupré, pp. 103–4.
2 *Mémoires*, 4, 2–3.
3 Brice and Bottet, pp. 178–9.
4 *Mémoires*, 4, 8.
5 Triaire, footnote p. 352.
6 Triaire, p. 352. (Letter dated August 9, 1812, from Larrey to his wife, written at Vitebsk.)

7 *Mémoires*, **4**, 30.
8 Triaire, footnote p. 357.
9 *Mémoires*, **4**, 36.
10 Triaire, footnote p. 354.
11 Murmurings in Russia that Barclay's retreat and scorched earth policy amounted almost to treason, compelled the Czar to replace him by the old, obese, one-eyed Kutuzov.
12 *Mémoires*, **4**, 40.

19. BORODINO *pp. 157–63*

1 *Mémoires*, **4**, 43–4.
2 *Mémoires*, **4**, 44–6.
3 Ségur. Philippe de Ségur was aide-de-camp to Napoleon on the Russian campaign and his memoirs of this particular part of his career were originally published in 1824. I have relied heavily on them for background information on the retreat from Moscow.
4 *Mémoires*, **4**, 49–50 and 57
5 *Campagnes*, pp. 379–80.
6 *Mémoires*, **4**, 58–9.
7 Triaire, footnote p. 369.

20. MOSCOW *pp. 164–8*

1 Ségur.
2 *Mémoires*, **4**, 72.
3 Triaire, p. 369.
4 *Mémoires*, **4**, 74–6.
5 *Mémoires*, **4**, 76–8.
6 Triaire, p. 372.
7 *Mémoires*, **4**, 78–9.

21. FROM MOSCOW TO THE BERESINA *pp. 169–77*

1 *Mémoires*, **4**, 80.
2 *Mémoires*, **4**, 80–3.
3 Ségur.
4 Larrey's journal of the retreat from Moscow (from Mojaisk to Königsberg) is given in Triaire, pp. 375–96. The story of this journey published in his *Mémoires* is an expurgated version of the campaign journal.
5 *Campagnes*, pp. 373–6.
6 Triaire, footnote p. 377.
7 Mme Bursay was killed by a bullet while in bivouac at Smolensk.

22. THE LAST DAYS OF THE GRAND ARMY *pp. 178–85*

1 Larrey's campaign journal. (See Note 4, Chapter 21.)
2 Triaire, footnote pp. 389–90. (Letter written on March 11, 1813, from Leipzig.)
3 *Campagnes*, pp. 404–5.
4 Soubiran, pp. 376–7.
5 Ségur.

23. THE PHOENIX RISES *pp. 186–9*

1 *Mémoires*, **4**, 121–2.

2 Triaire, p. 400.
3 Leroy-Dupré, p. 174.
4 Dulieu.
5 Triaire, footnote p. 402.
6 Triaire, footnote p. 402.
7 Triaire, pp. 402–3.
8 *Mémoires*, 4, 153–4.

24. SAXONY *pp. 190–8*

1 Leroy-Dupré, p. 179.
2 Triaire, footnote pp. 408–9. Bessières' behaviour towards Larrey in Spain during January and February 1809 is indicative of the sort of conduct that prompted Larrey's note.
3 Larrey's unpublished campaign journal of 1813 in the Wellcome collection. Strictly speaking, this is neither a diary nor a chronological account of events. Although Larrey seems to have started with the best of intentions the journal becomes a record of the most important events as they occurred mixed with later recollections of these earlier events, together with other thoughts and reflections. I have edited the journal so that, in this chapter and the next, it makes a continuous story. Among his doodles at the beginning Larrey wrote: 'This journal will only ever be seen by my son and after my death.'
4 Triaire, footnote pp. 411–12.
5 Triaire, p. 416.
6 *Campagnes*, pp. 338–9.
7 *Mémoires*, 4, 166.
8 Triaire, p. 421.
9 Triaire, footnote p. 421.
10 This was, in fact, a not unreasonable assumption. Self-mutilation to avoid conscription or in the training depots in France was well recognized.
11 Triaire, p. 422.
12 Leroy-Dupré, p. 187.
13 *Mémoires*, 4, 170–5.
14 Leroy-Dupré, p. 188.

25. SURGEON TO HIS MAJESTY *pp. 199–204*

1 Campaign journal of 1813 (Wellcome).
2 *Les Sépulchres de la Grande Armée, ou Tableau des Hôpitaux Pendant la Dernière Campagne de Bonaparte.* Paris; Eymery. 1813. (By an anonymous author—cited in Garrison.)
3 Triaire, p. 437.
4 Triaire, footnote p. 447.
5 Soubiran, p. 324. (Marchand's letter is in the Bibliothèque Nationale.)

26. A CAMPAIGN OF GENIUS *pp. 205–9*

1 Triaire, footnote p. 459.
2 Triaire, p. 460.
3 *Mémoires*, 4, 466.
4 *Mémoires*, 4, 467–8. *Campagnes*, p. 403.
5 *Mémoires*, 4, 470. *Campagnes*, pp. 395–7.
6 *Mémoires*, 4, 475–6.
7 *Mémoires*, 4, 476.

27. ET TU, LARREY ? *pp. 210–13*

1 Triaire, footnote p. 469. The suicide attempt took place, in fact, during the night of April 12/13. Larrey probably did not know about it at the time and thus based his note on second-hand evidence. Moreover, the poison had been provided by Yvan as long previously as 1812 at Malojaroslavitz—though this time lapse would not have affected its potency.
2 *Campagnes*, footnote p. 2.
3 Soubiran, p. 332.
4 Soubiran, p. 336 (Val-de-Grâce collection).
5 Soubiran, p. 339.
6 McGrigor, p. 355.
7 McGrigor, p. 353.
8 McGrigor, p. 265.
9 Soubiran, p. 337.
10 *Campagnes*, p. 3.

28. THE HUNDRED DAYS *pp. 214–20*

1 Triaire, p. 472.
2 *Campagnes*, p. 3.
3 Soubiran, notes pp. 506–7, quoting 'Journal de M. Jacob, docteur en médicine et pharmacien militaire sous le Premier Empire' and the views of André Gosse, a Geneva doctor in Paris from 1811–16.
4 In pouring rain, Blücher, then aged seventy-three, personally led a cavalry counter charge but his horse was shot from under him and he was ridden over several times. He was rescued, half-conscious, by his adjutant and carried off. He resumed command the next day.
5 Creasy, E. S. *The Fifteen Decisive Battles of the World*, **p.** 368. London; Dent (Everyman's Library). 1943.
6 *Campagnes*, p. 395.
7 Triaire, p. 478.
8 Marcy, H. O. Letter to the Editor: 'Anecdotes of Baron Larrey.' *Boston Medical and Surgical Journal*, **182**, 310. 1920.
9 Henry, **2**, 17–18.
10 *Campagnes*, p. 7. The Guard had been in action, though not until late in the day. Six battalions had been involved in the fighting against Bülow at Plancenoit, and a further nine in the final assault on the English. Only two battalions were still in reserve at the rout.
11 Triaire, p. 481. This story may well be apocryphal since Larrey gives no clue about who told it to him.
12 *Campagnes*, p. 10.

29. THE SECOND RESTORATION *pp. 221–6*

1 *Campagnes*, pp. 11–14.
2 Soubiran, p. 350.
3 Triaire, footnote p. 495.
4 Soubiran, p. 351.
5 *Campagnes*, pp. 16–17.
6 *Campagnes*, p. 17.
7 Soubiran, p. 353.
8 Triaire, p. 497.
9 Wellcome.
10 Triaire, p. 498.

30. THE LAST BATTLE *pp. 227–37*

1 In the Wellcome collection is a letter dated April 23, 1839, from the Abbé Grasset to Larrey. The Abbé must by then have been in his nineties, yet the letter is in a clear firm hand. Larrey had evidently written to his former tutor to find out what had happened to money he had sent for restoring his old home. The Abbé replied that he had gone to Beaudéan (from Bagnères) with a carpenter to examine in detail all the urgent work. The most pressing need had been to repair the roof which had been in a state of complete ruin. The Abbé continued to visit the house two or three times a week to oversee the repairs. Larrey's sister, he wrote, was looking after other work, and had arranged for a large number of fruit trees to be planted. She was proposing to go and live there in two or three months' time. Larrey or his son would be welcome, but they would find his sister much changed. (She died the next year, 1840.)

2 O'Meara, **2**, 251.

3 Triaire, p. 515. The tribute was paid during a conversation with Dr Archibald Arnott.

4 In April 1830 Larrey spoke up against the branding of forgers on the shoulder with a red hot iron. He succeeded in having the practice removed from the penal code, though he thereby made himself unpopular with authority (*Campagnes*, pp. 123–8).

5 Triaire, p. 522.

6 *Campagnes*, pp. 324–6. Larrey incorrectly referred to the Duke as Talleyrand's son.

7 Soubiran, pp. 400–2, quoting Briffault, E. 'M. le Baron Larrey á l'Hôtel des Invalides.' *La Presse*, July 16, 1836.

8 Da Costa.

9 Annan. In her article, Gertrude Annan mentioned that Larrey also sent the thorax of a soldier on whom he had operated for empyema, the result of a sabre wound. There was no knowledge of whether this relic ever arrived.

10 Triaire, footnote p. 523.

11 Triaire, p. 545.

31. VALE *pp. 238–40*

1 Leroy-Dupré, p. 245.

2 Triaire, p. 554. ('Notes de voyage médical en Afrique avec mon père du 5 mai au 15 juillet 1842' in Bèrenger-Féraud, L. J. B. *Le Baron Hippolyte Larrey*, Paris; Fayard. 1899.)

3 Campaign journal of 1813 (Wellcome).

Bibliography

Ackerknecht, E. H. *Medicine at the Paris Hospitals 1794–1848*. Baltimore; Johns Hopkins Press. 1967.

Annan, Gertrude L. 'Jean-Dominique Larrey and the "Academie de New York".' *Bulletin of the New York Academy of Medicine*, **7**, 921–3. 1931.

Begin. 'Discours prononcé sur la tombe de F. Ribes.' *Bulletin de l'Académie Royale de Médecine*, **10**, 421–7. 1844–5.

Bégin, L.-J. *Études sur le Service de Santé Militaire en France*. Paris; Rozier. 1860.

Bouchot, H. *L'Épopée du Costume Militaire Français*. Paris; May. Undated.

Brice and Bottet. *Le Corps de Santé Militaire en France, son Évolution, ses Campagnes 1708–1882*. Paris and Nancy; Berger-Levrault. 1907.

Busquet, P., Gilbert, A., and Genty, M. *Les Biographies Médicales*. (Larrey, pp. 49–76; Percy, pp. 105–28; Boyer, pp. 129–40; Dubois, pp. 185–212.) Paris; Baillière. 1929–31.

Cases. 'Art. IX. The case of Napoleon Bonaparte.' *Philadelphia Medical and Physical Journal*, **5**, 380–97. 1822.

Chaplin, A. Letter to the Editor: 'Napoleon's funeral.' *British Medical Journal*, **2**, 552. 1915.

Chevalier, A. G. 'Hygienic problems of the Napoleonic armies.' *Ciba Symposia*, **3**, 974–80. 1941.

Cilleuls, J. des, Pesme, J., Hassenforder, J., and Hugonot, G. *Le Service de Santé Militaire de ses Origines à nos Jours*. Paris; S.P.E.I. 1961.

Da Costa, J. C. 'Baron Larrey: A sketch.' *Bulletin of the Johns Hopkins Hospital*, **17**, 195–215. 1906.

Debénédetti, R. 'Eloge de Jean-Dominique Larrey à l'occasion du bi-centenaire de sa naissance.' *Bulletin de l'Académie Nationale de Médecine*, **150**, 489–505. 1966.

Desgenettes, R. *Histoire Médicale de l'Armée d'Orient*. Paris; Croullebois; Bossange, Masson, and Besson. 1802.

Dible, J. H. *Napoleon's Surgeon*. London; Heinemann. 1970.

Dulieu, L. 'Desgenettes à Montpellier.' *Histoire de la Médecine*, **9** (3) 8–53 (4) 8–51. 1959.

Ganière, P. 'Dominique Larrey chirurgien en chef de l'Hôtel Royal des Invalides.' *La Presse Médicale*, **73**, 1881–4. 1965.

Garrison, F. H. 'Notes on the history of military medicine.' *The Military Surgeon*, **49**, 481–501, 601–25; **50**, 1–30, 142–62, 318–37, 448–64, 578–602, 691–718; **51**, 201–19. 1921 and 1922.

Hassenforder, M. 'Relation historique des campagnes de Dominique Larrey a Austerlitz et en Espagne d'après une collection de lettres autographes inédites adressées par Larrey a sa femme.' *Société de Médecine Militaire Française, Bulletin Mensuel*, **51**, 242–53. 1957.

Hassenforder. 'Relation historique des campagnes du Chirurgien-major d'Héralde Dominique.' *Histoire de la Médecine*, **9** (5), 8–64. 1959.

Heizmann, C. 'Military sanitation in the sixteenth, seventeeth and eighteenth centuries.' *Annals of Medical History*, **1**, 281–300. 1917.

Henry, W. *Trifles from my Port-folio or Recollections of Scenes and Small Adventures During Twenty-nine Years' Military Service.* 2 vols. Quebec; Neilson. 1839.

Keith, A. 'An address on the history and nature of certain specimens alleged to have been obtained at the post-mortem examination of Napoleon the great.' *British Medical Journal*, **1**, 53–9. 1913.

Kemble, J. *Napoleon Immortal.* London; Murray. 1959. (Contains a large bibliography on Napoleon's health and illnesses.)

Larrey, D. J. *Relation Historique et Chirurgicale de l'Expédition de l'Armée d'Orient, en Egypte et en Syrie.* Paris; Demonville. 1803.

Larrey, D. J. *Mémoires de Chirurgie Militaire, et Campagnes.* 4 vols. Paris; Smith. 1812–17.

Larrey, D. J. *Mémoirs of Military Surgery, and Campaigns of the French Armies, on the Rhine, in Corsica, Catalonia, Egypt, and Syria; at Boulogne, Ulm, and Austerlitz, in Saxony, Prussia, Poland, Spain, and Austria.* From the French by R. W. Hall. First American Edition from the Second Paris Edition. 2 vols. Baltimore; Cushing. 1814.

Larrey, D. J. *Memoirs of Military Surgery.* Containing the practice of the French military surgeons during the principal campaigns of the late war. Abridged and translated from the French by John Waller, surgeon of the Royal Navy. In two parts. Part I. London; Cox. 1815. (In his introduction Waller wrote: 'On the whole, however, notwithstanding a tolerable proportion of disgusting egotism and vaunting, the book, as a system of military surgery, and containing considerable information on many diseases not common, is an undoubted acquisition to the medical world.' Nevertheless, Waller was horrified at Larrey's rapid evacuation of the wounded immediately after operation—as at Eylau: 'I knew that many of the French officers themselves considered it as an unnecessary, wanton act of barbarity'.)

Larrey, D. J. *Surgical Essays.* Translated from the French, by J. Revere. Baltimore; Maxwell. 1823.

Larrey, D. J. *Clinique Chirurgicale, Exercée Particulièrement dans les Camps et les Hopitaux Militaires, Depuis 1792 Jusqu'en 1836.* 5 vols. vols. 1, 2, and 3, Paris; Gabon. 1829. Vol. 4, Paris; Baillière. 1832. Vol. 5, Paris; Baillière. 1836.

Larrey, D. J. *Observations on Wounds, and their Complications by Erysipelas, Gangrene and Tetanus, and on the Principal Diseases and Injuries of the Head, Ear and Eye.* Translated from the French by E. F. Rivinus. Philadelphia; Key, Mielke and Biddle. 1832.

Larrey, D. J. *Surgical Memoirs of the Campaigns of Russia, Germany, and France.* Translated from the French, by J. C. Mercer, Philadelphia; Carey and Lea. 1832.

Larrey. *Relation Médicale de Campagnes et Voyages de 1815 a 1840.* Paris; Baillière. 1841.

Le Dran, H-F. *Observations in Surgery.* Translated by J. S. 2nd ed. London; Hodges. 1740.

Le Dran. *The Operations in Surgery.* Translated by Mr Gataker. 5th ed. London; Dodsley and Law. 1781.

Leroy-Dupré, L. A. H. *Memoir of Baron Larrey, Surgeon-in-Chief of the Grande Armée.* (Abridged and adapted from the work.) London; Renshaw. 1861.

Luckhardt, A. B. 'Historical background and introduction.' In *Medicine and War,* ed. Taliaferro, W. H. pp. 1–22. Chicago; University of Chicago Press. 1944.

McGrigor, J. *The Autobiography and Services of Sir James McGrigor, Bart.* London; Longman, Green, Longman, and Roberts. 1861.

Medical and philosophical intelligence. 'Report of appearances on dissection of the body of Napoleon Bonaparte.' *Philadelphia Medical and Physical Journal,* 5, 195–6. 1822.

Ministère de la Guerre. *Historiques des Corps de Troupe de l'Armée Française (1569–1900).* Paris; Berger-Levrault. 1900.

Murray, J. F. 'Napoleon—of what did he die?' *South African Medical Journal,* 45, 1005–9. 1971.

Naumann, W. 'Napoleon's medical legislation.' *Ciba Symposia,* 3, 991–2. 1941.

Obituary. 'Death of Baron Larrey.' *Lancet,* 2, 671. 1842.

O'Meara, B. E. *Napoleon in Exile; or, A Voice from St Helena.* 2 vols. London; Simpkin and Marshall. 1822.

Paré, A. 'Apologie, et voyages.' *Les Œuvres d'Ambroise Paré,* 11th ed. Lyon; Rigaud. 1652.

Pariset. 'Éloge de J.-D. Larrey.' *Bulletin de l'Académie Royale de Médicine,* 11, 217–51. 1845–6.

Percy. *Journal des Campagnes du Baron Percy Chirurgien en chef de la Grande Armée (1754-1825)*. Introduction by M. É. Longin. 2nd ed. Paris; Plon-Nourrit. 1904.

Pringle, J. *Observations on the Diseases of the Army*, 3rd ed. London; Millar, Wilson, Durham, and Payne. 1761.

Pringle. *Observations sur les Maladies des Armées, dans les Camps et dans les Garnisons*. Translated from the 3rd edition. Paris; Barrois. 1795.

Richardson, F. M. 'Napoleon and the doctors.' *The Scottish Society of the History of Medicine. Report of Proceedings*, 26–34. 1967–8; 1968–9.

Rieux, J. and Hassenforder, J. *Histoire du Service de Santé Militaire et du Val-de-Grâce*. Paris, Limoges, Nancy; Lavauzelle. 1951.

Rochard, J. *Histoire de la Chirurgie Française au XIXᵉ Siècle*. Paris; Baillière. 1875.

Ségur, Comte de. *Histoire de Napoléon et de la Grande-Armée*. 2 vols. 5th ed. Paris; Baudouin Frères. 1825.

Soubiran, A. *Le Baron Larrey. Chirurgien de Napoléon*. Paris; Fayard. 1966.

Spencer, W. G. 'Larrey and war surgery.' *Lancet*, 1, 867, 920–1, 962–3. 1919.

Triaire, P. *Napoléon et Larrey*. Tours; Mame. 1902.

Wiseman, R. *Eight Chirurgical Treatises*. 2 vols. 5th ed. London; Tooke and 15 others. 1719.

Further Reading

Coignet, J.-R. *The Note-Books of Captain Coignet: Soldier of the Empire*, 1799-1816. London; Greenhill Books. 1988. (Translated from the French by Mrs M. Carey and first published by Chatto and Windus, 1897.)

Elting, J.R. *Swords Around a Throne. Napoleon's Grande Armée*. London; Weidenfeld and Nicholson. 1988.

Esposito, V.J. and Elting, J.R. *A Military History and Atlas of the Napoleonic Wars*. Revised edition. London; Greenhill Books. Pennsylvania; Stackpole Books. 1999.

Griffith, P. *The Art of War in Revolutionary France, 1789-1802* London; Greenhill Books. Pennsylvania; Stackpole Books. 1998.

Lachouque, H. and Brown, A.S.K. *The Anatomy of Glory. Napoleon and his Guard. A Study in Leadership*. 2nd revised edition. Providence, Rhode Island; Brown University Press. London; Lund Humphries. 1962. (Republished by Greenhill Books, London. 1997.)

Appendix

The best that one can hope for when translating the ranks in Larrey's ambulance divisions is to select modern ranks whose functions are as close to equivalent as possible and would be readily recognized by the reader (always bearing in mind that we are dealing with a 'civilian' organization). But when writing for an English-speaking readership, even this is beset with difficulties: the British and American military terminologies do not always coincide. For example, in the American army, 'first sergeant' (the senior sergeant of a company) is the British 'company sergeant-major' (warrant officer, WO II) — in the text I have used the British term and put the American equivalent in square brackets. Similarly, the American 'sergeant-major' is the British 'regimental sergeant-major' (warrant officer, WO I).

Nevertheless, this was only a minor problem compared to the translation of *commissaires-ordonnateurs* and *commissaire général*. Americans are happy with commissaries and commissary-general. However, in the reorganization of the British Army Medical Department in the late 1870s, commissaries or purveyors became known as quartermasters, and quartermasters they have remained ever since. I hope my American readers will therefore understand why I use quartermasters (which has a different meaning for you) instead of your commissaries.

The situation was further confounded by the fact that the Napoleonic *commissaires* were civilians. Indeed, the administration of the army was in the hands of the civilian *Intendance* (Administration) who employed contractors to supply all the needs of men and horses. Not until the late nineteenth-twentieth century did the ancillary services become militarized — in the British army in the form of the Royal Army Medical Corps, the Royal Army Ordnance (now Logistic) Corps, the Royal Army Service Corps (now also Royal Logistic Corps), the Royal Army Catering Corps, etc.

* By courtesy of the Wellcome Trustees

Index of Personal Names

Abbatouchi, Charles (1771–1796), 25
Aboville, Augustin Marie d' (1776–1843), 142–144
Alexander of Macedon (the Great) (356 B.C.–323 B.C.), 39, 53
Alexander I of Russia (1777–1825), 109, 120, 147, 150, 164, 167, 188, 202, 208, 224
Antommarchi, Francesco (1780–1838), 227
Appiani, Andrea (1754–1844), 40
Arrighi, Toussaint, Duke of Padua (1778–1853), 67–68, 238
Augereau, Pierre François Charles, Duke of Castiglione (1757–1816), 39, 93

Bagration, Peter Ivanovitch (1765–1812), 96, 153
Bailly, Adjutant-General, 25
Baird, Sir David (1757–1829), 81
Barbier, Joseph Athanase (1767–1846), 30–31
Barclay de Tolly, Michael Bogdanovitch (1761–1818), 153, 155
Barras, Jean Nicolas Paul François (1755–1829), 30
Baste, Pierre (1768–1814), 140
Beauharnais, Alexandre (1760–1794), 24, 25, 26, 27
Beauharnais, Eugène Rose, Prince and Viceroy of Italy (1781–1824), 88, 149, 158, 169, 173, 182, 185, 187, 188, 189, 227
Beauharnais, Hortense Eugénie, Queen of Holland (1783–1837), 88
Beauharnais, Josephine, see Josephine
Belgida, Marquis of, 124
Bennigsen, Levin August Theophil (1745–1826), 110
Benoist, Pierre Vincent (1758–1834), 88, 224
Bernadotte, Jean Baptiste Jules, Prince of Ponte Corvo, Charles John XIV of Sweden and Norway (1763–1844), 39, 93, 110, 198, 201, 226
Berthier, Louis Alexandre, Prince of

Wagram and Neuchatel (1753–1815), 38–39, 65, 67, 73, 75, 76, 80–81, 100, 108, 111, 132, 168, 171, 182, 188, 216
Bertrand, Henri Gatien (1773–1844), 74, 218, 227, 238
Bessières, Jean Baptiste, Duke of Istria (1766–1813), 49, 92, 93, 105, 122, 131, 132, 185, 190
Blücher, Gebhard Leberecht von, Prince of Wahlstatt (1742–1819), 200–201, 205, 207, 216, 217, 221
Bodin (citizen), 30
Bon, Louis André (1758–1799), 45, 50, 59, 67
Bonaparte, Joseph, King of Naples then of Spain (1768–1844), 104, 125, 127
Bonaparte, Marie Anne Élisa (Mme Bacciochi) (1777–1820), 38
Bonaparte, Marie Annonciade Caroline, see Murat, Caroline
Bonaparte, Marie Letitia (Madame Mère) (1750–1836), 38
Bonaparte, Marie Pauline, Princess Borghese (1780–1825), 38
Bonaparte, Napoleon, see Napoleon I
Bourgeois (surgeon), 187
Boyer, Alexis (1757–1833), 89, 119, 226
Brueys d'Aigalliers, François Paul (1753–1798), 44, 46, 51
Brunswick, Karl Wilhelm Ferdinand, Duke of (1735–1806), 18–19
Bülow, Friedrich Wilhelm von, General (1755–1816), 221
Bursay, Aurore Domergue (?–1812), 176

Caffarelli, Maximilien (1756–1799), 45
Cambridge, Adolphus Frederick, Duke of (1774–1850), 219
Capron (surgeon), 189
Carlin, General, 26
Carnot, Lazare Nicolas Marguerite (1753–1823), 27
Casabianca (surgeon), 58, 72

Subject Index